WELSH REFORMATION ESSAYS

Welsh Reformation Essays

by

GLANMOR WILLIAMS

CARDIFF
UNIVERSITY OF WALES PRESS
1967

In Memoriam
GRIFFITH BEDDOE REES

CONTENTS

QUALITEX PRINTING LIMITED CARDIFF

ACKNOWLEDGEMENTS

All these essays have been published before. Numbers I and II, and the greater part of VII, appeared in the *Transactions* of the Honourable Society of Cymmrodorion for 1966, 1961 and 1948 respectively. Part of VII and the whole of VI were published in the *Journal* of the Historical Society of the Church in Wales, I (1947) and II (1950); II in the *Transactions* of the Caernarvonshire Historical Society for 1966; IV in *The Welsh History Review*, III (1966); V in the *Bulletin* of the Board of Celtic Studies, XV (1953) and XVI (1954); VIII in the *Transactions* of the Denbighshire Historical Society, XIV (1965); and IX in *History*, XXXVIII (1953).

Permission to reprint those articles in this form was readily given by the editors of these journals: Professor Idris Ll. Foster of the Cymmrodorion, Rev. Canon E. T. Davies of the Church in Wales, Mr. Emyr Gwynne Jones of both the *Bulletin* and the Caernarvonshire *Transactions*, Dr. Kenneth O. Morgan of *The Welsh History Review*, Mr. Frank Price Jones of the Denbighshire *Transactions*, and Professor Alfred Cobban of *History*. I am deeply grateful to them for their kindness.

I am much indebted to Mrs. P. M. Thomas and Miss Kathleen Lewis of the Department of History at the University College of Swansea for help in preparing the manuscript for the press. I should also like warmly to thank my friend, Dr. Brinley Jones, of the University of Wales Press Board for so generously helping me to see the volume through the press.

My greatest debt, as always, is to my wife who has helped me in innumerable ways, and not least by preparing the index.

In dedicating this book to the memory of Griffith Beddoe Rees, I pay tribute to one who was not only the kindest and dearest of friends but also who typified so much of what is best in the Welsh parish priest.

G.W.

I. WALES AND THE REFORMATION

THE HARTWELL JONES MEMORIAL LECTURE*

I

In Welsh historiography the Reformation draws attention to itself as the dog that hasn't barked. It seems almost incredible that it should have been the subject of no major study. There have been valuable monographs and articles, certainly.[1] But they have all been either relatively small-scale works like Archdeacon Lawrence Thomas's *The Reformation in the Old Diocese of Llandaff* or Arthur Pryce's *The Diocese of Bangor in the Sixteenth Century*. Or else they have been concerned with some limited aspect of the subject, like William Pierce's biography of John Penry or T. P. Ellis's studies of the Catholic martyrs. Many, perhaps most, of these publications have been partial in their treatment, in more senses than one. Admittedly, there are many facets of Welsh history still inadequately written up. Religion is, however, not in general among them. 'Ecclesiastical history', Professor A. H. Dodd has rightly observed, 'is notoriously a prickly subject; it is also one that has always interested Welsh historians'.[2] There have indeed been masterly studies of epochs in Welsh church history earlier and later than the Reformation. One thinks at once of Hartwell Jones's own splendid work on Celtic Britain and the pilgrim movement, of Conway Davies's studies of the period from 1066 to 1282, of Thomas Richards's detailed examination of seventeenth-century Puritanism, and of a veritable flood of literature of every kind on the Methodist Revival and Nonconformity since the eighteenth century. On the Reformation in Wales there has been nothing comparable. This is in sharp contrast to the copious and seemingly unending stream of literature on the Reformation elsewhere in Europe and in Britain.[3] We are at once prompted to ask why this should be so.

Part of the answer may be competition from other subjects in the history of Tudor Wales regarded as more exciting: the absorption of Wales into the Tudor state; the creation of new organs of administration; or the emergence of important new social and economic developments.[4] A powerful deterrent, too, has been the poverty of original sources. We are dependent in the main on what has survived in the central archives; but, useful as state papers and the records of the great courts are, they have their limitations. Episcopal registers are scrappy, chapter records hardly more satisfactory, and parish records scarcely exist.[5] There is only a handful of Welsh books available in print or manuscript, and the once-abundant harvest of Welsh verse becomes thinner in content and poorer in quality, without being conspicuously easier to interpret. Sermons, meditations, letters, diaries, and the like, if they ever existed, have virtually all disappeared. All this must be conceded. But we are still entitled to ask, 'Are such sources as we have for the Reformation less useful in bulk or quality than those which exist, say, for the history of the Celtic Church?' The answer must surely be 'No'. And yet major works of scholarship on this subject, considerably weightier than anything that has so far appeared on the Reformation, have been published and still continue to appear.[6]

The real reason for the neglect seems to have been that the Reformation in their own country has held little intrinsic attraction for Welshmen. They have tended to conceive of it as something alien and unheroic; an anti-climax, even a betrayal. 'Mute suffering Wales', wrote O. M. Edwards in that wonderfully persuasive way he had, 'apathetic while the world around was awakening to a brighter morning, suspected by rulers who thought that its very patriotism was tinged with a smouldering rebellion, betrayed by the reformers whose selfishness and insolence had brought the spirit of the Reformation in a degraded form to its mountains'.[7] This sums up what many Welshmen have thought, and continue to think, of the Reformation in Wales. So unappealing an assessment of it helps to explain why the subject as a whole has not been studied but only those aspects of it to which an author's sympathies have responded. Catholic writers have generally gone for the Catholic exiles, martyrs and recusants. Those with strong Protestant and Welsh sympathies have concentrated on the translations of the Bible. Dissenters have made John Penry or the early Stuart Puritans their heroes. In each instance they have singled out what, in their eyes, alone redeemed the Reformation in Wales from mediocrity or worse.

We may have here the aftermath of two revivals which imprinted themselves traumatically on the Welsh psyche: the Romantic Revival and the Methodist Revival. Each had its own vision of the Middle Ages as an Age of Faith. Admittedly there were wide differences between them. One saw it as an era of deep, unshaken, assured piety; the other as one of untroubled ignorance and super-stition never seriously breached until the fourth decade of the eighteenth century. But with the growth of national consciousness in the nineteenth century and after, these two apparently conflict-ing views of the past could and did fuse in writers so different, but so widely influential, as, for example, O. M. Edwards, or W. Llewelyn Williams, or W. J. Gruffydd, or Saunders Lewis. Reformation Wales appeared as a grey twilight world. The old warm sunlight of the Catholic faith in which Wales had so long lived secure and happy had vanished. Over the land hung the cold and meaningless clouds of Anglican formulae. Nor was it only a change of religious climate. 'Catholicism stood for more than the old religion; it stood also for Welsh nationality'.[8] The chill winds of anglicizing political influence also blew cheerless and blighting through Welsh social and cultural life. Views such as these are often allied to a mystique about the 'emotional temperament' of the Celt and his stubborn reluctance to conform to a religion imposed upon him.[9] In Wales he never found his soul again until the prophets of the 'Great Awakening' were able to recall him from a land of darkness.[10]

Assumptions, predilections, prejudices and values like these have powerfully shaped interpretations of the Reformation in Wales. There is no agreed view; certainly no classical statement, though perhaps one comes nearest to this in the writings of O. M. Edwards or W. Llewelyn Williams.[11] There are many differences of emphasis and some flat contradictions. Yet there seems to be a kind of broad consensus of opinion about what are held to be the main stages in the development of the Reformation in Wales and the nature of its impact (or lack of it). It is, perhaps, possible to construct, as it were, a traditional anatomy of the subject, though its component members may have to be drawn from a variety of sources. It may be useful first of all to present this in outline and then try to show at what points it needs fairly drastic revision.

II

First of all, there is the common attitude towards the condition of the medieval Church and religion. It presupposes that the whole of the Middle Ages was, for Wales and the rest of western Europe, the Age of Faith. This was a time when there existed in Wales a universal, unquestioning acceptance of the doctrine, practices and hierarchy of Latin Christendom. It was a fidelity untainted by serious doubt, criticism or heresy. A number of authors have gone further in their insistence that the Welsh were quite exceptionally fervent and devoted in adhering, as Hartwell Jones maintained, 'to the Old Faith as rigidly as Spain or Italy at the beginning of the nineteenth (century).'[12] Others, however, have occasionally found it impossible to squeeze a camel of anti-Roman feeling through the eye of an historical needle. They have tried to draw a distinction between the enthusiasm of the Welsh for the old Celtic Church and a tepidity in their response to Rome.[13] Understandably, such nuances have been hotly rejected by the champions of Rome; by none more flatly than a convert from Anglicanism like J. E. Hirsch-Davies. Admitting differences between Celtic civilization and Latin civilization, he nevertheless insisted that they 'cannot reach a point where they are likely to affect the essential character of Catholicism. They are purely external, incidental, subsidiary'. Only 'colour-blindness' could make them appear fundamental.[14]

There follows a second stage in the argument to the effect that when the Reformation came to Wales it sprang from no genuine desire for change. There was no conviction that much in the contemporary church was amiss, nor any deeply felt sense of spiritual deprivation. Innovations were imposed as an act of state by the *diktat* of a government insensitive to the wishes or the needs of the Welsh. This was, in O. M. Edwards's phrase, the 'unwelcome Reformation'. To those on whom it was foisted it came in an alien, unintelligible garb. And as *ffydd Sayson* ('faith of Saxons') it remained.[15]

Then it is usually recalled that the Reformation was introduced at much the same time as the Act of Union and with a common object.[16] Each was directed towards destroying the old Wales and absorbing the country into the new Tudor state and church. It is in fact commonly affirmed that an essential purpose of the Act of Union was to ensure that the Reformation statutes could be made applicable to Wales and safely implemented there.[17] Distasteful as these changes were, they were viable because they were acceptable to the landowning classes. The latter are depicted as selfish, grasping and unprincipled, turning their backs on the claims of nationality and religion in an eager pursuit of the loaves and fishes. In all this the dissolution of the monasteries is a key episode. The monks are generally treated sympathetically and the disappearance of their houses is regarded as a severe loss.[18] The gentry who benefited emerge as thinly-veiled robbers engaged in a desperate and unsavoury scramble for possessions and office, with no holds barred.[19] So naked a pursuit of wealth and power served only to alienate still further a bemused and sullen peasantry.

To that loyal and unshaken mass of 'mute suffering Wales' the new creed and worship remained thoroughly repugnant. Deterred from rebellion by their 'blind unreasoning loyalty' to their *soi-disant* Welsh dynasty and the perfidious gentry, they nevertheless showed their real allegiance by remaining loyal to Catholicism. Like Naaman they may have bowed the knee in the house of Rimmon, but in their hearts they remained true. They welcomed Mary with wholehearted rapture. In her sister's reign their conformity was hollow and brittle even by the Queen's own unexacting standards. It is not unsymptomatic that so much more work should have been done on the Welsh Catholic opposition to Elizabeth, at home and in Europe, than on any other aspect of the Welsh religious history of the period.[20] Here, it seems sometimes to be implied, lies the true history of the Welsh.

All this meant that the Church by law established in Elizabeth's reign was very largely a failure. There were, naturally, some honourable exceptions. A respectful cap is always doffed in the direction of the biblical translators. Their work is recusancy's only serious rival for attention.[21] John Penry, too, is for most writers the clarion voice of conscience whose life and death serve only to reveal more starkly than ever the moral bankruptcy of the Anglican Church.[22] But, these distinguished exceptions apart, the record of the Elizabethan and early Stuart Church has more often than not appeared as lamentably inadequate and uninspired. Broadly speaking, it is possible to isolate five key problems by which it is said to have been bedevilled and with which it never successfully coped. First, there was its crippling poverty, caused chiefly by the rapacity of an erastian state and unscrupulous lay impropriators. Secondly, and arising largely from this poverty, there were the inadequacies of the clergy, many of whom were time-servers, pluralists, and absentees, and almost all of whom were non-preachers.[23] Thirdly, it failed to produce a convincing body of Protestant literature. Fourthly, it was unable to eradicate the Catholic inclinations of the people, as revealed by the existence of a number of recusants and still more numerous secret sympathizers. Finally, the laity, or at least the gentry, continued to be avaricious and largely unmoved by principle. The net result was that the Anglican Church remained an alien plant which took no real root in Wales.[24]

The argument extends beyond the early Stuart period. There exists what might be described as a pervasive notion of a 'religious vacuum' stretching from the end of the medieval Church to the coming of the Methodist Revival. This came about because the initial failure of the Established Church was for the most part unredeemed by the inspiration of Puritanism in the seventeenth century. Wales was one of the most unillumined of the 'dark corners of the kingdom' which Puritan efforts strove to enlighten. After 1660, things became progressively worse. Aggravated by Restoration persecution, the desiccation of Dissenting sects, and Hanoverian latitudinarianism, the Church in Wales sank into ever more moribund state. By the first two or three decades of the eighteenth century it lay, like Florestan, immured in hopeless darkness, until the 'trumpet-call of Methodism' (a favourite metaphor!) brought it new hope of light and life.

This can, it is hoped, be taken as a reasonably fair summary, within its necessarily very restricted compass, of widely-held views about the course of the Reformation in Wales. Before proceeding to attempt any revision of them, it may be useful to make two preliminary points. First, this kind of interpretation is not only a coherent and readily intelligible one, but all its major arguments have some substance. Were this not so it would not have lasted as long as it has. Nor does it need to be entirely jettisoned. What follows in this chapter is not complete rejection so much as extensive modification. Secondly, a great deal of qualification of older views has already taken place. I am by no means the first seriously to question some aspects of traditional interpretation. A few examples only may here be cited. Two generations ago, Thomas Shankland questioned the validity of the supposition that the Church at the end of the seventeenth century and the beginning of the eighteenth was in an almost wholly moribund state.[25] In the 1920s, Professor R. T. Jenkins emphasized the hold which the pre-Methodist Church exercised over the affections of the people in Wales and the danger of applying to it standards of criticism which belong appropriately only to a later age.[26] In more recent years, Professor Dodd's studies have put the gentry and clergy of Elizabethan and Stuart times in much sharper focus, and in a short but penetrating essay he has offered many acute suggestions about the Reformation.[27] Nothing has been more valuable than some of the chapters in Professor David Williams's *Modern Wales*, where the whole subject has been treated with exemplary clarity, astringency and good sense.[28] This can only make us deeply regret that Professor Williams's many contributions to the history of Wales in the eighteenth and nineteenth centuries have never permitted him the time to write that book on the Reformation which was once a favourite project.

But it is now high time to proceed to a stage-by-stage reexamination of the views of the Reformation summarized earlier.

III

THE AGE OF FAITH

It ought to be said at the outset that it seems difficult to draw any valid distinction between a fervid Welsh loyalty to the Celtic Church and a lukewarm acquiescence in the Roman Church. The memory of the former was vividly alive and touched deep chords, but was not regarded as something distinct from or in any way hostile to the latter. It may be true that papal authority seemed to people in Wales to be somewhat remote, unreal and even unwelcome.[29] But this was not an attachment to the memory of an earlier Celtic loyalty so much as part of a common pattern of dislike of the pope's legal jurisdiction while accepting nevertheless his spiritual leadership. Nor, again, can one fail to agree that there was in Wales no doubt, anxiety or hostility to established modes of belief and worship. But, on the basis of protracted attempts to understand the nature of late medieval religion in Wales, I should like here to make three suggestions—very briefly, because the case has been argued at length elsewhere.[30] The first is that the Church of the fifteenth and sixteenth centuries should not be treated, as it so often is, as though it were identical with that of the thirteenth. The crises through which it had passed after 1300 had disastrously weakened some of its most vital institutions —the papacy, the hierarchy and the religious orders—while strengthening the relative position of secular rulers and the laity. Secondly, the very absence of questioning and misgiving in the face of so much that needed correction in the Welsh Church was a symptom of debility not vigour. Finally, it is a serious misconception to suppose that most Welshmen were fanatically devoted to the Roman Church. The faith was accepted unquestioningly by them but was dimly apprehended. Habit rather than conviction was its mainspring. It left them as ill-prepared to defend the old as to welcome the new. No better summing-up could be found than Professor David Williams's reminder that 'men will abandon so lightly only what they lightly hold'.[31]

IV

THE REFORMATION AS AN ACT OF STATE

It is undoubtedly true that the Reformation, particularly in its Henrician and Edwardian phase, was imposed on Wales from above and from without. But we should beware of assuming that as an act of state it was necessarily unwelcome. On the contrary, it was greeted by some Welshmen as a praiseworthy part of the general pattern of stronger and more effectual government which Henry VIII and his ministers introduced into Wales. A poet like Lewis Morgannwg could be as emphatic on this score as a royal servant like Sir John Price.[32] In this context, we should do well to note a very shrewd comment made recently by Professor A. G. Dickens. 'Alongside the Protestant Reformation', he writes, 'the Tudor dynasty undertook another sort of reformation—the conditioning of society to the rule of law . . . the Tudor rehabilitation of law and government has enormous importance . . . for the religious history of Englishmen',[33] and, he might have added, 'of Welshmen'. Because what is really remarkable is that, if the imposition of the Reformation was as unwelcome as has often been suggested, there should have been no rebellion or uprising of any kind in Wales, For it was, after all, in the 15 or 20 years between 1534 and 1553, the only major area of the conservative and Celtic north and west where there was no revolt against Tudor rule in which religion provided at least an excuse for opposition. Admittedly, fears of or hopes for such a rising were voiced in Henry VIII's reign and Edward VI's.[34] But they were never realized and, so far as we can now tell, never looked like coming to anything. In the light of the turbulence and tumult of fifteenth-century Wales this was astonishing. But this was not all. Not only

did Welshmen not themselves rebel, but they could be recruited
with apparently equal confidence to put down the conservatively-
minded westcountrymen who rebelled against Edward's Prayer
Book no less than the very differently orientated malcontents who
supported Wyatt against Mary's Spanish marriage.

Also in this context of an imposed and alien religious regime,
there is need to be more circumspect in the use of that deceptively
convenient catchphrase 'ffydd Sayson'. No doubt it does sum up
the reaction of many, probably the majority, of the Welsh to the
changes of Edward VI's reign when the English service book was
introduced. The Edwardian changes were too rapid and unmeaning-
ful to be acceptable in Wales. The religious verses of South Wales,
the *cwndidau*, and the poems of the north Wales poet, Siôn
Brwynog, are a clear enough index of that. Yet it must at the
same time be remembered that the *cwndid* in which the phrase
'ffydd Sayson' first occurs is a partisan propaganda poem,[35] presumably given circulation in Mary's reign when it was safe to do
so. It is doubtful whether the phrase can safely be applied to
Welsh popular reaction much beyond a limited phase in the reigns
of Edward and Mary. It certainly will not sustain the burden often
put upon it of summing up the attitude of nearly all the Welsh to
the changes of the whole Tudor period. There is a real danger of
carrying the notion of opposition to things English too far. After
all, nearly all the *cwndidau* themselves of the latter half of the
sixteenth century are reformist in tone. Moreover, amid Welsh
writers there is a long line of applause for the solicitude of the
English in bringing the truths of the Reformation to Wales from
John Price, Richard Davies and William Morgan through Vicar
Pritchard down to Charles Edwards, late in the seventeenth
century. In any case, during Elizabeth's reign, the charge of
'foreign-ness' was in large measure answered by the translation
of the Bible and the Prayer Book and also by the Protestant views
of early British history—of which more later.

V

THE REFORMATION WAS ACCEPTED ONLY BECAUSE IT PAID THE GENTRY TO ACQUIESCE

Perhaps it would be as well to deal first with the connexion that
is often traced between the Act of Union and the Reformation. No
Act of Union was needed to implement the Reformation statutes.
All the major measures passed between 1529 and 1534 for the
regulation of the Church and the establishment of the royal
supremacy had been made applicable to Wales and enforced there
before the Act of Union was passed.[36] They had not been contested on either religious or constitutional grounds.

As for the gentry before whom the bait was dangled, no one would deny that most of them were ambitious and acquisitive. This was nothing new among men of their class. The Tudor gentry had no more than a normal dose of original sin. Indeed, as compared with some of their predecessors in the fifteenth century,[37] they were slowly learning to behave with a growing sense of restraint and public responsibility. As for their cynicism in religion, there can surely be no simple equation which will cover them all. To illustrate this, let us take two examples of men of similar generation, training and background. Sir Edward Carne (c. 1500–1561) was a distinguished humanist, lawyer and diplomat. He ended his career as Queen Mary's ambassador at Rome. So deep and genuine were his Catholic loyalties that when Elizabeth came to the throne he did not wish to return home. He got the pope to keep him in Rome, and there he died. Here, it can surely be agreed, was a man loyal to religious principle. Look back at his career, however, and it will be found that he had served Henry VIII as an envoy in the 'King's great matter' and as one of those who took part in dissolving the monasteries. Not merely that; but he had been as eager as anyone in his native Glamorgan to acquire monastic estates and was one of the most successful in the quest for them.[38] Now set side by side with Carne another able lawyer and humanist. One of the most active of the King's visitors of the monasteries, he had also done very well out of monastic lands. He may well have been a key adviser on the policy of introducing the Act of Union. He became secretary of the Council of the Marches, a sheriff and a member of parliament. On the face of it he should have been a typical Tudor careerist with not too many scruples about religion. Yet this man was genuinely attracted to Erasmian reform. He, Sir John Price (?1502–1555), at his own expense published the first book ever to be printed in Welsh because of his deep concern at the religious ignorance of his fellow-countrymen.

It cannot be denied, nor is it necessary to try to do so, that many of the gentry were eager to get their hands on monastic land and tithe and that they succeeded. But this gives no infallible index of their religious loyalties and inclinations. The truly surprising correlation is that many of the families who benefited substantially from the dissolution remained distinctly conservative in their religious allegiance. Recent investigation into the disposal of monastic land in Glamorgan which, Monmouthshire apart, was the Welsh county with the largest and wealthiest monastic estates, shows that almost every one of the families who benefited there were, originally at least, Catholic in sympathy.[39] In neighbouring Monmouthshire, Tintern Abbey's lands provided the earls of Worcester with some of their richest estates, and they were the only family who got monastic land in Wales free or at bargain rates.

Yet it was the earls of Worcester whose influence made Monmouth-shire the staunchest recusant stronghold in Wales. Similarly, one of the most ironic twists in the religious history of north Wales is that tithe which once belonged to Bardsey Abbey should, in Elizabeth's reign, have gone to the support of the Catholic intelligencer-in-chief on the Continent, Hugh Owen.[40]

Much of the misunderstanding arises out of a misplaced senti-ment which the dissolution of the monasteries has aroused.[41] It fails to appreciate the extent to which the monasteries had declined by the 1530s. Nor does it take sufficiently into account the extent to which monastic property was already being farmed out to tenants great and small or the extraordinary lengths to which the government was willing to go to protect the interests of the tenants. Moreover, the gentry's view of what constituted their interests should not be interpreted in terms too narrowly economic. There was a whole complex of considerations, political and social as well as strictly economic, which made demands on their loyalty. To this point of crucial importance we shall have to return later.[42]

VI

REJECTION OF THE REFORMATION BY THE
MASS OF THE WELSH

It would be foolish to contest the view that many of the changes enforced by statute in the course of the Reformation went against the grain, when indeed they were not meaningless. Nor need any-one be surprised by the stubborn persistence of medieval habits and practices as reported by the Protestant bishops of Wales.[43] This is surely what might be expected in relatively poor, isolated pastoral communities. All too frequently in this context, however, the wrong sort of comparisons are made with conditions else-where. It gets overlooked that much of what is said about the pro-gress of the Reformation in England is applicable almost only to the most highly developed areas of the south and east. The appro-priate places for comparison with Wales are dioceses like Carlisle, or counties like Derbyshire, or European countries like Norway.[44] There, evidence is readily found of the same kind of survivals as occur in Wales.

Having agreed that there were plenty of vestigial remains of older beliefs and worship among the Welsh, it is necessary to make two reservations about their nature which are not always borne in mind. First, that the medieval practices most obstinately clung to were not always the ones that commended themselves to thoughtful Catholics any more than to Reformers. The weakness of late medieval devotion had tended to be overemphasis on the external mechanisms of grace and the consuetudinal performance of outward acts unaccompanied by as clear and positive an inward understanding of their significance as might have been wished. The persistence of customary practice alongside widespread ignorance brought down a double condemnation. The reforming bishops and others attacked the survival of what appeared to them as unenlightened superstition.[45] Welsh papist authors, on the other hand, deplored what seemed to their eyes to be the lapse of the population into abysmal ignorance of even the rudiments of the Christian religion.[46] This they blamed on the Reformation, and modern authors have frequently accepted their standpoint.[47] But there is good evidence for assuming that such ignorance was a great deal older than the sixteenth century, and it certainly continued far beyond it. It was censured by observers as widely different in time and standpoint as Archbishop Pecham in the thirteenth century, Siôn Cent in the fifteenth, John Price in the sixteenth, and Griffith Jones in the eighteenth.[48] It was a deficiency which was not attributable to the official creed adopted but one which arose out of social conditions. As long as such a high degree of illiteracy survived among the commonalty and so extensive a neglect of books among their social superiors—and this was the unfailing burden of complaint among Welsh religious authors—so, too, would an immense and ineradicable mass of ignorance and superstition. It was a condition which neither zealous Roman nor Anglican observers of Wales found tolerable, but which both were almost equally powerless to change significantly in the short run.

The second comment to be offered on these survivals is a suggestion that they have usually been mistakenly taken as a basis for postulating strongly Catholic sympathies in Wales. The relation of these vestiges to Catholic dogma was, however, very tenuous. They are far removed from the Council of Trent and the Catholic Reformation. They have almost nothing to do with papal authority or doctrinal certitude. They arise from no struggles of conscience or a painful search for salvation. What they do represent is the carry-over by an unchanging peasantry of a fixed round of custom and habit in an age of rapid, officially-enforced religious change. This routine was as age-old, familiar and reassuring as their agricultural operations. It was linked with the seasons of the year, health and sickness, and the great milestones of human existence: birth, marriage and death. Maintaining such customs could be, and usually was, far removed from recusancy. They could, with minimal stress or contradiction, be combined with outward conformity to the Established Church. All the more so when there was so much in the appearance, procedure and worship of that church that could be reminiscent of the old. Some of the practices were as much pagan as they were Christian. But they, too, survived happily in some rural areas of Wales down to our own century.[49]

VII

THE FAILURE OF THE ESTABLISHED CHURCH

Of the five key problems by which it was beset, the first noted was that of poverty. There can be no denying that the Church in Wales was poor or that its poverty gave rise to grave short-comings.[50] But then, it had been poor all through its history and it would be very difficult to prove that it was, relative to the Church elsewhere in the Queen's realm, any poorer than it had been before or that the abuses attributable to indigence were any worse. Admittedly, also, the Church suffered from lay rapacity in the earlier stages of the Reformation and was continuing to do so.[51] But the point so frequently made about the responsibility of lay impropriators for the poverty of the Church—Archbishop Edwards, the arch-enemy of Disestablishment, not unnaturally held this early act of disendowment to be primarily responsible for all shortcomings![52]—is one that is capable of serious misunder-standing. Lay impropriators had, for all practical purposes, existed long before the Reformation when monks farmed out to laymen the tithes of parishes appropriated to their monasteries.[53] Again it is argued that clerical marriage added greatly to the economic burdens of the clergy and their families. This is probably true; but we should remember that clerical marriage in pre-Reforma-tion Wales was so widely prevalent that legal sanction for the custom may have made remarkably little difference to the practical situation. The argument that inflation imposed a growing pressure on clerical incomes may well have much more relevance. The stipends of unbeneficed clergy and incumbents of unendowed livings probably did not keep in step with the rise in prices.[54] But where, as was usually the case, incumbents depended largely on returns in kind from glebe and tithe this must have provided for a distinctly greater element of elasticity in their income. For example, in 1583, Bishop Middleton of St. David's estimated that the incomes of his clergy had trebled in value since 1535.[55] Still more to the point is the notable success of the Church in attracting the younger sons of gentry and substantial freeholders to its benefices.[56] This it could hardly have done if the prospects it held out were utterly bleak and unremunerative.

The second shortcoming was the indifferent quality of the clergy. Once more, the criticisms made are in some measure justified. Dislodging tenacious incumbents of the old kind was virtually impossible. Poor livings unquestionably led to pluralism and failed to attract preachers and men of talent. Nevertheless, the general quality of clerical recruitment has probably been seriously under-estimated. Much of the criticism of it derives from the complaints of the Elizabethan bishops. But we should remember that resident and critical bishops of this kind were a relatively new pheno-menon in Wales. They were men setting a distinctly higher standard of training and achievement for their parish clergy than had previously been expected—and so, in fairness, were their antagonists in the Catholic seminaries on the Continent. The Elizabethan bishops were taking such steps as they could to achieve a higher standard, and not without some success. Before the end of the sixteenth century, an impressive and growing number of the clergy being ordained had been through grammar schools and universities.[57] There may possibly have been some danger of attaching too much value to this kind of education; but at least this was a recognizable improvement on the educational attain-ments of the clergy's medieval predecessors.[58] Another equally sharp contrast was that the majority of the higher clergy were now of Welsh origin, were resident, and were in a number of instances men of some distinction.[59] Neither should we overlook the worth of many of the parish clergy. The clerical patrons of the poets of north Wales emerge in a distinctly favourable light;[60] so, too, do their counterparts in the south as authors and patrons of the *cwndidau*. To the credit of the clergy in Wales it has to be recorded that, for the next century or two when the gentry were becoming almost wholly anglicized, they remained committed to teaching their flock in the only language that most of them understood. Whatever the clergy's shortcomings, they provided virtually the sole nucleus of a Welsh-speaking intelligentsia. The fact that they were married helped greatly in this respect because of the effective transmission of the tradition in clerical families. On the vexed question of how many of them were preachers, we have to remember that before a cleric could be licensed as a preacher, vastly more exacting qualifications would be required of him than would be the case today. 'A man was not then deemed worthy to be called a preacher unless he could hold forth for a length of time that would tire the patience of the most orderly modern congregation'.[61] This goes a long way towards explaining the fewness of official preachers. It may also explain the disparity between John Penry's estimate of fewer than twelve preachers in the whole of Wales and George Owen's indignant rejoinder that there were more than that number in Pembrokeshire alone![62]

On the third count, that of Protestant literature, no one could fail to agree that in terms of output the production of Welsh printed books during the century from 1547 to 1642 was meagre and ineffectual. This was true not merely by comparison with that of England and other European countries but also in the light of the standards and expectations of the Welsh humanists themselves. Their view of the need and opportunity created by the Renaissance and Reformation has been set forth in more detail elsewhere.[63] Here only a few main conclusions can briefly be indicated. First, the failure of Welsh humanists to achieve their ambition was not brought about by lack of insight or will on their part, but by the 'unripeness' of social and economic conditions in Wales, which were at this time almost certainly incapable of sustaining a prolific output of printed books. Again, it has to be acknowledged in their favour that their translation of the Bible and Prayer Book, and the other volumes they published, constituted a real triumph; and the seriousness of the obstacles they overcame in order to achieve this is far from being fully or generally appreciated.[64] In addition, they gave the Established Church a strongly patriotic appeal not only by the successful use of the vernacular in worship, but also by creating a version of early British history which represented the Reformation as a restoration of the Church of the Golden Age of their British forebears and so a consummation of the whole Tudor claim to have vindicated the messianic prophecies of a thousand years.[65] Finally, these efforts did constitute a decisive turning point insofar as they ensured that the Reformation was to be brought to Wales in Welsh. It should not be forgotten that there was nothing necessary or inevitable in this. There were, on the contrary, inimical forces of power and persuasiveness militating against such a decision, as many Welsh writers testified.[66] Admittedly, the task of making Reformation doctrines intelligible and acceptable was no more than begun. But it is hard to see how much more could have been achieved at this stage. To have made justification by faith, or the priesthood of all believers, or individual meditation on the Scriptures, a reality among large sectors of the population would have required a much higher degree of literacy and a much readier access to books than existed in Wales. No sufficient social stimulus existed to produce so desirable a state. Before it came about there had to be a century and a half of effort, much of it heavily subsidized from outside Wales, plus the spur applied by civil war and the fear of further social tumult. But at least it had been ensured, even before the end of Elizabeth's reign, that Wales would be spared the kind of cleavage that existed in Scotland or Ireland, where virtually no early effort was made to propagate Reformation doctrine in the Celtic languages spoken by large masses of the people. If this had been the fate of Wales, what would have happened? It is impossible to tell with certainty. The country might, like Cornwall, have been peaceably anglicized. But if, as befell Ireland and parts of the Scottish Highlands, it had had the effect of linking nationality, language and recusancy,

Wales might have been subjected to a repression even more savage than that which fell to the lot of Ireland or the Highlands.

Catholic exiles, recusants, 'fellow-travellers' and sympathizers were not, in reality, such a formidable opposition to the establishment in Wales as the very minute attention they have received at the hands of historians might suggest. If the Reformation in general is a dog that hasn't barked in Welsh history, recusancy may be one that has barked too much. This is understandable. The exiles and martyrs sacrificing comfort, security, even life itself, are extremely attractive figures; recusants defying the might of a persecuting state are hardly less appealing. Furthermore, the persecution of this minority has left so much more in the way of records than the undisturbed placidity of the majority.[67] But this should not conceal the fact that the Counter-Reformation was a resounding failure as far as Wales was concerned. For this, the coercive policy of the state was largely responsible. It outlawed the adherents of Roman religion, executing priests, excluding lay recusants from office and favour and threatening them with crippling fines and imprisonment. But there were other reasons for failure, too. The Counter-Reformers came up against many of the same daunting hurdles as the Reformers: the dire shortage of suitable priests; the difficulty of printing Welsh books; the still greater difficulty of getting enough people to read them; and a desolating lack of theological or controversial interest. There was no effective campaign in Wales for reconversion. Though the country produced a number of seminary priests, few of them came back to proselytize in Wales. There were damaging differences of view among the exiles and all too little sense of urgency. By the end of Elizabeth's reign there were only 808 known recusants as against 212,450 regular churchgoers. The number may have increased slightly during James I's reign, but continued to be no more than an insignificant fraction of the whole population.[68] This has led historians to postulate the existence of large numbers of secret believers.[69] But this thesis of a swarm of Nicodemuses is based on no very tangible evidence. It might be nearer the mark to suggest that the beliefs and practices of the majority were so custom-bound, ill-formed and unsophisticated as to be the despair of the earnest-minded of either religious persuasion. Even that small minority who were articulate in their expression of opinions and values in religious poetry offered little theology and less dogma. The greater part of the free verses, including those of Vicar Pritchard, consisted of simple biblical allusions and stern moral precepts which could have been largely applicable to men of any Christian persuasion. This helps to explain why the Established Church met with so little overt opposition. Not because there existed widespread and intelligent attachment to Protestant doctrine

as such, but because of a comparable absence of any deep and
discriminating regard for Catholicism. Only a successful campaign
among the gentry could have turned the tide in favour of the old
faith. But they showed no enthusiasm for opening their doors to
the seminary priests or their doctrines. And they had good reason
for their reluctance.

That brings us to a discussion of the relationship of the Church
with the laity, and that, for all practical purposes, means the
gentry. They have had, as Dr. Penry Williams has rightly said, 'a
discouragingly bad press'[70] from Tudor times down to our own.
In the first Elizabeth's day, and after, there was criticism a-plenty
of their indifference to religion. It came from widely diverse
quarters: recusant, Anglican and Puritan.[71] But all these critics
agreed that the gentry were, by and large, greedy, lax and devoid
of religious principle. No doubt much of this censure was deserved.
But there is another side to the case which ought to be put. The
rhetoric of ardent pulpit critics, of whatever complexion, is
partisan and highly-coloured. It ought not to be taken, as so often
it is, for gospel truth. For all that was said of the laity's deficiencies, if a share in producing religious literature be any guide,
they were nearly as active as the clergy. Take away men like
William Salesbury or Maurice Kyffin or Rowland Vaughan from
among the writers, or Humphrey Toy or Rowland Heylyn or
Thomas Myddelton from among the patrons, and the story of
Welsh literature would be sorely impoverished. There had been
nothing in the Middle Ages to compare with this degree of lay
initiative. It speaks well for the value of the Reformation's shift
of emphasis to the importance of lay commitment. However, the
key to the gentry's rôle lies not in religion but in government.
They could not separate the question of authority in the Church
from that of authority in the state and in society. Neither could
the laity anywhere else in Europe, in the long run.[72] What really
counted with most of the Welsh gentry was the security of the
political and social order from threats internal and external. Its
stability was guaranteed in their eyes by the successful liaison
between their pre-eminence in the locality and royal jurisdiction
at the centre. The relationship was not one of unbroken harmony
and there were often clashes of interest between private advantage
and public duty; but on the whole it was a successful working
partnership. That alignment was not imperilled by anything in the
Reformation changes of the Tudor state. On the contrary, the new
arrangements gained strength because they were being enforced
with the full backing of law and government, and were not being
agitated for in tumult and upheaval by dissident groups of nobles,
merchants or artisans. They brought about a settlement that was
the more attractive for being erastian, comprehensive and

undemanding. It offered the further incentive of a church over which the gentry could exercise a great deal of influence in terms of patronage and livings, choice and control of incumbents, and enforcement of statutes regulating attendance. The Church became associated with two kinds of patriotic loyalty; the one Tudor, the other Welsh. The Tudor loyalty sprang from participating in politics and local government, which led to a growing attachment to a whole complex of institutions, including the crown, common law, Parliament and the Established Church.[73] The Welsh loyalty was fostered by the use of the vernacular in worship and the acceptance of Reformed religion as a return to that great fountain-head of Welsh religious life, the Celtic Church. Conformist indoctrination was reinforced by the trend towards an increased measure of formal education for the gentry in grammar school, university, and Inns of Court. Conversely, the Roman religion was becoming increasingly synonymous with sedition and disloyalty, with external enemies, the menace of invasion and the fear of internal disorder. 'I protest I would sooner spend my living, and my life also, than the enemy should possess any part of Her Majesty's dominions' said a Pembrokeshire gentleman, Sir John Wogan, in 1599.[74] He spoke for most of his fellow-gentry. Whatever shortcomings may have defaced the Church in the eyes of ardent Puritans or even Anglican bishops, it was, in the eyes of the ruling classes, a prime bulwark of order and stability. And this was what mattered most to them. This closely-knit unity between squirearchy and Church is the key to understanding much of what happened in Stuart Wales.

VIII

THE 'SPIRITUAL VACUUM'

Now we come to the last and most difficult theme, that of the 'vacuum' thought to exist between the end of the medieval Church and the coming of the Methodist Revival. It can be treated only in the baldest and most sketchy way. But, however inadequately, dealt with it must be. Partly because the Methodist Revival is, in all important respects, the delayed impact of the Reformation in Wales. Partly because this idea of a religious vacuum seems to have been productive of more misunderstanding than almost anything else in Welsh historiography. This misunderstanding has grown out of one root cause: that insufficient account has been taken of the whole social context of which men's religious beliefs and allegiance are only a part. There has been a tendency in Wales to regard religious doctrines as self-evident truths which, once they were clearly grasped and effectively proclaimed by those responsible for promulgating Christian doctrine, would be widely accepted for their own sake and in their own right. This has led to four basic misconceptions. First, the 'failure' of the Elizabethan and Stuart Church has been over-stated. Second, the influence of Puritanism has been undervalued. Third, and perhaps most serious, there has been a thorough mis-conception of what was happening in the social and religious milieu of Wales from 1660 to *c.* 1740. Finally, the significance of the impact of the first great Methodist leaders has been over-emphasized. Let us take each of these suggestions in turn and examine them briefly.

The issue of the 'failure' of the Church between 1558 and 1640 has already been sufficiently aired. All that perhaps needs to be recalled is the serious underestimate of the limitations placed by social conditions upon the effective propagation of reformed doctrines, and inadequate appreciation of the issues of lasting consequence determined in Elizabeth's reign.

Puritanism is generally represented as having made only a restricted appeal because it came from England, whereas the real reasons lie in the unsuitability of the social not the national environment in Wales. Furthermore, Puritanism has become too narrowly and exclusively associated with Dissenters, when in truth the Puritan ethos could and did survive strongly among Anglicans and Dissenters after the Restoration. It, indeed, was the main-spring of the philanthropic and educational crusades—the Welsh Trust, the S.P.C.K., the Circulating Schools—launched among the Welsh during the period.

But probably the worst misconception arises from the undue emphasis which has been placed on the blemishes in the Church during the period from 1660–1730. The unlovely tableau of non-resident bishops, nepotism, pluralism, non-residence, neglected buildings, and the like, is too familiar to need recounting. (In passing, though, it is worth noting that it is not always realized how much this is drawn from the single source of Erasmus Saunders's *State of the Diocese of St. David's.*[75]) The undis-tinguished record of abuse and laxity may all be true. But it is not the real cause of the Methodist Revival, any more than similar corruption in the medieval Church was the cause of the sixteenth-century Reformation. A generation ago, the great French historian, Lucien Febvre, wrote a brilliant article, 'Une question mal posée: les origines de la Réforme française', precisely to make this point.[76] Exactly the same could be said of the origins of the Methodist Revival. It, also, is all too often 'une question mal posée'. Admittedly we have been getting much closer to posing the appro-priate question and getting a better answer in reassessing the importance and value of the efforts of the Welsh Trust or the S.P.C.K.[77] But even now, we have a long way to go in appreciating that this was not an age of torpor but an age of gestation. Attention should be increasingly directed to vitally important considerations often overlooked or undervalued. There was, first of all, an enormous increase in the number of books published in Welsh. Three times as many different titles were published between 1660 and 1700 as between 1540 and 1660. Between 1700 and 1740, there were about three times as many again as between 1660 and 1700. The overwhelming majority of the books published are concerned with religion. For the first time Welsh Bibles and Prayer Books became really widely diffused among people. Editions of as many as 10,000 Bibles were published at as modest a price as four shillings, and a great deal of literature was distributed free.[78] Until this had happened, how could the central doctrines of the Reformation have had much substance? Moreover, this religious literature tended to emphasize an individual's responsibility for his own soul,—favourite reading was Vicar Pritchard's *Canwyll y Cymry*, and Welsh translations of *Pilgrim's Progress* and *The Practice of Piety*. In many instances the books implied that religion was a matter of inward discipline and conviction rather than conforming to the external requirements of the visible Church. For the first time, there had been brought into being, by the beginning of the eighteenth century, the same kind of climate among a sizeable proportion of the Welsh-speaking population as had been created among large sectors of the population in parts of Europe in the fifteenth and sixteenth centuries when the printing press was first evolved. The basic characteristics are much the same: a dramatic extension of religious literature and literacy; an emphasis on individual responsibility and personal piety; an independence of formal means of religious instruction, which might often be corrupt or ineffective; and the nurturing of a need for a new and different kind of religious satisfaction: more immediate, subjective and intense.

In addition, it may well be that these cultural changes were interfused with displacements of considerable magnitude in the social structure. Our ignorance of these at the present time makes it impossible to do much more than speculate what they might be. There seem good reasons for concluding, however, that there was a growth in the size of landed estates, with a consequent depression in status of many families of minor gentry.[79] They now became reduced to the level of substantial farmers, professional men, or craftsmen.[80] No longer able to afford to send their sons to universities, or even to grammar schools in some instances, they tended to be excluded from cosmopolitan upper-class culture. They were turned in increasingly on what was available to them in Welsh: a staple diet, as far as printed literature was concerned, of piety and religion. The decline in the status of many of the smaller gentry was accompanied by a trend towards rather larger tenant holdings on the one hand and, on the other, towards a depression of a very large class of cottagers, labourers and poor. But it is essential to remember that it was not to the poor that Methodism made its appeal, but to those with a measure of respectability and a stake in property, however modest. It was precisely among these groups that literacy of the kind discussed earlier appears to have made its most striking gains.

Lastly there is the role of the early Methodist leaders. The historical stereotype is that of a group of men of genius, consumed with all the power of a heavenly inspiration, their message running like a flame through stubble. To this was added the further appeal of their effective use of the Welsh language—as though Morgan Llwyd, the seventeenth-century Puritan, knew no Welsh, or as though the Methodist, Hywel Harris, never preached in English! Of course, these first Welsh Methodists were men of outstanding gifts and one can no more explain Methodism without them than Lutheranism without Luther or Wesleyanism without Wesley. But in an excessive preoccupation with leaders our vision is in danger of becoming hopelessly out of focus. It is high time we looked longer and harder at their congregations. For success sprang only partly, and not primarily, from the evangelizers. Its true secret lay in those whom they evangelized. Had their ears still been stopped by the same wax of ignorance and illiteracy as those of their forebears, that trumpet-call of the Methodists, no matter how shrill and urgent, would have sounded in vain. As it was, however, it vibrated excitingly in the heads and hearts of a large audience of religious literates, capable of an appropriate response. With them the Reformation came of age in Wales.

NOTES

* Delivered before the Society in London, 25 January 1966. *Chairman*: Sir David Hughes Parry, Q.C., M.A., LL.D., D.C.L.

[1] A detailed bibliography will be found in *A Bibliography of the History of Wales* (2nd. ed., Cardiff, 1962), Sections G and H, *passim*; cf. also Supplement I (1963) and II (1966) in *Bulletin of the Board of Celtic Studies*, xx (1963), 126-64, xxii (1966), 49-70.

[2] Elwyn Davies (ed.), *Celtic Studies in Wales: a Survey* (Cardiff, 1963), p. 66.

[3] See, for example, *Bibliographie de la Réforme* (1450-1648). *Ouvrages parus de 1940 à 1955*. I. *Allemagne, Pays-Bas* (Leyden, 1958); II. *Belgique, Suède, Norvège, Danemark, Irlande, États-Unis*, (ibid. 1960); III. *Italie, Espagne, Portugal* (ibid., 1961); IV. *France, Angleterre, Suisse* (ibid., 1963); V. *Pologne, Hongrie, Tchécoslovaquie, Finlande* (ibid., 1965).

[4] Some of the best and most interesting work of recent years has been on these themes, e.g., Professor A. H. Dodd on the gentry and the Welsh interest in Parliament, Dr. Penry Williams on the Council of the Marches, Professor Ogwen Williams on Tudor Gwynedd, or Dr. Geraint Dyfnallt Owen on the social scene in Elizabethan Wales.

[5] For a general description of the records of the Church in Wales, deposited at the National Library, see J. Conway Davies, 'The records of the Church in Wales', *N.L.W. Journal*, iv (1945-6).

⁶ For instance, Hugh Williams, *Christianity in Early Britain* (Oxford, 1912); V. E. Nash-Williams, *The Early Christian Monuments of Wales* (Cardiff, 1950); E. G. Bowen, *The Settlements of the Celtic Saints in Wales* (Cardiff, 1954); Nora Chadwick (ed.), *Studies in the Early British Church* (Cambridge, 1958).

⁷ *Wales* (London, 1907), p. 347.

⁸ W. Llewelyn Williams, *The Making of Modern Wales* (London, 1919), p. 197.

⁹ G. Hartwell Jones, *Celtic Britain and the Pilgrim Movement* (Hon. Soc. of Cymmrodorion, London, 1912), p. 3; cf. W. J. Gruffydd, *Llenyddiaeth Cymru: Rhyddiaith o* 1540 *hyd* 1660 (Wrecsam, 1926), p. 136.

¹⁰ Iorwerth C. Peate, *Cymru a'i Phobl* (Cardiff, 1931), chapter viii; cf. Olivier Loyer, *Les Chrétientés Celtiques* (Paris, 1965), pp. 108-12.

¹¹ O. M. Edwards, *Wales*; W. Llewelyn Williams, *The Making of Modern Wales*.

¹² Hartwell Jones, op. cit., pp. 2-3; cf. David Mathew, *The Celtic Peoples and Renaissance Europe* (London, 1933), pp. 31-2; W. Ambrose Bebb, *Cyfnod y Tuduriaid* (Wrecsam, 1939), pp. 73-6.

¹³ J. W. Willis-Bund, *The Celtic Church of Wales* (London, 1897), was the foremost advocate of this view. There are more indistinct echoes of it in other later authors.

¹⁴ J. E. Hirsch-Davies, *Catholicism in Medieval Wales* (London, 1916), pp. 4-5.

¹⁵ ibid., p. 142; cf. Hartwell Jones, op. cit., p. 546; Lawrence Thomas, *The Reformation in the Old Diocese of Llandaff* (Cardiff, 1930), p. xiv.

¹⁶ ibid., pp. xiii-xv; cf. David Williams, *Modern Wales* (London, 1950), p. 46.

¹⁷ William Rees, 'The union of England and Wales', *Cymmrodorion Transactions*, 1937, pp. 27-100; cf. David Williams, *Modern Wales*, p. 34.

¹⁸ Thomas Parry, *A History of Welsh Literature*. Trans. Sir Idris Bell (Oxford, 1962), pp. 192-3; cf. also W. A. Bebb, *Machlud y Mynachlogydd* (Llandysul, 1937)—the only book, but not an adequate one, available on the dissolution in Wales.

¹⁹ Mathew, *Celtic Peoples*, p. 50; cf. Geraint Dyfnallt Owen, *Elizabethan Wales: the Social Scene* (Cardiff, 1962), pp. 216-7.

²⁰ For details see *Bibliography*, pp. 137-40, 176-9; cf. also *BBCS*, xx, 145-9

²¹ *Bibliography*, pp. 136-7.

²² Especially William Pierce, *John Penry* (London, 1923). For Archbishop A. G. Edwards on the other hand, Penry was a 'turbulent and unstable visionary', *Landmarks in the History of the Welsh Church* (London, 1913), p. 108.

²³ For an introduction to this subject, see below, pp. 173-5, 177-80.

²⁴ Gruffydd, *Llenyddiaeth Cymru*, pp. 136-7; Llewelyn Williams, *Modern Wales*, pp. 197-201.

²⁵ 'Sir John Philipps and the charity schools movement', *Cymmrodorion Trans.*, 1904-5.

²⁶ *Hanes Cymru yn y Ddeunawfed Ganrif* (Cardiff, 1931), ch. II.

²⁷ See particularly his articles in *Cymmrodorion Trans.*, 1942-8, *Studies in Stuart Wales* (Cardiff, 1952), ch. I., and his article on the Reformation in *The Welsh Church Congress* (*Llandrindod*) *Handbook* 1953, pp. 18-41.

²⁸ See especially chs. iv, v, viii, ix, and x.

²⁹ Dodd, *Welsh Church Congress Handbook*, 1953, pp. 25-6.

³⁰ See my *The Welsh Church from Conquest to Reformation* (Cardiff, 1962).

³¹ *Modern Wales*, p. 61.

³² Glanmor Williams, *Welsh Church*, pp. 545-6; cf. the introduction to *Yny Lhyvyr Hwn*, ed. J.H. Davies (Bangor, 1902).

³³ *The English Reformation* (London, 1964), p. 14.

³⁴ See Chapuys's reports, *Letters and Papers, Foreign and Domestic of the Reign of Henry VIII* . . . (23 vols. London, 1862-1932), vi, 902; vii, 957, 1057, 1141, 1193, 1534; cf. also the views of the rebel priests, Feron and Hales, ibid., viii, 567, 609 (iv); and Bishop William Barlow's claims of a link between some of the St. David's canons and the Pilgrimage of Grace, ibid., xii, 830. The changes of Edwards VI's reign also provoked fears of rebellion, see below, pp. 130-31.

[35] See 'Trigo yn ddwl, mewn tri meddwl', by Thomas ab Ieuan ap Rhys, in L. J. Hopkin James ('Hopcyn') and T. C. Evans ('Cadrawd'), *Hen Gwndidau, Carolau, a Chywyddau* (Bangor, 1910), pp. 33-4.

[36] For example, in the act of 1529 concerning mortuaries (21 Henry VIII, c. 6), special provisions were made in relation to Wales and the Marches, see Ivor Bowen, *The Statutes of Wales* (London, 1908), p. 50. Under the Act of Supremacy the clergy of the Welsh dioceses were required to take the oath in the same way as their English brethren. The returns for the Welsh dioceses will be found in P.R.O., E36/63, pp. 1-20.

[37] For one well-documented example, see R. A. Griffiths, 'Gruffydd ap Nicholas and the fall of the house of Lancaster', *The Welsh History Review*, II (1965), 213-32.

[38] See below, pp. 102-4.

[39] See below, pp. 104-7.

[40] E. G. Jones, *Cymru a'r Hen Ffydd* (Cardiff, 1951), p. 15.

[41] See, for instance, Ambrose Bebb, *Machlud y Mynachlogydd*, ch. x.

[42] Below, sect. VII.

[43] See, for example, Richard Davies's report of 1570 in D. R. Thomas, *Life and Work of Davies and Salesbury* (Oswestry, 1902), pp. 37-44, or that of Nicholas Robinson in David Mathew, 'Some Elizabethan documents', *BBCS*, vi (1931-3), 77-8; cf. also Pierce, *John Penry*, pp. 119-130.

[44] *V. C. H. Cumberland*, II (1905), 62ff; Kenneth Charlton, *Education in Renaissance England* (London, 1965), pp. 94-5, for conditions in Derbyshire. For Norway see G. R. Elton (ed.), *The New Cambridge Modern History*. II. *The Reformation* (Cambridge, 1958), pp. 142-4.

[45] See note 43 above; cf. also Bishop Middleton's articles for St. David's diocese, 1583, published in W. P. M. Kennedy, *Elizabethan Episcopal Administration* (3 vols. London, 1924), III, 145-52.

[46] For the introduction to *Drych Cristianogawl* (1585), see Garfield H. Hughes, *Rhagymadroddion, 1547-1649* (Cardiff, 1951), pp. 52-4; cf. Gruffydd, *Llenyddiaeth Cymru*, p. 140; and *Rhyddiaith Gymraeg: Yr Ail Gyfrol* (Cardiff, 1956), pp. 192-4.

[47] Cf. W. J. Gruffydd, cited in E. G. Jones, *Cymru a'r Hen Ffydd*, p. 7.

[48] Williams, *Welsh Church*, pp. 22, 237-9, 335; cf. W. Moses Williams (ed.) *Selections from the Welch Piety* (Cardiff, 1939), *passim*.

[49] D. Edmondes Owen, 'Pre-Reformation survivals in Radnorshire', *Cymmrodorion Trans.*, 1910-11, pp. 92-114.

[50] See the present writer's 'Ecclesiastical landholding in Wales' in Joan Thirsk (ed.), *The Agrarian History of England and Wales*, volume iv (Cambridge, 1967), 381-95.

[51] See below, pp. 173-4, 177-80; G. Williams, 'The Collegiate Church of Llanddewibrefi', *Ceredigion*, IV, iv (1963), 336-52; Edwards, *Landmarks*, pp. 102-7.

[52] ibid., p. 107.

[53] Williams, *Welsh Church*, pp. 350-2.

[54] In St. David's diocese in 1583, only 11 out of 79 curates' stipends were worth more than £10; and 33 were worth £5 or less. In Llandaff in 1603, only 7 curacies out of 31 were worth more than £5 a year. P.R.O., S.P.12/vol. 65, i; B.M. Harleian MS., 595.

[55] P.R.O., S.P.R.12/vol. 65, i.

[56] Pryce, *Diocese of Bangor*, p. xxx; Dodd, *Stuart Wales*, pp. 38-9.

[57] Pryce, *Diocese of Bangor*, pp. xxx-xxxi.

[58] For the doubts expressed, see Kenneth Charlton, *Education in Renaissance England*, pp. 129-30, 154-9, 167-8; for the medieval priesthood, Williams, *Welsh Church*, pp. 327-31.

[59] Pryce, *Diocese of Bangor*, pp. xxxv-vi; D. R. Thomas, *History of the Diocese of St. Asaph* (3 vols. Oswestry, 1908-13), I, 317 ff. For the higher clergy before the Reformation, Williams, *Welsh Church*, pp. 312-25.

[60] Enid Pierce Roberts, 'Canu Wiliam Cynwal i Glerigwyr', *Trafodion Cymdeithas Hanes Sir Ddinbych*, 14 (1965), 120-8.

[61] Edwards, *Landmarks*, p. 99.

[62] John Penry, *Three Treatises concerning Wales*, ed. David Williams (Cardiff, 1960), p. 39; George Owen, *The Description of Pembrokeshire* (4 vols. Cymmr. Record Ser., no. 1., London, 1902-36), III, 99.

[63] In the present writer's *Dadeni, Diwygiad a Diwylliant Cymru* (Cardiff, 1964).

[64] See below, pp. 202-4.

[65] See below, pp. 183-5, 212-3; cf. also Saunders Lewis, 'Damcaniaeth Eglwysig Brotestannaidd', *Efrydiau Catholig*, II (1947), 36-55.

[66] See especially Bishop William Morgan's Latin dedication to his translation of the Bible and and Maurice Kyffin's introduction to his translation of Bishop Jewel's *Apology*.

[67] It is noticeable that, because records of persecution have survived in some quantity, nearly all the volumes on ecclesiastical history in the Victoria County Histories give far more space and attention to Elizabethan recusancy than to any other aspect of the religious history of the period.

[68] E. G. Jones, *Cymru a'r Hen Ffydd*, pp. 38-9, 45-62.

[69] ibid., p. 40; A. H. Dodd, 'Wales and the Scottish Succession', *Cymmrodorion Trans.*, 1937, p. 206.

[70] 'The Tudor Gentry' in A. J. Roderick (ed.), *Wales through the Ages*, II (Llandybie, 1960), 31.

[71] For recusant criticism, see Hughes, *Rhagymadroddion*, pp. 52-4; for Anglican criticism, Thomas, *Life of Davies and Salesbury*, pp. 37-8, 41-4, 48-9: and for a Puritan view, Penry, *Three Treatises*, pp. 32-6.

[72] Joel Hurstfield, *The Reformation Crisis*, (London 1965), pp. 1-7.

[73] A. H. Dodd, 'The pattern of politics in Stuart Wales', *Cymmrodorion Trans.*, 1948, pp. 20-7.

[74] *Calendar State Papers, Domestic*, 1598-1601, p. 269.

[75] First published in 1721, it has been reprinted by the University of Wales Press in 1949.

[76] 'Une question mal posée: les origines de la Réforme française et le probleme général des causes de la Réforme', *Revue historique*, CLXI (1929), 1-73.

[77] See M. G. Jones, *The Charity School Movement* (Cambridge, 1938); John Davies, *Bywyd a Gwaith Moses Williams* (Cardiff, 1937); and Mary Clement, *The S.P.C.K. and Wales, 1699-1740* (London, 1954).

[78] For the books published in Wales during this period, see William Rowlands, *Cambrian Bibliography* (Llanidloes, 1869); for the editions of the Bible, John Ballinger, *The Bible in Wales* (London, 1906).

[79] A. H. Dodd, 'The landed gentry after 1600', *Wales through the Ages*, II, 78-85; Peter Roberts, 'The decline of the Welsh squires in the eighteenth century', *N.L.W.J.*, XIII, 2 (1963), 157-73.

[80] On the importance of craftsmen in the Methodist Revival, see Dafydd Jenkins, 'The part played by craftsmen in the religious history of modern Wales', *The Welsh Anvil: Yr Einion*, VI (1959), 90-7.

II. THE REFORMATION IN SIXTEENTH-CENTURY CAERNARVONSHIRE*

In 1567 one of Tudor Caernarvonshire's most famous sons, Bishop Richard Davies, came to survey the religious history of the Welsh in his celebrated prefatory letter to the first Welsh translation of the New Testament. It was a discouraging note that he had to strike: 'How great a loss of writings of all kinds—whether of the arts, or of history, or of genealogy, or the Scriptures—have the Welsh suffered? Wales has been completely deprived of them all.' The bishop's lament over the disappearance of the native sources for the history of Wales has been wistfully echoed by many later historians. The loss is particularly grievous for the period of the Reformation. Many of the sources which can be regarded as no more even than the basic minimum simply do not exist, or if they do, succeed in defying all attempts to bring them to light. Bishop Davies himself might have smoothed the path a little if he had not been quite so anxious to send so many of the documents relating to his diocese to William Cecil.[1] It would have been still more helpful if he and his fellow-bishops and their successors had contrived to preserve the records of their sees rather more carefully. In the circumstances with which we are now confronted it becomes difficult enough to piece together evidence for some picture of the Reformation in Wales as a whole. To scrape it together for a single county is a still more daunting operation. An individual county, indeed, is not the natural unit for a history of Tudor religion in the way that it can be for a history of Tudor politics or society. It might have been more appropriate in undertaking a survey of the Reformation to have taken Gwynedd as a whole, or possibly the diocese of Bangor. But before this introduction begins to sound too suspiciously like an alibi constructed carefully to explain away the inadequacies of what follows, it might be as well to begin our task with a brief survey of the ecclesiastical and religious condition of the county just before the Reformation.

I

CAERNARVONSHIRE ON THE EVE OF THE REFORMATION

The most important ecclesiastical institution within the county was the cathedral at Bangor. By the beginning of the sixteenth century its bishops had for more than a century not been Welsh.[2] Very often they were friars. These were usually royal confessors paid off with this small, remote Welsh bishopric—the poorest in

England or Wales and worth no more than £131 a year by the
valuation of 1535. This was too contemptible a remuneration as a
rule for the abler civil servants who could expect a bishopric as their
reward. But it would do well enough for a friar, or for a wealthy
abbot who could ignore the unremunerative nature of the see but
who coveted episcopal status in order to add to his dignity. The
immediate pre-Reformation bishop was just such a one. He was
Thomas Skeffington (1509-33) of Beaulieu in Hampshire—then
noteworthy for its abbey, not its vintage motor-cars or jazz festivals!
Skeffington was, like most contemporary Welsh bishops, an absentee.
That did not necessarily mean that he was indifferent to the welfare
of his cathedral church and diocese. Skeffington is best remembered
for his generous contributions towards the cost of building the tower
at Bangor cathedral. It cost him a 'goodly chestful of gold' and won
him a *cywydd* of praise by one of his priests, the poet Dafydd Trefor.[3]

Many of the bishop's cathedral clergy were, like himself,
absentees. Several of them were busy administrators in church or
state whose sole interest in the diocese was the yearly revenue they
drew from it. Other members of the chapter had, of course, to be
resident to manage its affairs. They had no thought of making the
cathedral the centre of diocesan religious life and activity as a modern
chapter normally seeks to do. The canons then thought of their
functions as being limited to maintaining the fabric and a proper
round of services at the cathedral and overseeing the chapter's
estates and revenues. Such responsibilities called for local knowledge
which could best be found in men drawn from the local families of
gentry. They were not as a rule remarkable for their sanctity or
their learning. Frequently they led a highly secularized existence
not noticeably different from that of their lay brethren. Typical
enough of them was Richard Kyffin, dean of Bangor from c. 1480
until his death in 1502. Of gentle lineage but dubious legitimacy,
Kyffin won his reward as an ardent supporter of Henry VII. As
became a high ecclesiastical dignitary, a wealthy canon lawyer and an
accomplished landowner and husbandman, he lived in considerable
state in his fine rectory at Llanddwynwen. He hunted with gusto
and kept a hospitality hardly rivalled by any of the local squires.
To his well-stocked table he attracted a number of the leading poets
who went into rhapsodies about traits in him that were virtually
indistinguishable from those of their secular patrons.[4] It was to
men like Kyffin that absentee bishops delegated much of their
jurisdiction. Not always with the happiest results; for some twelve
years between 1524 and 1536 the diocese of Bangor was torn by the
unedifying vendetta waged between Archdeacon William Glyn,
vicar-general of the diocese and a leading member of the house of
Glynllifon, and the formidable Sir Richard Bulkeley. The feud first
came into the open in 1524 with a quarrel over Glyn's right to succeed

as archdeacon of Anglesey another Richard Bulkeley, the announcement of whose death like that of Mark Twain had been much exaggerated! Glyn was much in favour with Bishop Skeffington, by whom he was described as a man 'right cunning, very virtuous and of very good fame and name'. When, in 1525, Archdeacon Bulkeley really did die, the bishop lost no time in naming Glyn as his successor. This promotion was regarded as a gratuitous snub not only by Sir Richard Bulkeley but also by Cardinal Wolsey. It did not go unremembered. In 1529 one of Wolsey's agents, Edward Johns, backed by Richard Bulkeley, was pushing the cardinal's interests in the diocese. Glyn and Skeffington promptly tried to block his moves. In the ensuing scuffles 'some had broken elbows'. Bulkeley leapt in on Wolsey's side—with more zeal than discretion, even Edward Johns had to admit.[5] Wolsey's own disgrace saved Glyn from any serious discomfiture, but the rancour between him and Bulkeley still smouldered.

Whatever their shortcomings, prelates of this kind nevertheless often had, as perhaps might be expected, a real pride in the cathedral and affection for it. Richard Kyffin was no paragon of the ecclesiastical virtues, but he did help repair the chancel during his lifetime and left a handsome endowment for a chantry there after his death. But it still remains true that men of this kind were unfitted by temperament or training to give a very positive lead in religious matters to the lesser clergy and the laity.

In addition to the cathedral at Bangor there were four houses of religion within the county: those of the Augustinian Canons at Bardsey and Beddgelert; the Cistercians at Maenan (formerly of Conway); and the Dominican friars at Bangor. Admittedly we know all too little in detail of their condition in the generation or two before the Reformation (though Conway's fortunes have recently been chronicled with great care and accuracy by the Welsh-American historian, Dr. R. W. Hays).[6] However, what evidence we have of them and other Welsh houses in general at this time adds up to a picture of decay. There appear to have been two main reasons for this: the decline of the monastic ideal, and the undue influence exercised by laymen over monasteries. The decline of the monastic ideal is shown most clearly in the reduced number of monks. Unfortunately, information concerning the actual number of monks in the Caernarvonshire houses at the time of the Dissolution is scantier than for almost any other part of Wales. But there is no reason to suppose that they were immune from the chronic manpower problem which beset all other Welsh houses at this time, when the average number of inmates in a Welsh Cistercian house was down to six or seven, in an Augustinian house to five or six, and in a house of Dominican friars to seven or eight.[7]

Partly the result of this decline, partly the cause of it, was the excessive influence of laymen over the life of monasteries. For a very long time—a century or more probably—the monks had taken little or no direct responsibility for the management of their estates. They had been content to lease the great bulk of them to laymen and to live on the rents. In Beddgelert Priory just before the Reformation it was said that the only time that Prior David Conway ever kept his two canons in the priory was when they were needed to sign leases of property.[8] The control which laymen thus gained over monastic possessions tempted them to extend it to other spheres of monastic life, notably the election of abbots. The extraordinary lengths to which this process of jockeying for position could go can be seen in the contest for influence over the choice of an abbot of Conway in 1536, when two such redoubtable opponents as Sir Richard Bulkeley and Dr. Ellis Price were bidding against one another for Cromwell's favour. Ellis Price's family, thanks to the pressure exerted by the formidable old Robert ap Rhys, almost monopolized the abbey's lands in Hiraethog. Just before his death Robert had managed to get his own son, Hugh, made abbot, though he was still a minor. Now, in 1536, though death had removed both Hugh and his father from the scene, the family was as active as ever in promoting the candidature of another son, Richard. This was something that Sir Richard Bulkeley was determined to prevent. He maintained to Cromwell that if Richard ap Robert were appointed abbot he would 'utterly destroy the said abbey within short space'. But if only Cromwell would lend his support to Bulkeley's favoured candidate, David Owen, 'an honest man and meet to be the ruler of such an house', he was promised £100 for his pains 'to be paid unto your hands at such a day as it shall please you to appoint'. Ellis Price's influence was, however, too strong—or his purse too long!—for it was his brother who was elected abbot.[9] The eagerness of each side to secure election of a favoured client was heightened by the imminent prospect of the dissolution of the smaller monasteries; and bitterness between them was exacerbated by the memory of a sharp clash of interest between them a few months earlier over the priory of Penmon, over which Bulkeley exercised a semi-proprietorial influence.[10] In the same way the family of Edward Gruffydd of the Penrhyn regarded the friary of Bangor as being something of a family appanage.[11] There is no need to labour the details, but simply to make one crucial point. The religious orders were no longer the *corps d'élite* of the Church. They had neither the moral nor the intellectual nor the economic independence to withstand the powerful pressures of the state and the laity. Moreover, they presented a standing temptation to appropriation by both.

But what of the ordinary parishes, and their priests and people? Nearly all the Caernarvonshire parishes were large in area, small in population and meagre in income. Most of them (some 74 per cent) ranged between £5 and £15 a year in value, though a considerable number (13 per cent) were worth less than £5 a year. In addition to the beneficed clergy there were usually about as many again who were unbeneficed—curates, chaplains, chantry priests. Most of these got less than £5 a year.[12] This poverty was bound to affect the quality of the clergy. Though there was no simple equation that a poor benefice meant necessarily a poor parson, it was true that, in general, the poorer the livings the more ill-educated and untrained were their incumbents. The large majority of the Caernarvonshire parsons had not been to a university; many—possibly the majority—had not even been to a grammar school. They had had virtually no systematic theological training, and they probably knew no more than the rudiments of Latin necessary to get through the services. This was bound to have detrimental effects on the quality of the religious instruction given by them. When confronted with the great doctrinal issues of the Reformation changes neither they nor their parishioners were likely to have a very clear understanding of their significance.

Of the nature of popular belief and devotion it is extremely difficult to generalize. But what evidence there is suggests that the forms of contemporary religious worship and teaching were widely accepted without question. The means of measuring the popular allegiance are crude and imprecise; bequests in wills, church-building, pilgrimages, and the like. All are well represented in pre-Reformation Caernarvonshire, and it is interesting to observe that bequests to friaries and pilgrimages to favourite shrines persisted right up to the very eve of their dissolution. For example, Rhys ap Gwilym of Llanbadrig left two shillings apiece to the friaries at Bangor and Llanfaes in May 1538; by the time his will was proved in August of that year, the friaries had already been dissolved.[13] Such indications as we have, therefore, indicate a ready acceptance of the faith. At its best it was sincere, earnest and deep-rooted. But within it there was a very large admixture of superstition, credulity and ignorance. Custom predominated over conviction, and was to prove as resistant to the efforts of Catholic Reformers as to those of Protestant Reformers. Official promulgation of the need for change wrought only very slow modifications in practice throughout the sixteenth century.

II

THE FIRST IMPACT OF THE REFORMATION ON
CAERNARVONSHIRE, 1534–1553

When King Henry VIII began his proceedings for annulling his first marriage the 'King's great matter' was probably not widely known or understood among the mass of the people. In so far as they did know anything about it, their sympathies were very often on the side of Catherine of Aragon as a wronged wife and against Anne Boleyn as a baggage who was no better than she should be. However, most men kept a discreet tongue in their heads. Those who had any knowledge of government and any share in it knew that the displeasure of the king's great servants, Wolsey, and later, Cromwell, was not lightly to be incurred. Even as lordly and domineering a figure as the chamberlain of North Wales, Sir Richard Bulkeley, had tremblingly to confess to Cromwell, 'I know right well it lieth in your hands to undo me for ever with a word of your mouth'.[14] And the wrath of the king was an even more terrible thing, as the young Rhys ap Gruffydd of south Wales discovered at frightful cost when he was executed in 1531. The consternation caused by his death sent ripples of alarm trembling into many other parts of Wales and roused flutters of apprehension among the servants of Sir Richard Bulkeley's wife.[15] So, in the years from 1531 to 1536 most men kept their own counsel whatever they may inwardly have thought of the king's proceedings. There was one Caernarvonshire priest, however, who gave vent to an unguarded outburst. This was one Sir William ap Llywelyn who was reported as having said on 4th July, 1533, that he wished 'to have the king upon a mountain in north Wales called the "Withvay", otherwise called "Snoyden Hill" saying that he would souse the king about the ears till he had made his head soft enough'. When remonstrated with by one Edward ap Richard, the priest 'made affray upon the said Edward saying that he would make him sore enough for telling any tales'. He was then promptly seized by the servants of Sir Richard Bulkeley who reported the whole matter to Cromwell.[16] William ap Llywelyn's may have been the voice of a mass of popular prejudice and misgiving. But if such sentiment did exist it found singularly little overt or effective expression.

The clergy seem to have accepted the policies leading up to and including the royal supremacy without demur. Admittedly we have no surviving return from the diocese of Bangor to show what the attitude of its clergy was towards the Act of Supremacy. But there is no reason to suppose that their reaction was any different from that of the rest of the clergy of Wales who were willing to take the oath almost to a man. Behind the complaisant formal acceptance, however, there arose some serious difficulties The bishop of Bangor, John Salcot, in June 1535 found himself sorely handicapped in his desire to 'accomplish the diligent setting forth and sincere preaching within the diocese of Bangor of the royal supremacy' because he himself was ignorant of the language of his flock; but he hoped he could accomplish this by means of other people.[17] For most of his diocesan clergy, paradoxically enough, one of the first effects of the breach with Rome was the tightening up of erstwhile Roman discipline in relation to clerical marriage. Canon Law forbidding the marriage of priests had widely been ignored in medieval Wales, nowhere more than in the diocese of Bangor. In January 1536 a petition from the clergy of the diocese reached Cromwell. It admitted that the petitioners had been 'detected of incontinency . . . and not unworthily'. They begged for 'remission or at the least wise of merciful punishment and correction; and also to invent after your discreet wisdom some lawful and godly way for us . . . to maintain and uphold such poor hospitality as we have done hitherto, most by the provision of such women as we have customably kept in our houses'. They explained that if they had to put away these women it would be to 'the great loss and harms of the king's subjects, the poor people, which were by us relieved to the uttermost of our power. And we ourselves shall be driven to seek our livings at alehouses and taverns, for mansions upon our benefices and vicarages we have none. And as for gentlemen and substantial honest men, for fear of inconvenience, knowing our frailty and accustomed liberty, will in no wise board us in their houses'. The petitioners also went on to complain that another effect of the religious changes had been to lead laymen to seize upon this as an excuse for not rendering to the clergy tithes and customary offerings. For this difficulty there is also some corroborative evidence from lawsuits in the Court of Chancery.[18]

Another complication was one which manifested itself in other dioceses besides Bangor. This was that the royal supremacy became an issue in faction struggles which really had very little to do with religion. Struggles for power within a diocese often became identified with an apparent zeal for reform or an alleged reluctance to accept change. That earlier contest between Bulkeley and Glyn already referred to, which goes back at least as far as 1524, became mixed up with questions relating to the royal supremacy and reform of the clergy. The feud between the two parties flared up again more violently than ever in 1535–36. Ostensibly it was a row over indulgences. The commissary of the bishop of Bangor, Robert Oking, who now held the post previously occupied by William Glyn under Bishop Skeffington, was accused by Richard Gibbons, registrar to the bishop, of allowing papal indulgences to be sold; indulgences which Gibbons caused to be seized by the bailiffs of Caernarvon.[19] But the root of the trouble was the old quarrel between Sir Richard Bulkeley on the one side and William Glyn and Edward Gruffydd of the Penrhyn on the other. Bulkeley was vice-chamberlain, later chamberlain, of North Wales, formerly Cardinal Wolsey's agent in Gwynedd, and now Cromwell's chief confidant in the area. His enemies accused him of overbearing pride and ambition; he complained to Cromwell that they had said 'that I would suffer no man to dwell in this country but myself'.[20] Bulkeley's advancement was certainly much resented by Edward Gruffydd, whose father, grandfather, and great-grandfather had all been chamberlains of North Wales. Glyn, too, though a cleric, was in Sir John Wynn's words a man 'of a stirring spirit and a great housekeeper, spent all and had a hand in all the great temporal affairs of the country as well as spiritual'.[21] Deprived now of the office and much of the influence he had enjoyed under Bishop Skeffington, he was keenly desirous of recovering both.

Both sides had access to Cromwell and each tried to convince him of its zeal and loyalty. Glyn had embraced, or assumed, marked reformist or anti-Romanist attitudes. He wrote to Cromwell on 2nd November, 1535 to the effect that in the diocese of Bangor the sale of indulgences and the mart of vice were now greatly decayed, and would be even more reduced if the great maintainer of them, the bishop of Rome, were expelled from men's hearts.[22] Predictably, it was Glyn who lay behind Richard Gibbons's denunciation of Oking for selling indulgences. Glyn's campaign put Bulkeley in a delicate position. He suspected Gibbons's intentions and was well disposed to Oking; but he knew he had to be careful not to become embroiled in any suspicion of pro-papal sympathies. He tried to get Gibbons to produce for him 'all such papistical scripts, muniments and writings as he had to allege' against Oking so that they could be sent to Cromwell. Gibbons—wisely perhaps—declined, saying that he would deliver them himself. Bulkeley therefore had to content himself with testifying to Oking's loyalty, claiming that he 'spake as much at all times in the annulling of the bishop of Rome's authority as any one man that I knew in these parts', and hinting darkly that the whole charge against Oking was a malicious conspiracy designed to recover Glyn's former office for him.[23] In a further letter to Cromwell dated a month later, June, 1535, Bulkeley returned to the charge of malice on the part of his enemies who had caused Cromwell to be 'untruly instructed of such things as I never thought nor wrought nor never intend to do. For they play with me "scogan", for they begin to complain because they know that I have special good matter to lay unto their charges'. He begged Cromwell not to believe his enemies' reports of him and sent Cromwell a bag formerly belonging to Wolsey which the great cardinal had given him as a memento.[24] Yet again before the end of 1535, in a letter dated 21st November, Bulkeley taxed his opponents with acting arbitrarily and illegally. This time he accused Glyn and Ellis Price of acting in collusion to imprison in his own priory the prior of Penmon, a house of which Bulkeley was steward.[25]

The net results of all these intrigues and counter-accusations were that in 1536 both sides were in trouble with Cromwell. It was

Glyn who was in the worst difficulty first. Bulkeley's most effective weapon against him was, no doubt, the charge of gross pluralism. In March, 1536 Glyn was summoned to London to answer charges against him (in which Bulkeley almost certainly had the chief hand) of simultaneously holding a number of benefices, of assessing himself for being liable to only 10s. in taxation when he should have paid £20, and of having been non-resident for sixteen years.[26] But Bulkeley on his side had cause to be gravely worried in the spring of 1536 by a more serious conjunction of religion, politics and royal matrimonial discord. On 2nd May, 1536 his brother, Roland, had written to give him the news of the downfall of Anne Boleyn and of the complicity in her disgrace of Henry Norris, chamberlain of North Wales, with whom Sir Richard had been on terms of close dependence. Roland urged Richard's immediate presence at court to safeguard his interests.[27] We do not know whether Sir Richard in fact repaired to London, but it seems quite clear that he rode out this storm very successfully, for in August, 1536 he was appointed to succeed Henry Norris as chamberlain of North Wales.[28]

Within a few months, however, he was in trouble with Cromwell. It arose over the living of Llangeinwen with the chapel of Llangaffo, which was also known as Clynnog Fechan, in the island of Anglesey. This was one of a number of livings held by William Glyn and there was apparently some move to deprive him of it in the autumn of 1536 on the grounds that it ought not to be held by the incumbent of Clynnog Fawr, of which Glyn was also in possession. Bulkeley must have acted quickly to induce the bishop to collate his kinsman, Dr. Arthur Bulkeley. In doing so he over-reached himself and seriously jeopardized his relationship with Cromwell, who intended that his own nephew, Gregory Williams, should be preferred there. Just how displeased Cromwell seems to have been may be gleaned from the tones of grovelling ingratiation employed by Richard Bulkeley in two letters to him dated 13th November and 17th December, 1536.[29] In the first Bulkeley declared that had he known of Cromwell's wishes, 'I would not have spoken one word against the simplest groom in your stable . . . for though I be not very wise I am not so stark mad to contend in anything that is appertaining to your lordship'. He would see to it that Dr. Bulkeley yielded up the living in favour of Gregory Williams, for he had always desired Cromwell's wealth and prosperity 'as the fowls would be glad to see day'. But Dr. Bulkeley was obviously not as pliant as either Cromwell or his kinsman would have wished to see him, and in the second letter Richard Bulkeley, conscious of Cromwell's deep and continuing displeasure wrote, 'Though he (i.e. Dr. Bulkeley) be lewd and froward there is no fault in me. . . . I have written to Doctor Bulkeley again that if ever he will claim me for his kinsman or have any good turn at my hand during my life to yield up his collation and interest

in the said benefice without any further tract of time. And if the said
doctor refuse thus to do I will take him for my uttermost enemy
during my life'. The rest of the letter went on to plead for the
restoration of Cromwell's favour and to recount how 'many salt
tears' had fallen from Bulkeley's eyes.

Bulkeley's troubles were far from over, however. The turn of
the year 1536–37 saw the quarrel between Bulkeley and his rivals
take a new and dangerous twist. For a large part of 1536 both Glyn
and Edward Gruffydd had been in London. In their absence,
Bulkeley claimed, peace and order had been maintained. However,
'within two or three days after their coming home', 'after All-
hallowtide last past' (i.e. November, 1536), 'divers persons of such
as were towards them made assaults and affrays'. Then at Christmas
time 1536, so Bulkeley alleged, there had been further clashes at
Bangor cathedral between them and Dr. Oking, whom 'they would
have murdered within the said cathedral' as he kept a consistory
court there. He further accused them of having caused another
affray at the cathedral on 21st February, with '100 riotous persons'
when an attempt was made to serve a writ of *sub poena* on them.
What made the whole affair still more sinister in Bulkeley's view was
the report that Glyn and Gruffydd were openly rejoicing in the
prospect that 'mortal war is like to be in England which words
and comfort have caused many light heads to pick many quarrels
and caused much mischief to be done in these quarters'. It had led
one of Glyn's servants to boast that his master was sure 'it would
be war and then his master and he trusted to be revenged of such
as were their adversaries'. Bulkeley wanted strong measures taken
against them, to bind them and their men over in large sums not to
go armed to church or markets or other places of assembly, 'nor none
other Welshman within the three shires', except on the king's service.
If this were not done 'the king shall have as much to do with his
subjects here in North Wales as ever he had in Ireland'.[30] The
reference to possible connections between Wales and the risings in
the north country was alarming, but it was the kind of accusation
freely and rashly made at this time with but little foundation.[31]
Much of the heat went out of these quarrels in the summer of 1537
with the death of William Glyn. When he died his collection of
benefices was carved up in a three-way split between the bishop,
Cromwell and Bulkeley.[32] The Bulkeley influence in the affairs
of the diocese continued to grow. The seal was set on it four years
later when Dr. Arthur Bulkeley became bishop.

For most of our knowledge of these dissensions we are dependent
on Sir Richard Bulkeley's highly partisan account of them. It puts
Glyn and Gruffydd in an unfavourable light, but we know from
another source that there may have been a good deal to be said for

them. One of the clergy of the diocese, Sir Dafydd Trefor, the poet, mentions the disputes in his poetry. He speaks for the ordinary parish clergy, 'poor terrified oxen' for whom it was 'madness to venture among such great bulls' as Glyn and Bulkeley. But as between the two, there was no doubt where Trefor's real affection lay. Glyn he referred to with real warmth, but in his approach to Bulkeley there was an unmistakable tone of apprehension and misgiving.[33] This may well have been representative of the attitude of most of the native clergy of the diocese, since a point regularly made by Bulkeley against his opponents was that they resented hotly the rule borne over them by an 'Englishman' like himself.

These struggles for power, though they often seem to have little to do with religion, have been recounted at length for a number of reasons. First of all they shed unusually clear light on the pressures which powerful lay patrons, in Wales and also at the centre of power in London, could in their own interests exert on the clergy. Again, they show how the Reformation changes could become little more than another stick with which to beat local rivals and to push family interests. Bangor is by no means an isolated instance of this; there are close parallels to be drawn in the other three Welsh dioceses. Finally, these episodes help to explain how difficult it was to give the Reformation any real meaning for the mass of the populace at this stage. In so far as it had any meaning for them at all, it was something to be fought over by distant potentates like the king and the pope, or by local magnates like Richard Bulkeley and Edward Gruffydd.

A further indication of the slowness with which the king's policy was being implemented in the diocese of Bangor comes in a letter written by the bishop to Dr. Arthur Bulkeley in 1537. Bulkeley maintained that Cromwell was dissatisfied with the way in which royal visitors had carried out their work in the diocese which 'was never visited but superficially by the King's authority and that it is not so ordered as other men's dioceses be throughout the realm', and better discipline was needed for excluding idolatry and the 'incestuous and abominable living as well of priests as of other laymen'. Bulkeley wanted to be appointed commissary in place of Dr. Vaughan. He thought he would do much good in that capacity and would not 'onerate' the clergy. Bulkeley's zeal for reform may have owed as much to his personal ambition and his need to placate Cromwell as it did to any concern for reform. Bishop Salcot was not greatly impressed. He contended that the royal visitors did their duty; certainly, 'they took no superficial procurations, but substantial and large'. His own episcopal visitation was undertaken in his absence, but he trusted that 'condign punishment with due reformation is taken and done, especially upon all abominable offenders as well as if I were there myself.'[34]

In other directions, however, important changes were going on apace. In 1535 the first steps towards the ultimate dissolution of the monasteries had been taken when a return on the value of ecclesiastical property throughout the realm was compiled. Sir Richard Bulkeley and other leading gentlemen were entrusted with the task of compiling the *Valor Ecclesiasticus* for the diocese. Bulkeley regarded the responsibility as a more than usually exacting one, knowing 'how barbarous and ignorant I and the gentlemen of the country are'. They had done their best to get the parson and four reliable persons in each parish to declare the true value of the benefice, but in some instances they found other people coming forward with evidence of higher value.[35] Later in the same year Cromwell's visitors were sent round to report on the state of morals and discipline in the monasteries. There is no evidence that they found any scandalous conditions in Caernarvonshire houses. But whether they did or did not find any delinquency made no difference to the ultimate fate of the houses. In the year 1536 the smaller monasteries were dissolved by Act of Parliament, and none of the Caernarvonshire houses was exempted from its provisions. Two years later, in August, 1538, the friary at Bangor along with the others of north Wales was surrendered to the crown.

Cromwell soon began to receive letters requesting him to take a favourable line of action in accordance with suitors' requests. Richard Price, abbot of Conway, and his brother, Ellis, pleaded that Cromwell should exempt his house from the Act of Parliament. 'If the house cannot be saved (which God forbid), I beg that one of my poor brethren may be the king's farmer of the house before any other'.[36] A little later, Edward Gruffydd of Penrhyn urged Cromwell that he should be allowed to buy outright the poor and dilapidated friary of Bangor. There was very little glass and iron there, and no lead, but Gruffydd humbly besought Cromwell 'to be so good lord unto me as ever you have been before this time, so that I and my heirs may have and enjoy the said friar house for the intent that I may make a dwelling house thereof'.[37] From 1537 onwards the Crown began leasing possessions formerly belonging to the monasteries. In the first instance it often seemed to be men from outside the county who were the chief beneficiaries. Some very unexpected figures appeared among the lessees, e.g. Beddgelert passed to Anne of Cleves and a grange of Conway was leased to William Stump of Malmesbury. But in the long run nearly all the former monastic lands passed to the local gentry. The rectory of Aberdaron, which was once part of the spiritual possessions of Bardsey, was first of all leased to Ralph Dodd of the Household and Thomas Jones of London, but by Elizabeth's reign it was in the hands of the Owens of Plas Du and by a twist of poetic irony its income went to maintain Hugh Owen, the famous Caernarvonshire recusant, and the 'intelligencer-in-chief' of Spain in Europe.[38] Or again, Bangor friary, after a chequered history in the hands of the Gruffydd family, was sold to Thomas Browne and William Breton of London; but it passed almost at once from them to Geoffrey Glynne, who founded Friars' School under the terms of his will.[39]

It would be inappropriate to try to discuss in detail how much loss to the religious life of the county the dissolution of the monasteries caused. There is really insufficient material available to strike any sort of balance-sheet. But there seems to be no indication that contemporaries in Caernarvonshire, or indeed anywhere else in Wales, made any vigorous protest against the disappearance of the monasteries. It does seem as if monastic life was so far decayed that its disappearance could hardly be the cause of great regret. What created more of a stir at the time was the suppression of shrines and pilgrimages, many of them closely associated with houses of religion. The destruction of these aroused much more popular indignation than the closure of the monasteries themselves, and strenuous efforts were made to save some of them. There was in Caernarvonshire no shrine which compared in intensity of popular esteem with that of the Virgin Mary at Pen-rhys in south Wales or Winifred's Well at Holywell or Derfel's image at Llandderfel in neighbouring Merioneth. But the bishop of Dover, when he suppressed the friary at Bangor, reported that he found there the 'holiest relic' in north Wales. It was a considerable pilgrim attraction and was worth 20 marks a year to the friars before the friary was suppressed and the relic packed off to London.[40]

All in all, what strikes one most about Henry VIII's reign is how little impact the great politico-religious changes made on ordinary people. There does not appear to have been any real danger of the waves of protest which broke upon Tudor policy in the North of England. Far-reaching as the consequences of the break with the papacy or the dissolution of the monasteries were, they were not of a kind to affect every-day life very much. The pope was a remote figure, a symbol chiefly of power rather than spirituality. But the king's jurisdiction, on the other hand, and that of his representatives was real and immediate. His orthodoxy was undoubted and many of his actions were approved as an urgently-needed pattern of strong government. Such changes as he had introduced had made remarkably little practical difference to the worship, appearance or language of the Church.

That could not, however, be said of the drastic and dramatic changes which were to be introduced in the next phase of the Reformation, the short reign of Edward VI, 1547–53. The boy-king was under the influence of advisers who, from conviction or self-interest, drove the country far and fast along the road to religious change. The changes now enforced had a triple impact, which struck home much more palpably and unavoidably at all sections of the populace. There were, first of all, the attacks on church property; secondly, the extinction of many of the features of medieval worship; and thirdly the attempts to establish Protestant forms of belief and worship by means of a Book of Common Prayer enforced by Acts of Parliament.

The attacks on church property were directed chiefly against the collegiate churches, chantries, guilds and fraternities. There were comparatively few of this sort of institution in north Wales generally, though there was the quite large Kyffin chantry in Bangor cathedral and the relatively wealthy collegiate church at Clynnog.[41] Following a survey of the endowments of this sort in 1549, they were all now swept away—except for those which escaped detection by the chantry commissioners. But the collegiate church of Clynnog Fawr was the subject of a fierce legal battle. Its incumbent was John Gwynedd, a man of more than ordinary interest. A former monk of St. Albans, he was a well-known author of religious books in English, one of which was one of the earliest books to be printed at the abbey of St. Albans. He was also a musician of some distinction. Faced with drastic measures for the royal appropriation of his church on the grounds that it was a collegiate institution, he fought doggedly to maintain its rights. In answer to a suit brought against him in the Court of Augmentations by the Crown in 1550–1, he contested the royal claims on the grounds that his church was a college in name only, that it had no corporate lands or buildings and no chapter seal, and that it never exercised its rights in a corporate capacity. He was supported in this by the testimony of a number of local witnesses, lay and cleric. The best informed of these appeared to be Morgan ap Rees, perpetual vicar of Clynnog. In his deposition he testified emphatically that 'by the space of xxii years last past the said church hath not been reputed a collegiate church but a parish church'.[42] There is no indication of how the verdict went; but perhaps it is worth recalling that Rowland Meyrick, the incumbent of Llan-ddewibrefi, also reputed to be a collegiate church, successfully defended his title in just such a lawsuit as that fought by John Gwynedd.[42a] The expropriation of the chantries was followed in 1552–3 by a wholesale confiscation of church plate and vestments by government commissioners. Unfortunately, returns for this act of spoliation have survived for only one Welsh county—Glamorgan. But if the consequences in that county are typical, then we must assume that most Welsh churches were deprived of treasured possessions. This can hardly fail to have led to some resentment against 'Reformers' who seemed chiefly concerned to line their pockets at the expense of the parish.

In the meantime there had also been a determined assault on many of those features of medieval worship that were obnoxious to Protestants. Images and pictures in churches were shattered or removed, and roods and roodlofts mutilated. Pilgrimages, holy days, and practices such as creeping to the cross on Good Fridays or burning candles at Candlemas were abrogated. Worst of all in the eyes of many, altars were thrown down and replaced by tables— though perhaps we ought at the same time to remember that one distinguished north Walian, William Salesbury, published a pamphlet sharply censuring traditional medieval teaching concerning the altar and defending the Reformers' attack on it.[43] But in general these measures were likely to have inspired an indignation and hostility quite without precedent in Henry VIII's reign. For example, the leading Catholic poet, Siôn Brwynog, who had spoken of Henry VIII in terms of warm admiration, assailed the Edwardian changes with tremendous contempt and vigour. After some harsh words on the married clergy he went on:

Ni sôn am fferen y sul	Côr ni bydd cŵyr yn y byd
Na chyffes mwy na cheffyl . . .	Na channwyll yn iach ennyd;
Oerder yn yn amser ni,	Yr eglwys a'i haroglau
Yr ia glas yw'r eglwysi.	Yn wych oedd ein hiachau.
On'd oedd dost un dydd a dau	Yr oedd gynt arwydd a gaid
I'r llawr fwrw'r allorau?	Olew yn eli enaid.[44]

("He speaks not of mass on Sunday, nor of confession, any more than would a horse. The coldness in our times, the churches are as cold as ice. Was it not a bitter blow to have cast down the altars within a day or two? There is no wax nor a single candle for a moment in the chancel of any church; the church that with its incense well healed us. There was once oil as a symbol of balm for the soul.")

These and other similar onslaughts, like those in the *cwndidau* of Glamorgan, give a firm impression of the offence offered to ordinary men's susceptibilities by these changes. Many people undoubtedly felt a strong sense of loss of those things which had been interwoven with the fabric of their lives since childhood. Nor could they as yet have been much compensated or consoled by the introduction of reforming doctrines and ideals.

The most important aspect of the introduction of Protestant worship was the publication of the first English Book of Common Prayer in 1549 and the enforcement of its use universally within the king's domains by an Act of Uniformity. But this created a special problem for those parts of the realm where English was not the language of everyday use—the Channel Islands, Calais, Ireland, Cornwall and Wales. Nor was the government entirely indifferent to it. A French translation was provided for Calais and the Channel Islands. A Worcester printer, John Oswen, was given the right to print prayer books for Wales; but it seems probable that this

meant printing English books for use in Wales.[45] No official translation into Welsh was provided, but in 1551 William Salesbury
published his version of the epistles and gospels of the Prayer Book
in his *Kynniver Llith a Ban*. How widely this book was known or
used in Caernarvonshire it is impossible to say. Nor can we say
with any degree of certainty how the English Book of Common
Prayer was used and received by priests and people. Siôn Brwynog
gives a contemptuous hint that some of the Edwardian priests had
very little understanding of the new service:

> Ni all ddeall a ddowaid,
> Ynte yn ffôl eto ni ffaid.[46]

('He understands not what he says; he is foolish and yet will not be
silent.')

Many of the priests must have had some knowledge of English,
since they frequently figure as witnesses or executors to English-
language wills for instance. But many of the humbler incumbents
and curates among them must have found English at least as difficult
as Latin to manage, without the advantage of knowing it by rote as
they knew the Latin. It may be that some of them resorted to the
same subterfuge as priests are known to have employed elsewhere,
i.e. of mumbling the service in a low and indistinct tone so that no
one knew for certain what language they were using! As for their
parishioners, English services must have been almost completely
incomprehensible to the overwhelming majority of those who lived
outside the old garrison towns.

Summing up the effect of these first phases in the introduction of
the Reformation we see that it had either made very little impression
at all or that it had, indeed, evoked a reaction of marked hostility and
resentment at the loss of old familiar things. Very few genuine
converts to Reformed doctrines appear to have been created. True,
some exceptional individuals like Richard Davies, the future bishop,
who had been attracted to the new ideas while a student at Oxford,
or his uncle the poet, Gruffydd ab Ieuan ap Llywelyn, had gladly
embraced Protestant teaching.[47] But the mass had remained unmoved, largely because no effective or concerted effort had been
made to present the new doctrines in the only language that was
intelligible to most of the inhabitants of Caernarvonshire. Until
such an effort was launched, as all the early Tudor writers of Welsh
books were agreed, Reformed religion could never hope to record
any worthwhile progress.

III

THE MARIAN REACTION, 1553-58

Mary's accession was undoubtedly popular. It is true that Lady
Jane Grey was actually proclaimed queen at Beaumaris and Denbigh

—and probably at Caernarvon and other places in north Wales.[48] But her triumph was short-lived. At Beaumaris Mary was proclaimed queen on the very day after she had been denounced; at Denbigh her reinstatement took place on the afternoon of the self-same day. The return to older forms of worship after the rapid and ill-prepared changes of Edward's reign was probably well received. Siôn Brwynog's well-known *englyn* probably sums up the reaction of very many:

> Wele fraint y saint yn neshau—eilwaith
> Wele'r hen 'fferennau;
> Wele Dduw â'i law ddehau
> Yn gallu oll yn gwellau.[49]

("Behold once more the privilege of the saints draw near, behold the old masses; behold God making us all whole with His right hand.")

In general, restoration seems to have been accomplished smoothly enough among the laity.

But among the clergy Mary's changes created something of an unheaval. In the diocese of Bangor, as elsewhere, they found the reintroduction of an earlier clerical discipline relating to wives more than a little embarrassing. Before the Reformation many of them had had 'wives' from whom they had been very reluctant to part in 1535–6. During Edward VI's reign when they had, by law, been allowed to take wives many of them had availed themselves of the opportunity of doing so—or perhaps had done no more than officially acknowledge long-standing liaisons! The first Parliament of Mary's reign had repealed the statutes allowing clerical marriage. This was quickly followed by a decree forbidding any married priest to say mass or minister. But the actual deprivations did not begin until March, 1554. If a married cleric agreed to part from his wife— and most of them did!—he was allowed to minister elsewhere after doing penance. All over England and Wales the result was a general post of the formerly married clergy. Bangor is the only Welsh diocese where we can see in detail something of what went on.[50] Here we can trace fifteen priests ejected for marriage, and at least ten of these were found other livings within the diocese. Sometimes there was a straightforward exchange, as when Peter Tudor of Llanllechid and Robert Evans of Llanengan were deprived and simply changed places. Others played a kind of game of 'musical benefices', for example when Thomas Hughes, deprived of one portion of Llaneli-dan, was moved to another portion, from which Thomas Griffith was turned out. Griffith in turn was moved to Aber, where he took the place of another deprived cleric.

In Wales it is only for the dioceses of Bangor and St. David's that we have any idea of what proportion of the clergy were deprived for marriage.[51] It seems fairly certain that in each instance the estimates of deprivations based on the episcopal registers are too low and that we have no more than an incomplete picture. Even so, the upheaval caused among the clergy during the year April, 1554 to March, 1555 was far greater than that caused by any other change in religious policy during the whole century. What is more, the number of deprivations in both Welsh dioceses is unexpectedly large. Broadly speaking, the greater the distance between the diocese and London, the fewer should be the number of deprivations. But in Bangor the ratio of one deprivation to eight clergy, and in St. David's the ratio of one to six, is distinctly higher than might have been expected on the basis of figures for the English dioceses. So that in these two Welsh dioceses most remote from England, in a land where Protestant influences had been slow to penetrate, we find that the proportion of deprivations is unaccountably high in terms of English conditions. The only way in which we seem to be able to account for this is the widespread prevalence of unofficial clerical marriages in Wales before the Reformation. It also leaves us wondering how far this practice predisposed some Welsh clerics to accept a religious regime which, among other novelties, legalized clerical marriages.

However, as opposed to a fairly large number of clerics turned out for marriage only a tiny minority were deprived for heretical beliefs. Only one cleric of Caernarvonshire origins, Richard Davies, found it necessary to go into exile on the Continent on account of his convictions; and he, of course, had been ministering not in his native county but far away in Buckinghamshire.[52] Most of the clergy were able to conform to Mary's requirements with the same obliging pliability which they were able to evince in all the bewildering changes of policy during the century. In some instances their readiness to conform is a little surprising. One noteworthy example of this from Caernarvonshire is Thomas Davies, chancellor of Bangor and incumbent of a number of livings in the diocese. When Mary came to the throne he was almost certainly a married man with a family, yet he contrived not only to accept the Marian restoration but also to keep his preferment intact. Nevertheless, in Elizabeth's reign, when he became bishop of St. Asaph, he was an active Reformer. The tactics of higher clergy of this kind are the ones we can most readily trace. Beneath them were dozens of humbler clerics of whose repeated tackings before the gusts of changing winds of policy and pressure we can know nothing; nor of their parishioners' reactions either.

But of one thing we can at least be reasonably sure; there were no burnings for religion in Caernarvonshire. As is well known, there were only three in the whole of Wales, and they all in south Wales. This is often cited as the most decisive proof of the lack of Protestant sympathisers in Wales. And so it is up to a point. But too much importance should not be attached to it. The intensity of persecution varied very widely, depending not only on the numbers of heretics but also on the persecuting zeal of bishops and on the social status of the heretics. Still, it remains true that Wales was spared most of the fury of the persecution.

Before leaving the subject of Marian reaction, there is one other aspect, rarely ever commented upon, which merits treatment. This is the attempt made to introduce Catholic reform. It is essential to realize that Cardinal Pole was not just seeking a return to the 'good old days'. In the light of the Catholic reform programme to which he and his lieutenants were dedicated the 'good old days' appeared far from good. In trying to implement his aspirations for reform he was, paradoxically enough, faced with not a few of the same problems as those which were to contront the Elizabethan Protestant reformers. He knew that to achieve his ends he must take action at diocesan and parish level. To replace the existing parish clergy *in toto* was impossible, but a great deal more might be hoped for where the bishops and cathedral clergy were concerned. The first effect of his influence in Bangor was the election of a new bishop in a see that had been kept vacant since 1551 in order to enrich the royal treasury. Pole's choice was a significant one. The new bishop, William Glyn,[53] was a distinguished Cambridge theologian of Anglesey origins. As Lady Margaret Professor of Divinity he had defended the doctrine of transubstantiation, and in 1554 he was one of those chosen for the responsible task of debating with Ridley and Latimer at Oxford. At Bangor he tried to carry out Pole's programme by summoning regular synods of his clergy and carefully instructing them, as he was peculiarly well fitted to do, in the doctrines of the Church. That great bardic champion of the old faith, Siôn Brwynog, as might have been expected, warmed in praise of Bishop Glyn, whom he described as a 'shepherd of souls' and a 'pillar of the faith'.[50]

Two of the brightest young Welshmen associated with this Catholic revival were Caernarvonshire men, Morris Clynnog and Gruffydd Robert,[55] and each was destined to play a distinguished role in the history of the Welsh Catholic exiles of Elizabeth's reign. Clynnog was to have succeeded Glyn as bishop of Bangor, had not Queen Mary's death intervened. Gruffydd Robert was already archdeacon of Anglesey and was also no doubt destined for higher office had the queen lived. Short-lived and largely unfulfilled as was this first attempt to introduce reformed Catholicism into Wales, it was not without its consequences for the future. Its leaders refused to compromise and went abroad to direct the campaign for re-conversion from exile. At home in each of the dioceses where it had made itself felt it left a hard core of resisters among clergy and laity, a nucleus around which the recusancy of the Elizabethan period crystallized.

IV
THE ELIZABETHAN CHURCH

We now come to the third and, as it turned out, decisive phase
in the history of the Reformation—the establishment of the
Elizabethan Church. But though we know now that it proved decisive we have to keep reminding ourselves that no one in the Wales of
the 1560s could know that this would be so. Indeed, the likelihood
was that it would not be. This, oddly enough, was one of the most
important reasons for the general acceptance of the Elizabethan
settlement. This, and the profound respect that existed for any
regime enforced by law, help us to understand the temporizing,
the compromising, the not-very-profound conforming that otherwise
seem largely inexplicable. This was particularly true of the first
ten years or so of the Queen's reign.

In the spring of 1559 Elizabeth revived the Second Prayer
Book of Edward VI's reign with a few significant conservative
amendments. Its use was enforced by the now familiar procedure
of an Act of Uniformity. To ensure that this act was implemented,
groups of visitors were sent round the country.[56] Two of the three
visitors who came to Bangor had close connections with the diocese.
The one, Richard Davies, was the son of a Caernarvonshire curate
and was soon to be bishop of St. Asaph and St. David's successively,
and the other, Rowland Meyrick, was the son of a well-known
Anglesey family and was to be the first Elizabethan bishop of Bangor.
The visitors were not confronted with any large body of resisters
among the clergy. Probably the only one who was deprived by them
was Gruffydd Robert, archdeacon of Anglesey, and he had probably
already fled to the Continent some months before the visitors arrived.
The only other local cleric deprived about this time was John Herde,
M.D., rector of Llanenddwyn, but it is not at all certain that he lost
his living for his beliefs. What does stand out unmistakably in the
course of this visitation is the general readiness of the clergy and
laity alike to conform—outwardly at least—to the new settlement.

The new Elizabethan bishops cherished no illusions that this
acquiescence carried with it any deeply felt conviction of the truth
of Reformed doctrine in many instances. From almost every diocese
in Wales in the 1560s we get rather pessimistic reports from the
bishops concerning the state of their dioceses. An early report by
Bishop Meyrick to Archbishop Parker[57] told of widespread
absenteeism and non-residence among his clergy. He had only two
licensed preachers among his clergy, though he hopefully added a
list of some thirty names of 'such as be able to preach, and may do
good'. The bishops also reported the widespread survival in Wales
of traditional medieval religious practices among the people. Bangor
diocese was no exception and Bishop Robinson's description of his

diocese in 1567 is well-known.[58] He describes how 'ignorance continueth many in the dregs of superstition' and comments sharply on the 'images and altars standing in the churches undefaced, lewd and indecent vigils and watches observed, much pilgrimage-going, many candles set up to the honour of the saints, some relics yet carried about, and all the country full of beads and knots'. This parallels almost exactly what Richard Davies had to say about the state of St. David's.[59] Robinson's diagnosis of the causes of these survivals is also almost identical with that of Davies. They both attribute them to three causes. First, there was the slackness, indifference, or even hostility on the part of the officers of local government among the laity. Secondly, the clergy suffered from all the shortcomings attendant upon poverty and ignorance. Finally, and most important, was the slow progress made towards circulating a knowledge of the Scriptures and order of service in Welsh. All these considerations are well-known and need no elaboration.

What does merit closer attention is the nature of these Catholic survivals. These vestigial remains were certainly widespread and tenacious; of that there can be no question whatsoever. But there is a real danger of misinterpreting their true nature and significance. They have been well summed up as being 'less concerned with doctrinal affirmations or dramas of conscience than with a set of ingrained observances which defined and gave meaning to the cycle of the week and the seasons of the year; to birth, marriage and death'.[60] This sort of attitude did not by any means necessarily involve recusancy. It was perfectly compatible with outward conformity which need make no pretence of concealing distaste for the religion by law established. This is perhaps an essential clue to a puzzle which has so often troubled historians in Wales: 'Why did Wales, apparently so conservative and disinclined to view reformed doctrines with favour, nevertheless provide so few hard-core recusants?'

It may also supply the answer to another awkward question: 'Why were the Catholic exiles often so profoundly critical of conditions in Wales, and yet why did they in fact make so little effort to re-convert their native country?' That they were critical comes out clearly in an important letter written by a Catholic exile from Caernarvonshire, Robert Gwyn.[61] A young scion of the Bodvel family, it seems likely, he was an Oxford graduate and a friend of Robert Owen of Plas Du. He had fled to Douai in 1571 and he wrote his letter three years later. In it he criticizes the Welsh gentry for being selfish, quarrelsome and materialistic, in terms remarkably similar to those of episcopal critics. He further condemns them for their reluctance to harbour in their households priests who could instruct them and minister Catholic sacraments. In other words,

Robert Gwyn, like most of the Welsh and English priests and exiles who had come under the influence of the reformed Catholicism of the Counter-Reformation was far from satisfied with the haphazard, undogmatic, ill-instructed clinging to the past from custom rather than conviction which characterized so many of his fellow-countrymen. He and the men of the Catholic Resistance envisaged the need for a much more positive and militant attitude towards their faith. They were the dedicated and informed minority who, from the mid-1570s onwards, tried to introduce the dynamic and disciplined ideas of the post-Tridentine Roman Church into Wales.

On the face of it, Caernarvonshire ought to have been a most fertile field for their operations. In Mary's reign it had already produced two of the brightest young hopes of the Marian reform movement, Morris Clynnog and Gruffydd Robert. These two were to be followed in Elizabeth's reign by some of the ablest and most resolute of the Welsh seminary priests: Morgan Clynnog, Robert Owen and Robert Gwyn.[62] In John Jones, Caernarvonshire gave Welsh Catholics one of their noblest martyrs.[63] And of the Welsh Catholic laymen who went into exile there was not one who gave longer, more loyal or more committed service to the political wing of Welsh Catholic activity than Hugh Owen[64] of Plas Du, intelligencer-in-chief to the Spanish government among the emigrés. At home in Caernarvonshire itself were two particularly notable recusant households—Plas Du in the Llŷn Peninsula, and the home of the Pughs in Creuddyn. Both these *plasau* provided shelter and comfort for the clandestine seminary priests, the former as a landing-place for them, and the latter as an important staging-post on their route from Llŷn to the recusant strongholds in Flintshire and Lancashire. It was the Pughs, too, who were responsible for helping to establish that secret printing-press at Rhiwledyn, where the first Welsh book ever to be printed in Wales, *Y Drych Cristionogawl*, was hurriedly and incompletely produced.[65] With all this in mind we might have expected Elizabethan Caernarvonshire to have been a hotbed of recusancy.

Yet in fact it was not. There were within the county only a handful of recusants, as Mr. Emyr Gwynne Jones has shown; a markedly smaller number than were found in the north-eastern counties of Wales.[66] Why should this have been? Partly it may have been due to the vigilance of the bishops, especially Bishop Robinson. In a letter of 1582 he wrote, 'I am termed by letters from my countrymen beyond the seas a persecutor; for that of long time I have laid wait for their massing priests and such as hear them'.[67] Partly it was on account of the ripples of alarm and confusion that spread along the exposed nerves of gentry families after the revelations of the Llŷn recusancy case of 1578–80 involving the

Owens of Plas Du, or the still more widely ramifying aftermath of the Babington conspiracy of 1586.[68] These considerations already mentioned are in themselves testimony to the heavy and in general successful pressure which the regime brought to bear on the gentry in the 1580s and 1590s. It demanded more than usually strong nerves and an even stronger purse to withstand indefinitely, especially when the government made it plain that all it required was conformity, not necessarily conversion. We can also discern profound differences among the exiles themselves. Hugh Owen might place himself wholeheartedly at the service of Spain; but others of his co-religionists at home and in Europe viewed such political alignments with distaste. Morris Clynnog's letter to William Cecil giving him advance warning that Elizabeth might be excommunicated is a well-known example of the acute conflict of loyalties that a man of un-impeachable Catholic belief could experience.[69] There was, further-more, a marked difference of attitude which could conceivably arise between Catholic gentlemen at home and those clerics who came from seminaries in Europe. The gentry, to quote Lord Vaux of Harrowden, 'did each claim his house to be a parish by itself'.[70] The gentleman wanted control over his priest no less than his dependants and tenants. Such values could hardly commend them-selves to priests who came over deeply imbued with notions of sacerdotal privilege. The potential rift between them and the gentry could be seen clearly enough in Robert Gwyn's letter of 1574. (In passing, it might be noted that the more erastian Elizabethan settlement offered the average gentry family rather better prospects of control over the Church.) But perhaps the most significant reason of all for the failure of the Roman Church in Elizabethan Caernarvonshire, and indeed Wales in general, was that although the country was very propitious for Catholic survivalism of the kind mentioned earlier, it was not really a very fruitful sphere for Catholic conversion. There were, after all, only three main instruments by which this could be achieved—by political weapons, i.e. conspiracy or invasion; by literature; or by seminary priests. Not one of these three proved very practicable in Elizabethan Wales as it turned out. As far as political weapons were concerned Caernarvonshire's geographical position put it too far out on the periphery for it to be of primary importance. Literature of any kind could be produced only with tremendous effort in face of the most daunting odds;[71] to have to print and circulate clandestine contraband Catholic literature increased the difficulty twenty-fold. The Rhiwledyn venture is a most romantic and interesting episode, but the fact remains that it was a tragic failure. As far as seminary priests were concerned, they should have offered the best prospect of success. Wales produced a relatively large number of priests; and there was a disproportionately large number of Caernarvonshire men among the most distinguished of them. Yet of these only a small fraction came back to Wales, and an even smaller proportion back to Caernarvonshire itself. One of the chief reasons for this was the fewness of recusant households able and willing to take itinerant priests. Any home that was going to do so had to be not merely devoted but also prosperous, influential and secure. There were very few such, as was made plain in Robert Gwyn's letter of 1574. Nor was the author of *Y Drych Cristionogawl* any happier about the prospects in his preface to this Catholic book published in 1585. Yet strangely enough the Welsh Catholic exiles seriously and persistently overestimated their real numerical strength in Wales. As late as 1602 the Catholics at Douai were reliably reported as believing that Wales was 'almost all recusants, and as it were their own, and say no Queen's officers dare apprehend any man there.'[72] This was an assessment hopelessly out of touch with realities in the Wales of 1602. It simply failed to recognize the advantages which the Established Church enjoyed after nearly half a century of having been legally in possession of the religious field.

The Elizabethan Catholics were not the only people to have failed to take account of the way in which the Established Church had been able to capitalize its assets during Elizabeth's reign. Many more recent historians have tended towards a similar under-estimate. It may help to gain a clearer perspective by contrasting the state of affairs reported by Bishop Robinson in 1567 with conditions at the end of the century.

The first of the difficulties noted by Robinson was the reluctance of the gentry to show any enthusiasm for the Reformation. They had had strong political, social and economic incentives to accept any changes introduced into religion and worship by the State ever since Henry VIII's reign. But this did not necessarily involve them in any profound religious convictions. They were able to accept quite happily Mary's return to Rome. But during Elizabeth's reign the pressure of secular considerations inducing them to conform in religion increased. The long-drawn-out cold and hot war with Spain had conditioned men to associate Catholicism increasingly with subversion, treason and the overthrow of the established order. The gentry, as Professor Dodd has pointed out, were evolving a new kind of political loyalty to a whole nexus of associated institutions— Crown, Parliament, Common Law, and, not least, the Established Church.[73] So we need not be surprised to discover Caernarvonshire justices like Richard Vaughan showing 'energy and ruthlessness in prosecuting the opponents of the religious policy of the Government'. In the process he gained for himself the hatred 'of all papists that know him for because he doth correct their errors and goeth about to bring them to amendment of life'.[74] Nor should we, either, underestimate the force of cultural transformation which was making the laity, or at least the more well-to-do sections of it, better educated and more articulate. The old clerical monopoly of grammar-school and university education, crumbling in the fifteenth century, was finally shattered in the Tudor period. Within the county of Caernarvonshire the grammar school at Bangor and later at Botwnnog provided new educational opportunities for laymen and would-be clerics alike. Not far away were the schools at Beaumaris and Ruthin, while for those who could afford its facilities Shrewsbury attracted the sons of gentry from all over north Wales, and there were boys from the county going even further afield to Bedford, Westminster and Winchester.[75] Not a few of them proceeded from school to university or inn of court. In all these institutions they were likely to encounter Renaissance learning strongly tinged with Protestant values and loyalties. A large part of the literature for which they now acquired a taste was devotional or religious in character.[76] From their acquaintance with it sprang an ambition in some of them to provide a comparable diet for their fellow-countrymen in their own Welsh tongue.[77] But because of the immense difficulties facing any would-be author and publisher of Welsh books only a handful were published. One of the more interesting manuscripts of this kind prepared but not actually published by a layman was that written by Rowland Puleston of Caernarvon entitled *Llefr o'r Eglwys Christnogedd* (1583).[78] It was an attempt, in the absence of a complete Welsh Bible, to provide a summary of the books of the Old Testament. But its most interesting feature was its violently anti-papal, even Puritan, tone in the introduction. Precisely how many more there were in Caernarvonshire with views in sympathy with those of Rowland Puleston it is impossible to tell, and it may be significant that he found himself unable to publish his manuscript, perhaps from lack of support. But, initially at least, he must have been hopeful that there were enough of his fellow-Welshmen in sympathy to want to buy it if it did appear. Moreover, the very existence of a prominent layman with Protestant affiliations as strongly-developed as his ought to make us pause carefully before assuming too solid and unbreached a conservative outlook or too complete an apathy on the part of the rest of the laity of the county. Particularly is this so when we link it with another consideration, the improvement in the quality of the clergy.

It will be recalled that the second of Bishop Robinson's criticisms was of the indifferent calibre of his clergy. Yet in fact, as A. I. Pryce pointed out a long time ago, there was a dramatic improvement in the quality of the clergy during the Elizabethan period.[79] They took their tone to some extent from the bishops, in whom the diocese of Bangor was singularly more fortunate than it had been for centuries. Its Elizabethan bishops were, on the whole, a notable succession of good men: Rowland Meyrick, Nicholas Robinson, Hugh Bellot, Richard Vaughan and Henry Rowlands. They were, without exception, men of learning, local connections, and, in marked contrast to their medieval predecessors, resident pastors. Their cathedral clergy, too, numbered among them men of considerable distinction, like Richard Parry, afterwards bishop of St. Asaph and responsible for the Welsh Bible of 1620, Edmwnd Prys, translator of the Psalms, Henry Perry, author of a well-known Welsh book on rhetoric, or Hugh Lewys, rector of Llanddeiniolen and author of *Perl mewn Adfyd*, a translation of Miles Coverdale's *A Spiritual and Most Precious Pearl*.[80] Among the parish clergy, also, there was a sharp increase in the number of graduates, coming from the now almost wholly Protestant climate of the universities, and in the number of those described as preachers. Not a few of them showed their enthusiasm for education by making provision for it in the form of gifts or bequests. Many of these clergy were drawn from among the younger sons of families of gentry like Glynn of Glynllifon, Gruffydd of Penrhyn, Brickdall, Holland and Hookes of Conway, and Wynn of Gwydir. Between men of this kind and their kinsmen among the lay gentry there existed a close liaison and a common interest. There was coming into existence among the clergy of the diocese the nucleus of an articulate, well-trained intelligentsia. In any dialectical contest with them it must have become increasingly difficult for laymen with Catholic susceptibilities to hold their own largely unaided by systematic and regular instruction from clerics of their own persuasion. This is not to say that all was well with the clergy of the diocese of Bangor, and that there were no ignorant, negligent or poverty-stricken clerics left among them; of course there were, as the reports of Stuart bishops and the comments of Puritan critics make plain.[81] But it is to argue that, in comparison not merely with the beginning of Elizabeth's reign but also with the pre-Reformation period, the standard of training and accomplishment of men being ordained into holy orders was greatly improved. This can be reasonably expected to have had a beneficial effect on the amount and merit of religious instruction being given to parishioners, particularly when it had become possible to do this increasingly in their own tongue.

That brings us to the third of Robinson's basic criticisms, the absence of effective means for instructing the people in the vernacular. The translation of the Bible and the Prayer Book into Welsh was at once the supreme need and the paramount achievement of the Elizabethan Church in Wales. It was greatly to its credit that the project begun in 1567 with the publication of the New Testament and Book of Common Prayer had been completed in 1588 with the appearance of the whole Bible. To that task, two Caernarvonshire men—Richard Davies and William Morgan—had made invaluable contributions. As a result, ever since 1567 the people of Caernarvonshire, like the rest of the Welsh-speaking population, had been

hearing, week in and week out all the year around, church services in
their own language. The effects of this in the long term were two-
fold. First, it was the appeal in the mother-tongue which everywhere
in Europe triggered off the most dynamic Protestant energies and the
deepest loyalties to reformed religion. It made its own profound
and special contribution to the emphasis on the religion of the Word,
as against the religion of the Mass, which was how the contest
between Reform and Rome tended to reduce itself in the simplest and
most basic terms. Secondly, the parish church and its pulpit were
still much the most powerful medium of persuasion and propaganda
as far as the mass of the populace was concerned. They provided the
Established Church in every corner of the country with a regular
and all-pervasive means of influencing opinion completely denied
to the few Catholic priests who succeeded in penetrating into Caernarvonshire. Admittedly, in the face of an overwhelmingly illiterate
population, the impact made on the masses was slight and superficial.
But on that small minority in the ruling class that was literate and
articulate we should certainly not underestimate its influence.
Furthermore, that same group was exposed to the influence of an
attempt which went on, parallel with the translation of the Bible
and the Book of Common Prayer, to create a Protestant literature
and a Protestant church history. The actual number of Welsh books
printed for this purpose was extremely small–much smaller than the
Welsh Protestant humanists had hoped for. But Caernarvonshire,
as we have seen, had made its contribution to them; and the fullest
statement of the Protestant view of Welsh church history was made
by Bishop Richard Davies in his prefatory letter to the Welsh New
Testament of 1567.[82] In it he sought to show that in the Golden
Age of British history the Church had based its belief and worship
solely on the authority of the Scriptures. It had been diverted from
the true path only when forced to do so at the point of the sword
by the Anglo-Saxons who had been converted to the corruptions of
Roman Christianity. The result had been disastrous for the Welsh—
politically and culturally, no less than in religion.

The whole literary and apologetic campaign launched by Welsh
humanist reformers was characterised by three principal sources of
inspiration. The first and most important was the fusing of the
Renaissance and the Reformation so as to make the Welsh language
a prime handmaiden of the new ideals. The second was a strong
sense of the need for a return *ad fontes*, to the sources of the Celtic
Church, believed by the Reformers to have been a church whose
worship and creed were based on scriptural authority in the same way
as they were seeking to make those of their own church. Finally
there came a powerful stimulus from what was believed to be the
historic destiny of the Welsh—the notion that they could recover the
greatness of the Golden Age of the ancient empire of Britain by

returning to the pristine religious purity of that epoch; that this, in fact, would achieve the full and final vindication of the age-old Welsh prophecies of recovery and restoration. Much of this inspiration, it can rightly be argued, was not peculiar to the Protestant Reformers. Who, for instance, better exemplified the blending of Renaissance learning and religous idealism than the Catholic Reformer, Gruffydd Robert? Much of the content of the appeal may also have been of doubtful historical validity. Had they, for example, more right to claim the Celtic Church for their own than had the papists? The latter clearly did not think so and said as much. But when all such reservations have been allowed, the fact remains that this was an immensely potent patriotic appeal which the Reformers had launched, and what was more they were in control of all the media through which it might be propagated. While it expressed in an agreeable way the loyalties expected of up-and-coming servants of the Tudor state in Wales, it was also rooted in the primordial instincts—linguistic, historic and prophetic—of the centuries-old patriotism of Wales. And in no part of the country were these more deep-seated and tenacious than in Caernarvonshire.

NOTES

*Address delivered at the Annual General Meeting of the Society at Caernarvon, 31st October, 1964

[1] For details see the present writer's *Bywyd ac Amserau'r Esgob Richard Davies* (Cardiff, 1953), pp. 84-7 and refs. given there.

[2] See the present writer's *Welsh Church*, pp. 299—305.

[3] Ibid., pp. 307-8.

[4] Ibid., pp. 319-20.

[5] Ibid., pp. 309-10; based on P.R.O., S.P. 1/30, p. 291 and S.P.1/53, pp. 286-7.

[6] R. W. Hays, *The History of the Abbey of Aberconway* (Cardiff, 1963).

[7] Williams, *Welsh Church*, p. 390. In a letter to Thomas Cromwell in 1538 Edward Gruffydd of the Penrhyn said that Bangor Friary 'never kept past two friars at the most nor were able to find any more', P.R.O., S.P.1/133, pp. 246-7. But it was in Gruffydd's interest to play down as far as possible the importance and value of the house, so he cannot be regarded as a completely reliable witness.

[8] P.R.O., C1/1447/49-53.

[9] Hays, *Aberconway*, pp. 160-1; cf. Williams, *Welsh Church*, pp. 406-7.

[10] P.R.O., S.P.1/99, pp. 79-81.

[11] Glyn Roberts, 'The Dominican Friary of Bangor', *The Dominican* (Fourth Centenary Number, Bangor, 1957), pp. 17-8.

[12] Williams, *Welsh Church*, pp. 283, 288.

[13] Roberts, *The Dominican*, 1957, pp. 15-6.

[14] P.R.O., S.P.1/112, p. 261.

[15] David Mathew, *The Celtic Peoples and Renaissance Europe* (London, 1933), p. 42.

[16] P.R.O., S.P.1/77, pp. 203-4.

[17] *Letters and Papers . . . of the Reign of Henry VIII*, VIII, 832-3.

[18] P.R.O., S.P.1/101, pp. 205-6 for the petition. For the Chancery suits, P.R.O., C1/1977/23-4; 932/60-1; cf. also Williams, *Welsh Church*, p. 552.

[19] Letter dated 5th May, 1535, P.R.O., S.P.1/92, pp. 134-5.

[20] Letter dated 25th June, 1535, P.R.O., S.P.1/93, pp. 175-6.

[21] John Wynn, *The History of the Gwydir Family* (Cardiff, 1927), p. 65.

[22] B.M., Harleian MS. 604, f.69; cf. *Letters and Papers*, IX, 748.

[23] P.R.O., S.P.1/92, pp. 134-5.

[24] Ibid., 93, pp. 175-6.

[25] Ibid., 99, pp. 79-81.

[26] P.R.O., S.P.1/102, pp. 184-6; C/66/667, m. 12.

[27] *Letters and Papers*, X, 785.

[28] Ibid., XI, 385 (16).

[29] P.R.O., S.P.1/111, pp. 89-90; S.P.1/112, pp. 260-1.

[30] Ibid., 116, pp. 117-8; 117, pp. 10-1.

[31] Cf. Bishop Barlow's accusations against some of his canons at St. David's, below, pp. 117-8.

[32] A. I. Pryce, *The Diocese of Bangor in the Sixteenth Century*, p. 8.

[33] Williams, *Welsh Church*, pp. 310-1.

[34] P.R.O., S.P.1/122, pp. 250-1.

[35] *Letters and Papers*, VIII, 599.

[36] P.R.O., S.P.1/104, pp. 108-9; cf. Hays, *Aberconway*, pp. 176-7.

[37] P.R.O., S.P.1/133, pp. 246-7; cf. Roberts, *The Dominican*, 1957, pp. 17-8.

[38] Emyr Gwynne Jones, *Cymru a'r Hen Ffydd* (Cardiff, 1951), p. 15.

[39] Roberts, *The Dominican*, 1957, pp. 18-9.

[40] T. Wright (ed.), *Three Chapters of Letters relating to the Suppression of the Monasteries* (Camden Society, 1843), p. 212.

[41] Williams, *Welsh Church*, p. 292; cf. P.R.O., E301/74-6.

[42] P.R.O., E321/38/9; cf. also E321/37/32; 46/98; 46/142; 519/7-8; cf. E.A. Lewis and J. Conway Davies, *Records of the Court of Augmentations relating to Wales* (Cardiff, 1954), p. 63. For Gwynedd, see Williams, *Welsh Church*, pp. 331n, 449, 504, 532.

[42A] See the present writer's The Collegiate Church of Llanddewibrefi, *Ceredigion*, IV, iv (1963), 336-52.

[43] In the pamphlet known as *The Baterie against the Popes Botereulx* (1549). For further details about this interesting work see the present writer's article on the subject in *BBCS*, XIII (1949), 146-50.

[44] Quoted by Dafydd J. Bowen in 'Y Gymdeithas Gymreig . . . fel yr Adlewyrchir Hi yn y Farddoniaeth Uchelwrol' (M.A. Thesis, Wales, 1951), pp. 101-2; cf. also similar complaints by another poet of North Wales, Owain ap Gwilym, ibid., p. 102.

[45] See Melville Richards and Glanmor Williams (ed.), *Llyfr Gweddi Gyffredin* 1567 (revised ed., Cardiff, 1966), pp. xx-xxi.

[46] Bowen, 'Y Gymdeithas Gymreig', p. 101.

[47] Willaims, *Richard Davies*, pp. 8-9.

[48] Jesus College MS. 18; cf. W. Ambrose Bebb, *Cyfnod y Tuduriaid* (Wrecsam, 1939), pp. 92-3.

[49] Ibid., p. 93.

[50] Pryce, *Bangor*, pp. 12-4.

[51] For a more detailed analysis of the evidence, see the present writer's 'The Episcopal Registers of St. David's, 1554–65', *BBCS*, XIV (1950), 45-54, 125-38.

[52] See below, pp. 155-6.

[53] *The Dictionary of Welsh Biography* (Honourable Soc. of Cymmrodorion, 1959), *s.n.*

[54] Bebb, *Tuduriaid*, p. 94; cf. also the complimentary *englynion* by Siôn Tudur in N.L.W., Mostyn MS. 131, p. 29.

[55] *D.W.B.*, *s.n.*; cf. also Griffith John Williams, *Gramadeg Cymraeg Gruffydd Robert* (Cardiff, 1939), introduction.

[56] See below, pp. 142-6.

[57] Published in Browne Willis, *Survey of the Cathedral Church of Bangor* (London, 1721), pp. 262-71.

[58] Published in David Mathew 'Some Elizabethan Documents', *BBCS*, VI (1931-33), 77-8.

[59] Published in D. R. Thomas, *Life of Davies and Salesbury*, pp. 37-44.

[60] John Bossy, 'The Character of Elizabethan Catholicism', *Past and Present*, 1962, p. 39.

[61] The text is available in *Rhyddiaith Gymraeg: yr Ail Gyfrol* (Cardiff, 1956), pp. 191-209; cf. also W. Alun Mathias, *Llên Cymru*, III, 63-73.

[62] For further details see Emyr G. Jones, *Cymru a'r Hen Ffydd*, pp. 14-6, 24, 34-6, 65, 85.

[63] T. P. Ellis, *The Catholic Martyrs of Wales* (London, 1933), pp. 63-7.

[64] Jones, *Cymru a'r Hen Ffydd*, p. 94, fn. 22, for detailed references; and also A. J. Loomie, *The Spanish Elizabethans* (London, 1963), ch. 3.

[65] Geraint Gruffydd, 'Gwasg Ddirgel yr Ogof yn Rhiwledyn', *Journal Welsh Bibliog. Society*, IX (1958), 1-23.

[66] Jones, *Cymru a'r Hen Ffydd*, pp. 13-31.

[67] Ibid., p. 17.

[68] Mathew, *Renaissance Europe*, pp. 64-72; A. H. Dodd, 'North Wales in the Essex Revolt of 1601', *Eng. Hist. Rev.*, LIX (1944), 348-70; Emyr Gwynne Jones, 'The Lleyn Recusancy Case', *Trans. Cymmrodorion*, 1936, pp. 97-123.

[69] Text of letter printed in *Rhyddiaith Gymraeg*, II, 21-3.

[70] Bossy, *Past and Present*, 1962, p. 41.

[71] See the present writer's *Dadeni a Diwygiad a Diwylliant Cymru*, pp. 21-6.

[72] *Calender of State Papers, Domestic*, 1601-3, p. 181.

[73] 'The Pattern of Stuart Politics', *Trans. Cymmrodorion*, 1948, pp. 9-29. cf. above, pp. 26-7.

[74] Quoted in Geraint Dyfnallt Owen, *Elizabethan Wales*, p. 217.

[75] For Welsh grammar schools generally, ibid., ch. v, and also L. S. Knight, *Welsh Grammar Schools to 1600* (Newtown, 1926).

[76] See Louis B. Wright, *The Middle Class Culture of Elizabethan England* (Chapel Hill, 1935) for the important place occupied by religious works in contemporary English publications.

[77] Williams, *Dadeni, Diwygiad*, pp. 13-21.

[78] The original MS. is N.L.W. Plas Power MS. 1. Valuable extracts from the introduction are printed in *Rhyddiaith Gymraeg*, II, 53-5.

[79] *Bangor*, pp. xxxi-xl.

[80] For their literary activities see Thomas Parry, *A History of Welsh Literature*, trans. H. Idris Bell (2nd ed. Oxford, 1962), ch. viii; cf. W. J. Gruffydd, *Llenyddiaeth Cymru : Rhyddiaith o 1540–1640* (Wrexham, 1926), ch. vii.

[81] Thomas Richards, *The Puritan Movement in Wales, 1639 to 1653* (London, 1920), ch. i.

[82] See below, pp. 184-5, 212-4.

III. TWO NEGLECTED LONDON-WELSH CLERICS: RICHARD WHITFORD AND RICHARD GWENT

In 1594, that canny and observant Pembrokeshire historian, George Owen of Henllys, looking back on a century of careers thrown open to Welsh talents, wrote of the great numbers of Welshmen 'brought up and maintained at the universities of Oxford and Cambridge . . . where some proved to be learned men and good members in the Commonwealth of England and Wales; some worthy labourers in the Lord's vineyard'.[1] Two of the earlier of such labourers form the subject of this chapter. Each has found small but honourable mention in the general histories of the period. Neither, it goes without saying, is absent from the Cymmrodorion Society's *Dictionary of Welsh Biography*. But it remains true that both have been neglected—perhaps unduly neglected—in the memory of their fellow-countrymen generally.[2] Each is interesting for his own sake. Added piquancy is given to their careers by the contrast between them as minor figures caught up on opposite sides in the great events of that epoch-making decade from 1530 to 1540. Both became London-Welshmen and each has attracted the writer's attention for some years, so that they seemed to provide for him an eminently suitable subject on which to be privileged to address the Society of Cymmrodorion.

RICHARD WHITFORD

As his name suggests, Whitford was a native of the parish of the same name in Flintshire. The terms of the will of his uncle, also a Richard Whitford,[3] indicate that they belonged to a family of substantial landowners holding estates in Lancashire as well as north-east Wales. The exact date of the younger Whitford's birth is unknown to us, though the circumstances of his university career point to his having been born *c.* 1470. We know nothing about his early life or schooling, but he was obviously intended for the priesthood and, to prepare for his vocation, he proceeded to the university. Nearly all the Welsh students of his time went to Oxford, and Whitford may have been no exception. He is claimed as an Oxford man by Anthony à Wood[4]; but apart from this there is no record of his having been there. The first authentic reference to his university career is his election to a fellowship of Queens' College, Cambridge, in 1495.[5] This makes it almost certain that he had spent part, if not all, of his career as a student at Cambridge.

In view of the marked attraction which humanism is known to have had for Whitford, it may have been the earlier welcome given to the new learning in Cambridge which attracted him thither, whether as a matriculant, or as a migrant from Oxford. At all events he was still at Queens' College in March, 1498, when he was given leave of absence by the President and Fellows of the College to go abroad in attendance on William Blount, Lord Mountjoy, as chaplain, confessor and tutor.[6] At the university of Paris, Whitford was received as B.A. on his Cambridge degree, being then described as a man from the diocese of St. Asaph; and he proceeded M.A. in 1499.[7] His young charge and master, Lord Mountjoy, was an enthusiastic student and in consequence of his attainments was afterwards appointed by the King to direct the studies of the young Prince Henry (later Henry VIII). When Mountjoy returned to England in 1499[7] he and Whitford brought back with them the most famous scholar in Europe, none other than the illustrious Erasmus. Mountjoy remained Erasmus's patron for the rest of his life, and Whitford, too, was on terms of very close friendship with him.

Soon after his return to England Whitford became chaplain to Richard Foxe, bishop of Winchester. Foxe, though far from being an altogether lovable character, was nonetheless a generous patron of the new learning being, among other things, founder of Corpus Christi College, Oxford. A curious episode involving Foxe, Thomas More and Whitford is related by Roper in his life of More. In the Parliament of 1504 More, then a 'beardless boy', had been foremost in opposing Henry VII's demands for taxation. Some time afterwards Bishop Foxe promised to restore More to the King's favour 'if he would be ruled by him'. But, having left the bishop, More, so Roper tells us.

> fell in communication with one Master Whitford, his familiar friend, then chaplain to that bishop, and after a Father of Sion, and shewed him what the bishop had said unto him, desiring to have his advice therein; who, for the passion of God, prayed him in no wise to follow his counsel: 'For my lord, my master', quoth he, 'to serve the king's turn, will not stick to agree to his own father's death'. So Sir Thomas More returned to the bishop no more.[8]

The story is almost certainly exaggerated; it may very well be apocryphal. It says little for Whitford's loyalty as a servant, but speaks eloquently of his friendship for More.

Of that friendship we have still more striking testimony in a letter from Erasmus a little later. On 1st May, 1506 Erasmus wrote 'from the country' to Whitford. He enclosed a Latin declamation of his own composition against Lucian's *Pro Tyrannicida*[9] and asked Whitford to compare it with a similar effort by More and decide which was the better. 'Both of us certainly you equally love,' said Erasmus, 'to both you are equally dear'.[10]

Soon after this letter was written, Whitford took a decision which shaped the whole of the subsequent course of his life: he entered the convent of Sion of which his uncle was already a member.[11] The house of Sion lay near the Thames on the outskirts of London between the villages of Isleworth and Brentford. Founded in 1431, it belonged to the Order of the Bridgettines which, together with that of the Observant Friars and the Carthusians, was the only order in England to maintain the monastic rule in all its strictness. Enjoying an annual income of £1,735, it was tenth in order of wealth among all the religious houses of the kingdom, and its possessions far exceeded those of any other nunnery. Its wealth, strict piety, and reputation as a centre of devotional literature, attracted to it recruits from some of the most distinguished families in the land. Sixty nuns were maintained there and twenty-five religious men, who acted as chaplains, confessors, and spiritual directors. The latter were drawn from an élite of learning and sanctity. Nearly all were former fellows of Oxford or Cambridge drawn to Sion by a yearning for strict religious observance, austere living, and dedicated scholarship. 'They formed', says Professor Knowles, 'a group without parallel in Tudor England, men who combined personal austerity of life with theological or devotional competence, and who, by their books, by their direction of a fervent and aristocratic nunnery, and by their influence as counsellors and confessors of leading laymen, were a power to be reckoned with in a religious world which contained all too few centres of enlightened piety'.[12] To have been a member of this group at all would in itself be some claim to distinction. Whitford, however, was for the next thirty years or so to be one of its two most brilliant luminaries.

During that time, apart from the publication of his books, we hear nothing of him. We must suppose that he found contentment and satisfaction in a steady round of spiritual counsel, prayer, meditation, and writing. Then, in 1534, the inmates of Sion became caught up in the toils of the pressing issues of Henry VIII's second marriage and the royal supremacy. The unique position of this influential and widely-known 'Orthodox Port Royal', as Dom David Knowles has so aptly described it, made its acquiescence in the King's proceedings a matter of much concern to Henry and his ministers. From January 1534 onwards a succession of Cromwell's agents visited Sion and tried by a mixture of blandishments, persuasion, sophistry, and threats, to break down the resistance of its inmates. They met with little success. The nuns and brethren found in Richard Reynolds their most learned, eloquent, and immovable champion, a man prepared to go cheerfully to a martyr's death. Next to Reynolds, Richard Whitford was rated by Cromwell's men as their most stubborn opponent. One of Cromwell's more insensitive and heavy-handed lieutenants, Thomas

Bedyll, was at Sion in December, 1535 and gave Whitford a rough passage: 'I handled Whitford after that in the garden,' he reported to Cromwell, 'both with fair words and foul, and showed him that through his obstinacy he should be brought to the great shame of the world for his irreligious life and for his using bawdy words to divers ladies at the time of their confession, whereby (I said) he might be the occasion that shrift shall be laid down through England'. Whitford was hardly a man to flinch at such crude threats and grossly untrue accusations. 'He hath a brazen forehead,' complained Bedyll, 'which shameth at nothing'.[13]

Nevertheless, early in 1536, Sion seems to have capitulated and to have subscribed to the royal supremacy.[14] Thereafter, until its dissolution the house was treated with a kind of gingerly mildness by the authorities—Whitford, for example, seems to have had no restraint placed upon him in the matter of publishing books. But the inmates refused to surrender voluntarily in 1539, and the house had forcibly to be suppressed in November of that year. Whitford was still there then, and was awarded a pension of £8. He was presumably required to take an oath to maintain the King's title as Supreme Head, but it seems impossible to tell whether in fact he did so. All that can be said with any degree of certainty is that he now retired to the household of Charles, Lord Mountjoy, the son of his former charge, and lived in seclusion. He was now an old man, probably in his late sixties, and had not long to live. But from Mountjoy's household he continued to publish devotional books wholly conservative in character.

Little, then, is known or is likely to be known of the events of Whitford's life. It is his writings which matter; his books are his biography.[15] Whitford must have begun writing seriously soon after he entered the convent of Sion, for he tells us in the preface to one of his books published in 1537 that it had originally been written more than twenty years previously at the request of Dame Elizabeth Gybs, then abbess of Sion. The book had become popular and Whitford literally had to rewrite it again and again. He adds feelingly, 'and because that writing unto me is very tedious: I thought better to put it in print'.[16] Almost all his books, in fact, we learn from their prefaces, had been written by him for the benefit of the community at Sion long before they were published.

Some of his books appeared to have a strictly vocational appeal to members of a religious community. Such was his translation of the rule of St. Augustine which was published in 1525 and was, as far as is known, the first of his works to be printed.[17] This, also, was a translation which had been undertaken seven years before it was put into print. Another work similarly designed 'for the edification of certain religious persons unlearned that daily did read' it in Latin, 'not understanding what they read', was *The martiloge in English after the use of the church of Salisbury/ & as it is read in Syon / with additions*,[18] which was first published in February, 1526–7. Possibly its chief interest for us in this context is the careful way in which Whitford insisted upon including some of the saints of his own native Wales, among them Cenydd, Teilo, David, Brychan, Caradog (*sic*), and Padarn.

But works of this kind, although first undertaken for the benefit of the convent of Sion, had a wider appeal. Nothing was more symptomatic of changing social attitudes and values in the fifteenth century and the early sixteenth century than the growing numbers of educated lay men and women. Literacy often went hand in hand with piety and inspired a craving for devotional and didactic literature. This demand had not been created by the printing press; the press had rather been brought into existence to supply it. Of the early books which began to pour from the presses of Europe, by far the greater number were religious in nature.[19] And so, Richard Whitford's writings, designed originally for the community at Sion, found a much wider market among those earnest men and women who aspired to edification and rectitude though their paths had been cast in the world and not in the convent.

Whitford himself was given an added impetus to publish his books by the alarm he felt at the spread of heresy in England. In a number of his works published in the 1530s he specifically referred to the need to combat the seditious doctrine of heretics. He prefaced his book called *The Pipe / or Tun / of the life of perfection*[20] with these words to his 'devout readers':

> This work was written years ago, and now thought necessary to be sent forth, because of these new fangled persons, which indeed be heretics, although they will not so be called, that do write new opinions and do not only deprave all religions that commonly be called by that name religion. But also do corrupt the high religion of all religions, the New Testament of Christ, against whom they fare.

This book was one which defended the monastic vocation with skill and subtlety but in the process made many damaging admissions of the low state of observance of the monastic rule in contemporary England and Wales. The copy of it to be found in the British Museum is preserved in its original handsome binding with the arms of England on the cover and those of Castile and Aragon on the reverse. It is believed to have been bound for Henry VIII and Catherine of Aragon—one must suppose that the latter derived more comfort and instruction from it than the former.

Two other books which were very popular and which ran through a number of editions in the 1530s were more specifically directed to a lay audience. The one was the *Dialogue or Communication between the Curate or Ghostly Father and the parochian or ghostly child for a due preparation unto houseling.*[21] This was a commentary on the sacrament of the altar and the best ways of preparing for it. Wholly and emphatically conservative in tone, it was not originally written as a controversial work but it does contain occasional references to the spread of heretical doctrine, such as:

> I beseech you take no heed unto these heretics that do move the simple people to require to have and to receive the sacrament in both forms, that is to say of bread and wine as the priest doth.[22]

The other book, known as *The Work for Householders*,[23] was designed to strengthen private devotions in the home and took the form of a dialogue between the householder and the household. It is full of sound and practical advice, effectively presented and refreshingly free from the kind of unawareness of the realities of everyday life that might have been expected from an author who had been so long immolated in a convent of strict observance. About the practical difficulties of fostering private devotions in the average Tudor household, Whitford had no illusions. He puts a pathetic answer to his own pleas into the mouth of one of his speakers in the work:

> Sir, this work is good for religious persons and for such persons as be solitary and do lie alone by themselves, but we do lie two or three sometimes together, and yet in one chamber divers beds and so many in company. If we should use these things in presence of our fellows some would laugh us to scorn and mock us.[24]

Two of the last books published by Richard Whitford may be specially related to the events through which he had lived since 1534. He tells us that each of the two books had been written many years before, but it is difficult not to suppose that the enforcement of the royal supremacy had not given them a new relevance. The one was *A Daily Exercise and Experience of Death* and the other *A Devout Work of Patience.* In the work on death there was nothing unwholesome or morbid. Whitford sought to bring comfort to the many who had so paralysing a dread of the 'horrible, ugly and fearful' sight of death and especially of sudden death. The burden of his argument was that by regularly remembering in life the prospect of death, and understanding that it was something 'only to be desired' wherein man might hope to 'change this wretched life for another more precious and joyful',[25] the terrors of mortality could be overcome. The martyrdom of his friend, Thomas More, his fellow-monk, Richard Reynolds, and others, had given Richard Whitford himself ample occasion for meditations of this kind.

The Devout Work of Patience was included in the last-known of his publications and appeared in 1541. The abrupt ending at this date of Whitford's activities as an author, after some fifteen years or more of actively publishing, suggests that he must have died in or soon after 1541, though we do not certainly know when his death occurred. The final paragraph of the work is worth quoting. It shows Whitford patiently resigned to the worst that the world could do to him, though, in keeping with the whole tenor of his life, there is a certain passive submissiveness and unmilitancy about it:

> For in this life if you in all persecutions, passions, adversities, troubles turn and apply your heart, mind and thought unto the example of our Saviour Jesu, you shall not only have patience, but also you shall be glad and joyful to suffer for his sake as he did for you and so shall you be rendered and made quiet, and restful in your mind and conscience, And for your good example in the edifying of your neighbour, you shall with our saviour be exalted and have good name and fame above other.[26]

There may be some surprise at this point why nothing has as yet been said about Richard Whitford and the *Imitatio Christi*. If and when Whitford is remembered at all it is chiefly as the author of the most famous and, many would insist, the best English translation of that great book.[27] I have not mentioned him in that context because I do not believe he was responsible for the translation. Since, as far as I know, I am the first to question Whitford's authorship, perhaps I may be allowed briefly to outline why.

Whitford made it almost a fetish to publish under his own name. In the preface to the second of his published works, *The Martiloge*, he gave his reasons for doing so. First, because although it was usual to publish anonymously, Whitford acknowledged his authorship not for 'any manner thanks, praise, or other temporal or worldly reward', but only for the 'spiritual profit of the readers', so that he might offer himself unto 'just correction'. Secondly, because the authors of some anonymous tracts were suspected of 'not holding and keeping the right path of Christianity'. By the 1530s, Whitford had become deeply concerned about the way in which heretics publishing anonymous tracts might mislead the orthodox. He complains in the introduction to the edition of his *Work for Householders* published in 1537 that in one volume entirely attributed to him 'is one of my works left out, which work is numbered among the contents of the same volume and book. And instead of my book is another . . . heretical work set in place'. In view of Whitford's strongly-held and repeatedly-expressed opinions about the need to acknowledge authorship of published works, it would be very risky indeed to accept anything as his work unless he himself attested his responsibility for it. This is not done in any one of the many editions of the English translation of the *Imitatio Christi* attributed to him. Yet the book has regularly and confidently been assumed to be his. Why should this have been so?

The mistake arose as a result of the edition of the *Imitation of Christ* published in 1556.[28] Bound up with it was a translation of the 'Golden Epistle' of St. Bernard of Clairvaux. The epistle is rounded off with the following paragraph by its translator:

> This was brought unto me in English of an old translation, rough and rude, and required to amend it. I beseech you to take all unto the best, and pray for the old wretched brother of Sion, Richard Whytforde.

This last sentence is Whitford's characteristic leave-taking of his readers and there can be no doubt that this translation of the epistle is his own work, for at least three editions of it appeared in 1530 and 1531 in his name.[29] And it was this last sentence which led people to attribute to Whitford the translation of the *Imitatio* as well as the *Epistola*.

This coupling of the *Epistola* with the *Imitatio* was not new. In each of seven editions published between 1530 and 1541[30] the two works had been published together. But, although the text of the *Imitatio* in each of the earlier editions is identical with that of the edition of 1556, the text of the *Epistola* is not. There were in fact two independent English translations of the *Epistola* being published in the 1530s. They are quite distinct and there can be no question of both having come from the same pen. The one was Richard Whitford's. The other was an anonymous translation first published separately by Thomas Godfrey in (?)1530.[31] It is this anonymous version of the *Epistola* which was bound with the *Imitatio* in each of the many editions which appeared between 1530 and 1541 which I have been able to see. Moreover, in every edition of the anonymous translation of the *Epistola* known to me there is also included a translation of the revelation of St. Bridget which is not found in Whitford's work. Knowing Whitford's pronounced views on acknowledging the authorship of his books it seems almost inconceivable that, having gone to the trouble of translating the 'Golden Epistle' himself, he would be content to have another man's translation of it bound up with his own version of the *Imitatio*. The conclusion would therefore seem to be that it was not Whitford who translated the *Imitatio* at all, but someone else—very probably the anonymous translator of the 'Golden Epistle'. Many editions accustomed readers to having the two works published together between 1541 and 1556. When Cawood came to publish it in 1556 it was Richard Whitford's translation of the *Epistola* which he included, for the first time, with the *Imitatio*. Later readers, seeing the ascription of the *Epistola* to Whitford, also attributed, erroneously, the *Imitatio* to his pen.

That is the crux of the argument against Whitford's authorship. It is, I believe, confirmed by internal stylistic evidence, especially one highly distinctive idiosyncracy. This is Whitford's inordinate fondness for archaic forms of the third person plural present tense of the verb, e.g. "been", "doon", etc. Abundant examples are found in all those works indisputably his, but do not occur in the English translation of the *Imitatio*.

To deprive him of what has been regarded as his chief mark of distinction may seem a strange way of honouring a neglected figure, but Whitford was not the sort of man who would have wanted to be remembered for the wrong reasons. Even if this beautiful translation of the *Imitatio* has to be denied him, there remains much to commend him to the regard of his fellow-countrymen. He was the loved and respected friend of two of the greatest men of his age; he was one of the most distinguished members of a religious community pre-eminent in its combination of austerity and scholarship; and he was a writer of English of no mean talent. Most of his work consists of translation and adaptation, it is true. But he approached his task with ripe commonsense as well as admirable equipment as scholar and writer. He found many contemporary religious writings, as he himself tells us, to be archaic and unreadable—'old, scabrous, rough, and not of the English commonly used in these parts'.[32] He himself aimed at a simple, intelligible, and fluent idiom—'a plain style without inkhorn terms'.[33] In this he succeeded. He wrote with the sparkle and directness which characterized so much writing in this age when the bloom of youth still lay soft and unrubbed on the English language.

Whitford represents, better than any other Welshman I know, the *devotio moderna* of the closing Middle Ages. Earnest, intense, scholarly; unwearying in its patient search for sanctity, it sought painfully and slowly to mount the ladder of perfection, that *scala perfectionis*, which was the subject of one of the books which John Fewterer, prior of Sion, began to translate and Whitford completed.[34] It was a kind of piety which was already being left behind by the tide of tumultuous events. But Richard Whitford lived and died amid the odour of medieval piety. He had in his make-up much of the medieval man's uncritical love of the spectacular and the legendary. Though a friend of Erasmus and More, he had a deep affection for the *Legenda Aurea* and did not hesitate to borrow from it for his own purposes. Yet in his own dedicated and self-renunciated fashion, 'the poor wretch' or the 'old wretch' of Sion, as he delighted to call himself, was an attractive figure whose striving after the life of perfection was, to quote his own metaphor, 'much like unto a pleasant, precious and wholesome wine'.[35]

RICHARD GWENT

Traditionally, Richard Gwent is said to have been a farmer's son from that province of south-east Wales whose name he bore.[36] This seems very probable. Throughout his career he maintained close connexions with south Wales and the border country, and the executor of his will bore the unmistakably Welsh name of Thomas ap Howell.[37] But the date of his birth and the circumstances of his upbringing, like those of almost every comparable personality of early Tudor times, remain obscure. The first certain record that we have of him is when he was elected a fellow of All Souls College, Oxford, in 1515. This suggests that he was probably born during the last decade of the fifteenth century. At the university he pursued a distinguished career as a lawyer. He became a Bachelor of Civil Law in December 1518 and of Canon Law in February 1519. By 1525 he had become a doctor of both laws,[38] and for a time was chief moderator of the Canon Law school at Oxford. A long connexion between him and the nunnery of Godstow is first signalled by his being instituted by the abbess and convent to the vicarage of St. Giles, Oxford, a living in their gift.

After leaving the university, Gwent appears to have done what many of the brightest and most aspiring graduates of his time were doing; he entered Wolsey's service. He can have served him only in lowly capacity for we know almost nothing about his activities during this period. We get a glimpse of his having acted as a commissioner on behalf of the cardinal to settle some quarrels in the monastery of Winchcombe. But the whole episode is obscure and is mentioned only incidentally many years after it had taken place.[39] More interesting is the inclusion of Richard Gwent as one of the counsel chosen to act for Catherine of Aragon in 1529[40] when the 'King's great matter' was being brought for hearing before Cardinals Campeggio and Wolsey. Gwent can have been no more than a very junior counsel. John Fisher, bishop of Rochester, Henry Standish, bishop of St. Asaph, and Nicholas West, bishop of Ely, were briefed as the Queen's chief defenders, though of these only Fisher was prepared to make any serious stand on her behalf. We learn nothing of Gwent's part in the trial from the contemporary proceedings, but some ten years later, in 1539, when one of Lord Montague's servants, Anthony Roke, was giving evidence at his trial for treason, he gave some interesting details about contacts he had had with Gwent during the proceedings against Catherine of Aragon. Roke was, at the time of the trial, a servant to the Queen and he testified that when certain writings came from Rome he was sent post-haste from Reading to bring Dr. Gwent from Gloucester and Llanthony for urgent consultations with the Queen at Woodstock.[41] Roke gave no indication what the contents of these 'writings' were—he contented himself with saying that Gwent knew what was in them—and it has not been possible to discover what they can have been. The interest of Gwent's part in all these proceedings is two-fold: first, it suggests that he was already being recognized as a jurist of more than ordinary skill; and, second, that he probably served the King better than the Queen, for it is quite evident that he suffered no check in his career as the result of his part in the proceedings. On the contrary, when next we hear of him in 1532, he is already the King's chaplain and a trusted royal servant.

The years 1530–2 in Gwent's career, as indeed in much else of the history of this period, are obscure. But we must probably assume that when, on the fall of the great cardinal, Wolsey's household of trained and experienced servants was transferred to the King,[42] Gwent was included among them. What was more, as one of Wolsey's men, Gwent had probably been in touch with Thomas Cromwell, who was soon to be, under the King, the most powerful man in the realm. As Cromwell's fortunes rose, so did Gwent's. The year 1532 saw Cromwell attain a position of ascendancy among the King's advisers.[43] It can hardly be a coincidence that it is in that year that Gwent's name begins to figure in Cromwell's correspondence or that in September of that year Gwent is put forward for the responsible office of dean of the Arches.[44] Nor would he be likely to have appeared early in February, 1533 in a list of leading ecclesiastics appended to one of Cromwell's *aide-mémoires*[45] unless he had been regarded by the latter as an able and trusted subordinate.

The choice of Gwent as dean of the Arches would at any time have been of some importance. The Court of the Arches was the consistory court of the province of Canterbury, combined with which was the archbishop's Court of Peculiars. The dean of the Arches was, therefore, the archbishop's official principal. In September 1532 the responsibility was weightier than usual. The see of Canterbury had just been made vacant by the death of Archbishop Warham. Warham was an old man who had occupied the see since 1504. Although at first be had bowed before royal pressure he had, in the last few months of his life, given every indication of putting up determined resistance to any suggestion by the King and his ministers that the divorce proceedings should be heard at Canterbury after the Pope had removed them to Rome.The archbishop had been referring pointedly to the precedent set for him by his martyr-predecessor, Thomas à Becket, and giving every sign of preparing to act upon it, when in August 1532 death intervened. The situation was critical; a compliant archbishop had to be found, and in the meantime a skilful and reliable man had immediately to be put in as dean of the Arches. Hence the importance of Gwent's appointment. From a letter to Cromwell by Thomas, prior of Christchurch, Canterbury, it appears that Gwent had wasted no time in getting down to Canterbury to be present in person at a presentation required by Cromwell.[46]

As dean of the Arches, Gwent was much employed during subsequent years. In addition to the considerable amount of routine work which he heard at the Court of the Arches and in the Court of Delegates, his ability as a jurist was frequently called upon by Archbishop Cranmer when he was faced with unusually tangled or delicate actions involving ecclesiastical administration, or matrimony, or probate.[47] Cromwell, too, had his uses for Gwent in this respect. It was Gwent, for instance, who granted a dispensation for marriage acting as deputy to Peter Vannes, the King's secretary and papal collector; and there exists one of Cromwell's memoranda for 1535 in which he adumbrated a scheme whereby Gwent should be given licence to wind up in the King's name the causes already being heard in the court of the archbishop of Canterbury. More significant was the suggestion that Gwent and three or four others should be given a commission to hear and determine in the King's name many important causes previously reserved to ecclesiastical courts. The kinds of actions specially singled out in the memorandum, which is very strongly erastian in tone, are those concerning probates, testaments, and tithes.[48]

Gwent was also extensively employed by archbishop and secretary in enforcing the royal supremacy between 1533 and 1535. In the summer of 1533 he was associated with Cranmer in the delicate task of interrogating Elizabeth Barton, the nun of Kent.[49] This nun, who had had a reputation for holiness since her mysterious illness of which she had been reputedly healed by miracle in 1525, had steadfastly and openly expressed her opposition to Henry's divorce proceedings. She was widely known and much respected on account of her trances and visions, the exact nature of which we are, luckily, not called upon to try to determine in the present context. She was, we may note in passing, a frequent visitor to Sion and must have been well known to Whitford. By 1533 her opposition was too dangerous to the Government to go unchecked and her trial, which followed, became a *cause célèbre*. Cromwell sent down interrogatories, on which she was examined by Cranmer and Gwent and others. In a letter to Cromwell, Gwent makes it plain that their technique was to lead the nun on to make increasingly damaging confessions that would destroy her completely, as indeed they did.[50] In the same letter Gwent suggested ways in which the King might direct his appeal to the archbishop's court and also desired Cromwell to thank the King for the buck given him at Cromwell's instigation—a further token of how rapidly he was rising.[51] Late in the same year Gwent was at Lichfield carefully supervising the election as bishop of Coventry and Lichfield of his friend Rowland Lee, another of Cromwell's most trusted agents. Gwent was here applying his legal expertise in searching out precedents so that no objection could later be raised to Lee's election.[52]

The following year, 1534, saw Gwent taking part in the peace negotiations between England and Scotland and signing the peace treaty as one of England's signatories in May 1534.[53] In the summer he was busy as one of Cranmer's visitors at the cathedral of Lincoln. As the archbishop's commissary he visited Merton College, Oxford, in September 1534 and altered many of the ancient customs there.[54] The year 1534 was also one in which he was rewarded with valuable ecclesiastical preferment, becoming archdeacon of London, archdeacon of Brecon, and a prebendary at Lincoln. The following year he was energetically enforcing the royal supremacy and ensuring that the Pope's name had been duly expunged from service books.[55] Writing to Cromwell after a tour of this kind in the diocese of Chichester, he had some revealing suggestions to make about the smaller monasteries. Commenting sadly on the ignorance of the inmates of such houses 'where be not . . . past 3, 6 or 9 in number', he suggested 'it were better such small houses were knit together in one that there might be a convenient number and so at the least two or three learned, and specially the master to teach the other'.[56] This sounds as if Gwent already had a shrewd suspicion of the way the wind was blowing in relation to the monasteries.

If he did not, early in 1536 he was given further pretty clear indications of the trend of events. He had been appealed to by monks for assistance with Cromwell before. Now he got more urgent appeals that he should use his good offices with the vicar-general. The abbots of Hayles and Evesham and the prioress of Catesby thus used him as their liaison with Cromwell[57]; and between the years 1537 and 1539 Gwent acted as the agent for a number of the larger houses in paying over fees and gifts to Cromwell.[58] However, Gwent was not, as far as one can tell, employed in the suppression of the smaller monasteries. He seems only to have been given the unsavoury task of giving one more twist to the relentless screw brought to bear on the inmates of the London Charterhouse in May 1537.[59] For two years or more the Carthusian monks, inspired by John Houghton, had stood out firmly against the royal supremacy. Their outstanding members had already been removed by martyrdom or dispersion, and the remnant had been subjected to persuasion, blackmail, and subversion. It was, therefore, hardly to be wondered at that in May 1537 many took the oath of acknowledgement of royal supremacy; what was surprising was that after all the pressure to which they had been subjected there were still many who refused.[60]

The reason why Gwent was not engaged on the work of dissolving the monasteries was no doubt that he was being entrusted with the more responsible task of acting as prolocutor of the lower house of Convocation which was meeting in June 1536. Richard Gwent himself makes it plain that this was a task thrust upon him against his will. A short but forceful letter from him to Dr. Richard Layton urges the latter 'this be most heartily to desire you (touching the prolocutor) that you will not only abstain from provoking any man to name me to it but also to do your best that some other may be, for if you knew what hangs upon it and what displeasure it would be to me I do not doubt but you would friendly help to rid me from it'.[61] What did hang upon the choice, and why was Gwent so eager to avoid the responsibility? The answer may well be that when this letter was written its author already had some inkling of what Convocation would be called upon to undertake. The opening sermon was preached by Latimer on 9th June and he struck a keynote of denunciation of papal usurpations and the slowness of Convocation to reform ecclesiastical and doctrinal abuses.[62] Such themes were certainly acceptable to Thomas Cromwell, and may even have been approved beforehand by him. But the response of the lower house of Convocation, as presented by its prolocutor, Richard Gwent, who was chosen for the office despite his unwillingness, was anything but in agreement with Latimer's eloquent declamation. Instead, it brought forward a long memorandum of sixty-seven *mala dogmata*, severely critical of the degradation of popular belief, the open blasphemy of holy things, and the widespread penetration of heretical doctrines, as the result of tacit or avowed sanction given by certain members of the council to the spread of heretical books.[63] We may be sure that Gwent, no matter what his personal views about religion were, had no relish for being associated with so outspoken a criticism of much that had Cromwell's connivance, if not his active instigation, especially at a time when he was already in some difficulty with Cromwell over another matter concerning the deanery of Lichfield. Two other issues of great delicacy had also been raised in this Convocation. The first was the declaration that Henry's marriage to Anne Boleyn (executed while Convocation was sitting) had been null and void. The second was Cromwell's claim to preside, through his proctor, Dr. Petre, over Convocation, from which laymen had hitherto been excluded. Here were matters enough for any man who had an inkling of them to be worried about how they should be steered through a not very sympathetic lower house of Convocation.[64]

Gwent may also have been involved in some minor difficulty as a result of the quarrels in the diocese of St. David's at this time. He had been archdeacon of Brecon since 1534 and as one of the most powerful members of the chapter, and one who had influence with Thomas Cromwell, he was drawn into the disputes between the chapter and its bishop, William Barlow.[65] It would be tedious to go into detail beyond a reminder that Barlow, an advanced reformer, was one of Cromwell's most trusted agents in Wales. In the course of his conflict with the canons he depended heavily on his close links with Cromwell, and Gwent may not have improved his own position by acting, as he appears to have done, as an intermediary between Cromwell and the somewhat conservatively-minded canons of St. David's.[66]

There is no reason to suppose that Gwent's stock appeared to have dropped in Cromwell's estimation at this time because he was himself out of sympathy with the Protestant trends which for the time being appeared to be given considerable freedom and encouragement. What reliable indications we have of Gwent's personal attitude towards the progress of reform—and extremely few they are—point to his having been of a reformist turn of mind. Nonetheless, his activities, for whatever reason, seem to have been much reduced in scope and importance during the whole of 1537 and the first half of 1538. Obviously he had not entirely lost favour, but he appears only very rarely in the records of the period.[67]

When Gwent reappears with some degree of prominence in 1538 and 1539, he does so as a searcher-out of heretics. In July 1538, John Longland, bishop of Lincoln, a diocese much troubled by heretics, sought advice from Gwent on how best to deal with a stubborn one.[68] On 1st October he was included in a strong commission appointed by Cromwell to search out Anabaptists.[69] Having been consulted early in 1539 about the Six Articles Act,[70] Gwent was much occupied during the later months of the year in helping Cranmer to discover and examine Anabaptists and sacramentaries in Calais, who were clearly being viewed with no little alarm.[71] The examinations at Calais were no sooner over than Gwent was plunged into the task of receiving the surrender of the larger monasteries in the border counties and assigning pensions to their inmates.[72] The three others associated with him in this work were all of Welsh origin—John Price of Brecon, Edward Carne of Glamorgan, and John Arnold of Monmouthshire. The very first monastery of which he took possession was the nunnery of Godstow, a house with which he had been closely associated for at least fifteen years. One would give much to know what his reactions were when he received the surrender from Katherine Bulkeley, who had on more than one occasion sought to influence Cromwell through him. The tour of the monasteries lasted for three months and was not completed until the end of 1540.

As is well known, the year 1539 and the first half of 1540 saw English politics deeply divided between two factions, the one led by Norfolk and Gardiner and the other by Cromwell and Cranmer. Gwent, though no more than a secondary figure, could hardly have avoided taking sides, but we have no certain indication where his affiliations lay. It is true that he had been included with Cranmer in 1539 on the commission dealing with heretics; but that body also included Richard Sampson, bishop of Chichester, who was, without doubt, a formidable enemy to Cromwell and Cranmer. Again, Gwent was required to undertake important responsibilities almost immediately after Cromwell's fall in June 1540. But this need not necessarily mean that he had been opposed to Cromwell's policies, for none of the latter's party followed him to the scaffold and Cranmer still retained his strategic position. Indeed, it may have been Cranmer's influence which had earlier ensured Gwent's re-election as prolocutor in April 1540, when there seem to have been two prolonged sessions before he was finally agreed upon and presented by Polydore Vergil.[73] The nature of the first task assigned to Gwent after Cromwell's fall suggests that he was at least acceptable to the conservative faction or that Cranmer's power was still strong enough to keep his dean of the Arches well placed. Gwent was now to play a leading part in getting rid of the King's fourth wife, Anne of Cleves, who had been Cromwell's worst miscalculation, and for pressing whom on the King he had very largely come to grief. It was Gwent who, on 7th July, 1540, presented the King's letters of commission under the Great Seal to begin the process of nullity, and it was Gwent, along with Gardiner, Tunstall, bishop of Durham, and Thirlby, the elect of Westminster—all three of whom belonged to the conservative wing—who were empowered to take the depositions of witnesses. The result was a foregone conclusion; three days later, Gwent, as archdeacon of London and prolocutor of the lower house of Convocation, signed the judgment against Anne.[74]

Gwent seems now to have been firmly established as prolocutor of the lower house of Convocation. He was elected to the office again in 1542 and presided over the sessions held in that year and in 1543. The Convocation which met in January 1542 proved to be the most important to have been held for some years.[75] The issues placed before it were those of the fallen and ruined state of religion (*de rebus religionis lapsis et ruentibus*), the remedies to be prescribed for abuses, the need to deal with the specially pressing problem of simony, and the examination of the text of the permitted version of the English Scriptures, the Great Bible. The lower house of Convocation, through its prolocutor, made suggestions for the reform of practical abuses. Gwent also presented his colleagues' notes on the existing translation of the Old Testament. The session of 1543 was chiefly taken up with the delicate and responsible task of revising the formulary known as 'The Institution of a Christian Man'. Prepared by the bishops and approved by the lower clergy, the new version, known as the 'Necessary Doctrine and Erudition of a Christian Man' and distinctly more conservative in tone than the 'Institution', was published in May 1543.

Gwent's services as a heresy-hunter were equally in demand. He was commissioned to hunt for heretics in London, to examine Portuguese who were charged with Judaism, to try the Lutheran Simon Haynes, dean of Exeter, accused of 'lewd and seditious preaching and sowing of erroneous opinions'; and the last glimpse of him that we get before his death in 1543 is of his part in having assisted Cranmer (and how the archbishop needed help!) in the prodigiously lengthy examination of heretics in Kent.[76] By this time, Gwent was patently failing in health. On 18th July, 1543, he was given permission by the King, whose chaplain he still was, to wear his bonnet in the royal presence because for 'divers infirmities which he hath in his head he cannot conveniently without danger be discovered of the same'.[77] Three days later he made his will, which was proved on 11th February, 1544. He committed his soul to 'Almighty God and His holy hands', and requested that his body should be buried in the middle of St. Paul's church in front of the sacrament which hung on the high altar. Careful stipulations were made for his funeral, including precisely-graded amounts to be spent on black gowns for the mourners. But he left nothing for prayers for his soul—an omission which confirms the reformist tone of the opening committal to God only and not to the Blessed Virgin and the whole company of Heaven as well. The provisions of the will suggest that he and Cranmer were on terms of some intimacy: he left the archbishop his best gelding called 'grey baker' and noted among his debts that the archbishop owed him £40. The bulk of his estate was to be divided into six parts: two were to go to his father and mother; two to his brother Thomas and his wife; and two to his brother John and his wife. Gwent's most pressing concern in his will seems to have been that his estate should not be unduly burdened with dilapidations, 'for I have been at much cost upon them save only my archdeaconry of St. David's, where I could get no dilapidations, for Fetherston, my predecessor, was attainted and his goods given to the king.[78] I could never get a farthing of his and I trust my successor of his conscience will ask me none'.[79] Gwent had reason to be apprehensive, since at the time of his death he held the archdeaconries of London, Huntingdon, and Brecon, as well as three prebends and six rectories.

In his constant immersement in government and his acquisition of a large and miscellaneous plurality of livings, Gwent was in many respects typical of the late Middle Ages, although of facets of it very different from those which Whitford represented. Gwent belonged to the civil-servant ecclesiastics of the fourteenth and fifteenth centuries. He was a lawyer-cum-administrator-cum-cleric of a type as yet far from extinct but becoming steadily less characteristic as laymen took an increasing share in government. Clerics of Welsh origin had rarely had his chances in earlier centuries; they were usually not sufficiently trusted by English governments. But a number of them had, like Gwent, thriven prodigiously in the sun of Tudor favour and trust.

Gwent was also representative of a newer trend among educated Welshmen. Like many other gifted and ambitious graduates he was influenced by the new learning at the universities. Humanists in sympathy, they were, in addition, men of affairs. Service to the King made them solid Henricians and ardent upholders of the royal supremacy. This they could be without having any more radical notions in religion. Bishops like Gardiner or Bonner or Tunstall were excellent examples of it and, at first sight, Gwent looks uncommonly similar to them. He was a lawyer, out of sympathy with papal claims or the grosser superstitions of medieval religion; but he was also chosen as spokesman of the conservatively-minded lower clergy and was a convinced heresey-hunter. Was he, then, a Henrician, willing to embrace royal supremacy but otherwise conservative in doctrine? It is difficult to tell when he always seems to be involved in all the controversies only as a bureaucrat not called upon to declare his personal allegiances. But the more one looks at Gwent the more one tends to see in him someone whose sympathies were closer to the reforming wing of the clergy. There is that long, close, and constant intimacy with Cranmer; this looks like something more than any official contact required. Then there are the wording and provisions of his will, distinctly un-Romanist in tone, and that at the most solemn hour when a man came to consider more profoundly than usual the destiny of his soul and where he placed his hope of salvation. It is impossible to tell with certainty, but Gwent's reactions look very like those of men who later became leading Welsh bishops—Thomas Young, Rowland Meyrick, or Richard Davies, or those of laymen like John Price, or Elis Price, or William Thomas, all of whom became convinced anti-papists. It is a pity he died so soon, before the crucial divide of Edward VI's reign. Had he lived a few years longer his career suggests he would have been raised to the episcopal bench. We should then have known with much greater certainty just where his sympathies lay.

Both Whitford and Gwent found wider scope for their interests and talents by emigrating. Whitford would not have found in Wales any strictly observant house nor any community of ascetics and writers such as existed at Sion. Gwent could not have gained such opportunities as a jurist and administrator in the small and insignificant dioceses of Wales. Whitford went up to the university in the spring-time of the new learning before it knew the cross-winds of heresy, and found the faith of his boyhood strengthened by humanism. Gwent belonged to a later generation of students among whom new tendencies were coming in but there is little sign that he was then much moved by them. Whitford withdrew into a seclusion which hardened his tenacity to the old ways. He remained unmoved by pressing considerations of politics and diplomacy. Gwent plunged into the maelstrom caused by the swiftly flowing tide of political and religious change and, seemingly, loved it. Neither could escape pressure of great contemporary issues. Whitford might have wished to; Gwent probably would not. Whitford's eyes looked back, Gwent's forward. For good or ill the future belonged to those who, like Gwent, aligned themselves with the Tudor state rather than the old church.

But each was a talented Welshman and each a 'successful emigrant. As such they may be thought to have earned some small commemoration by a Society founded on the strength of just such a combination.

APPENDIX

A LIST OF RICHARD WHITFORD'S WRITINGS IN ORDER OF PUBLICATION

Only those works of which Richard Whitford acknowledged himself to be the author are listed below. Many other books attributed to him on little or no evidence will be found listed in A. O. Evans's articles in the *Journal of the Welsh Bibliographical Society*, IV and V.

1. The rule of saynt Augustyne / bothe in latyn and englysshe / with two exposicyons. And also ye same rule agayn onely in englysshe without latyn or exposicyon.

Printed by Wynkyn de Worde, November 1525.
Another edition, by de Worde, 1527.

2. The martiloge in Englyshe after the vse of the chirche of salisbury / & as it is redde in Syon with addicyons.

Printed by Wynkyn de Worde, February 1526/7.

3. A werke for housholders, nowe newly corrected and set forthe into a dyaloge betwene the housholder and his housholde / by a professed brother of Syon Rycharde Whytford with an addicyon of pollecye for housholdynge / set forth also by the same brother.

Printed by Wynkyn de Worde, 1530.
Another edition by de Worde, 1533.
Another edition by P. Treveris (n.d.).
Another edition by R. Redman, 1537.
Another edition by Redman (n.d.).

4. The contētes of this boke. A werke of preparation / or of ordinance vnto cōmunion / or howselyng. The werke for housholders with the golden pistle and alphabete or a crosrowe.

Printed by Robert Redman, August 1531.
Another edition by Redman (n.d.).
Cf. also no. 6.

5. Here begynneth the boke called the Pype / or Tonne / of the lyfe of perfection. The reason or cause wherof dothe playnely appere in the processe.

Printed by Robert Redman, March 1532/3.

6. A dialoge or cõmunicacion bytwene the curate or ghostly father, & the parochiane or ghostly chyld. For a due preparacion vnto howselyng. The werke for housholders w^t the golden pystle and Alphabete or a crosrowe called an A.B.C.

Printed by J. Waylande, 1537.
This was acknowledged by Whitford to be a new and fuller edition of the works listed 4 above.

7. A dayly exercyse and experyence of dethe / gathered and set forth, by a brother of Syon, Rycharde Whytforde.
Printed by J. Waylande, 1537.
This work was bound up with 6 above.

8. Here foloweth dyuers holy instrucyons and teachynges very necessarye for the helth of mannes soule, newly made and set forth by a late brother of Syon, Rychard Whitforde.

The Contentes of this Boke.
Fyrste a deuoute worke of pacience.
A worke of dyuers impedimentes and lettes of perfectyon.
An instruction to auoyde and eschewe vyces and folowe good maners of Detraction.

Printed by William Myddylton, 1541.

NOTES

* An address given before the Society on 11th March, 1960. *Chairman*: Sir David Evans, O.B.E., D.Litt., Keeper of the Public Records.

[1] *Pembrokeshire* (Cymmrodorion Record Series, 1906), III, 56.

[2] No book or article has been written on either, though A. O. Evans devoted much attention to Whitford in his articles on the *Imitatio Christi* in Wales in *Journal of Welsh Bibliographical Society*, IV, 7-14, 28-9; V, 57-9.

[3] Like his nephew, he was also a clerk and a member of the community at Sion. His will was executed on 14th February, 1511, and proved on 24th January, 1512, Somerset House, Prerogative Court of Canterbury, 5 Fetiplace; cf. extracts from it in D. R. Thomas, 'Old Welsh Wills', *Arch. Camb.*, 1880, 221.

[4] *D.N.B.*, s.n.; cf. Joseph Foster, *Alumni Oxonienses* (Oxford, 1892), IV, 1621.

[5] C. H. and T. Cooper, *Athenae Cantabrigienses* (Cambridge, 1858), I, 79-80.

[6] *Opus Epistolarum Des. Erasmi Roterodami*, ed. P. S. Allen (12 vols., Oxford, 1906 ff.), I, 225-6.

[7] Ibid.

[8] Quoted by R. W. Chambers, *Thomas More* (London, 1938), 97-8.

[9] This was eventually printed in *Luciani Opuscula . . . ab Erasmo Roterdamo et Thoma Moro in Latinorum linguam traducta* (Paris, 1506).

[10] Nostram declamationem ita leges vt eam me pauculis diebus lusisse cogites, non scripsisse. Hortor autem vt et Moricam conferas, itaque iudices numquid in stilo sit discriminis inter nos quos tu ingenio, moribus, affectibus, studiis vsque adeo similes esse dicere solebas, vt negares vllos gemellos magis inter se similes seperiri posse. Vtrunque certo ex aequo amas, vtrique vicissim ex aequo charus. Vale, meum delicium, Richard festiusssime, Allen, *Opus Epistolarum*, I, 422-3.

[11] For Sion, see G. J. Aungier, *History and Antiquities of Syon Monastery* (London, 1840); see also David Knowles, *The Religious Orders in England* (3 vols., Cambridge, 1948-59), II, 176-81; III, 212-21.

[12] Op. cit., III, 213.

[13] B.M. Cotton MS. Cleop. E. iv, f. 109; text printed in T. Wright, *Three Chapters of Letters relating to the Suppression of the Monasteries*, pp. 48-50.

Richard Whitford and Richard Gwent 87

[14] *Letters and Papers of Henry VIII's Reign*, VIII, 77; cf. Knowles, op. cit., III, 219, n.

[15] A full list is given in the appendix on pp. 85-86.

[16] *A dayly exercyse and experyence of dethe gathered and set forth by a brother of Syon, Rycharde Whytforde*. Published by R. Redman, London, 1537, sig. A. ii; see *S.T.C.*, 593.

[17] *The exposicyon of saynt Augustynes rule*. Printed by Wynkyn de Worde, London, 1525; *S.T.C.*, 593.

[18] Published by Wynkyn de Worde on 15th February, 1526/7.

[19] J. M. Lenhart, *Pre-Reformation Printed Books* (New York, 1935). P. Janelle, *L'angleterre à la veille du schisme* (Paris, 1935), pp. 14-24. F. A. Gasquet, 'The bibliography of some devotional books printed by the earliest English printers', *Trans. Bibliog. Society*, new series, VII, (1904), 163-87. H. S. Bennett, *English Books and their Readers*, 1475-1557 (Cambridge, 1952).

[20] Printed by Robert Redman 23rd March, 1532/3.

[21] First printed by Robert Redman in 1531, it went through a number of editions in the 1530s.

[22] Sig. H. iiii.

[23] First published by Redman in 1531.

[24] Edition of 1537, printed by J. Waylande, sig. B. ii.

[25] Sig. C. iii, verso.

[26] Folio 48.

[27] See A. O. Evans, op. cit., and cf. Edward J. Klein, *The Imitation of Christ* (New York, 1941), and references given there.

[28] *The following of Christ, translated out of Latin into Englishe, newely corrected and amended*. Published by Cawood, 18th September, 1556.

[29] For details, see *S.T.C.*, nos. 1912-14.

[30] For details, see Klein, *Imitation of Christ*, xxxiv ff.

[31] *An Epistle of Sait Bernarde / called the Golden Epistle / whiche he sēt to a yōg religyous man whom he muche loued. And after the sayed epistle / foloweth four reuelations of Saint Birget.*

[32] The preface to *The Rule of Saynt Augustyne*.

[33] Ibid.

[34] *A devoute work of pacience*, f. 47.

[35] *The Pype or Tonne*, f. ii, verso.

[36] *D.N.B.*, *D.W.B.*, s.n.

[37] *P.C.C.*, 3 Pynnynge.

[38] *Register of the University of Oxford*, ed. C. W. Boase and A. Clark (Oxford Hist. Soc., 1884-9), I, 107.

[39] *L. and P.*, IX, 52 (2) ; X, 216.

[40] Ibid., IV, iii, 5768, 5866.

[41] *L. and P.*, XIV, 190.

[42] G. R. Elton, *The Tudor Revolution in Government* (Cambridge, 1953), p. 82.

[43] Ibid., pp. 96-7.

[44] *L. and P.*, V, 1326; cf. also V, 1530, 1540, 1672.

[45] Ibid., VI, 150.

[46] Ibid., V, 1530.

[47] Ibid., VI, 864, 880-1, 1092, 1246, 1259, 1568; VII, 1605, 1650; XV, 1027 (45); cf. *Miscellaneous Writings and Letters of Thomas Cranmer* (Parker Soc., 1846), pp. 250-1, 253-4, 256, 261, 275; Lambeth Palace Library, Reg. Cranmer, ff. 39, 67; see also Public Record Office, Court of Delegates; Act Book, 1538-44 (Del. 4/1), *passim.*

[48] Public Record Office, S.P. 1/99, p. 231; for summary see *L. and P.*, IX. 1071.

[49] Knowles, op. cit., III, 182-91.

[50] *L. and P.*, VI, 967; Public Record Office, S.P. 1/78, p. 119.

[51] Ibid.

[52] *L. and P.*, VI, 1579.

[53] Ibid., VII, 647, 1032 (i).

[54] *D.N.B.*

[55] Letters from him to Cromwell, *L. and P.*, IX, 25, 549, 690.

[56] Public Record Office, S.P. 1/95, p. 20.

[57] *L. and P.*, X, 192, 383; XI, 582.

[58] Cromwell's accounts, ibid., XIV, ii, 782—included among them were Godstow, Battle, Ely, Evesham, and St. Augustine's Bristol.

[59] *L. and P.*, XII, 1232-3.

[60] E. M. Thompson, *The Carthusian Order in England* (London, 1930), pp. 480-1.

[61] Public Record Office, S.P. 1/104, p. 86. *L. and P.*, X, 1018.

[62] *Sermons* (Parker Soc., 1844), pp. 33-57.

[63] B.M. Harl. MS. 419, f. 117. Wilkins, *Concilia*, III, 804. J. Strype, *Ecclesiastical Memorials* (Oxford, 1820-40), I, ii, no. 73. *L. and P.*, X, 1184.

[64] Public Record Office, S.P. 1/104, p. 86.

[65] I have recounted the course of this quarrel at length elsewhere, see below, pp. 116-24.

[66] See Cromwell's accounts, *L. and P,*. XIV, ii, 782, where Gwent is recorded as having paid 200 marks to Cromwell on behalf of Thomas Lloyd, precentor of St. David's, in May 1537; and £20 on behalf of the chapter in June 1538. These payments coincide with crises in the St. David's quarrel, and are probably best explained as presents designed to procure Cromwell's goodwill. Barlow on his part was making comparable bids for Cromwell's continued favour, see below, pp. 116-20.

[67] He was employed at the Charterhouse in May 1537, *L. and P.*, XII, 1232-3; and he acted for Katherine Bulkeley, abbess of Godstow, in March 1538 to secure acceptance by Cromwell of the stewardship of her nunnery. Ibid., XIII, i, 492; see also Cranmer to Cromwell, 12th June, 1538, 379-1.

[68] *L. and P.*, XIII, i, 1434.

[69] Ibid., XIII, ii, 498.

[70] Ibid., XIV, i, 1065.

[71] Ibid., XIV, i, 1209, 1210, 1238. Cf. also *Cranmer's Letters*, pp. 390-2.

[72] See the letters from Gwent and others, then in the west country, Wright, *Suppression*, p. 236; cf. *L. and P.*, XV, 19. Gwent assigned pensions at Gloucester on 5th January, 1540, at Tewkesbury and Great Malvern on 12th January, at Worcester on 18th January, at Pershore on 21st January, Cokehill on 26th January, and Evesham on 27th January. *L. and P.*, XV, 24, 49, 51, 81, (cf. also 868-9), 92, 110, 118.

[73] *L. and P.*, XV, 921. D. Wilkins, *Concilia Magnae Britanniae* (London, 1737), III, 850. Strype, *Ecc. Memorials*, I, 553.

[74] *L. and P.*, XV, 860-1. Wilkins, *Concilia*, III, 850.

[75] For this Convocation see Wilkins, *Concilia*, III, 860, ff.

[76] *L. and P.*, XVI, 494; XVIII, i, 255, 477, ii, 546 (pp. 332, 359).

[77] *L. and P.*, XVIII, ii, 907.

[78] Richard Fetherston, archdeacon of Brecon from 1523 to 1534, was a member of Princess Mary's household. He espoused Queen Catherine's cause and was attainted and executed in 1540.

[79] P.C.C., 3 Pynnynge.

IV. THE DISSOLUTION OF THE MONASTERIES IN GLAMORGAN

The chapter-house of Margam Abbey, with its exquisitely foliated capitals and delicately arched ribs, was one of the superlative architectural achievements of the religious orders in medieval Wales. On 20th June, 1536, it was the scene of the first step in transferring the Glamorgan monasteries to the possession of the Crown. A group of half a dozen men—an auditor, a receiver, and a clerk, together with two or three of the local gentry—were bringing to an end some four hundred years of monastic history in Glamorgan. Not much greater a span of time separates us from the dissolvers than separated them from the founders.

As far as is known, this ending of what had been an auspicious chapter in Glamorgan's religious history caused no upheaval or serious protest. There is no surviving record that a voice was raised, or a hand lifted, on behalf of these once influential houses. Indeed, if the reactions of the leading Glamorgan poet are at all typical, there were some who rejoiced at seeing the monasteries go. This poet, Lewis Morgannwg, had once extolled the virtues of Neath Abbey in the most mellifluous verses. After the Dissolution, however, he hailed Henry VIII as a 'prince ever to be remembered' for his masterly handling of the religious issue and especially for his suppression of the 'false religious orders'.[2] It might, at first sight, seem all very odd and puzzling that the monks could at this time command so little support and loyalty from a laity to whose forebears the houses of religion had meant so much. It was certainly not for lack of sympathy with traditional ways; for when a popular shrine like that of the B.V.M. at Pen-rhys was to be destroyed, serious trouble was expected,[3] and later in the century Glamorgan produced more than its share of Catholic recusants.[4] Yet the monasteries, as far as can be judged, found no such stalwart supporters.

Perhaps an essential key to unlocking this puzzle lies in remembering more clearly than is usually done the implications of the fact already noted: that some 400 years had elapsed between the founding of the monasteries and their dissolution. There is still a tendency to think of medieval monasteries in too static a way; to suppose them to have been much the same sort of places in Henry VIII's reign as they had been in their great days in the twelfth and thirteenth centuries. They were not, of course. They had in fact been subjected to some desperate crises during the intervening centuries: economic

depression; pestilence among men and beasts; spiritual and intellectual decline; long wars and crippling taxation; broken contacts
and relaxed discipline; the Glyn Dŵr Rebellion and prolonged
devastation. It is not always realized that these disasters had brought
some religious houses to the verge of destitution and extinction.
The largest and wealthiest Glamorgan house—Margam—was, in a
papal petition of 1412, described as utterly destroyed so that abbot
and monks were forced to wander the countryside like vagabonds.[5]
This was an exaggeration, no doubt; but it was symptomatic of
genuine and widespread distress and dislocation among Welsh
monasteries at this period. Such tribulations left the monasteries
permanently scarred and mutilated; they never fully recovered their
earlier health and vitality. These points have been argued and
illustrated at length elsewhere,[6] and it would be tedious to go
over this ground again except perhaps to recall two essential
considerations. First, laymen were exercising an excessive and
unhealthy control over many aspects of monastic life, and second,
the appeal of the monastic vocation, and respect for it, had suffered
a marked eclipse among all classes of laymen. When plans for
dissolving the monasteries were put forward in the 1530s, the
monks had few friends to uphold their interests at court or in the
country. By contrast, there were many who were inclined to think
that their extinction would be no loss to the common weal; might
indeed be a positive gain. Particularly were they encouraged to hold
so comfortable and convenient an opinion when the Crown was at
such pains to confirm the validity of all agreements and leases
entered into by the many monastic tenants, great and small.

For those who had had eyes to see, the flaccid collapse of the
Glamorgan monasteries might not have been unexpected in view of
the way in which the royal supremacy had been so smoothly enforced
within the county in 1534. Apart from the bishop of Llandaff,
George de Athequa, a Spaniard by origin and a man with little or
no local influence, no one had opposed the policy. Once the
supremacy had been pushed through, exploitation of its financial
possibilities could be quickly followed up. Already the Act in
Restraint of Annates of 1534 had decreed that annates (i.e. the first
year's revenue of an ecclesiastical benefice) were not to be rendered
to the papal curia, while another act of the same year, the Act for
First Fruits and Tenths, provided that these payments were now to
be made to the Crown. But some of Thomas Cromwell's memoranda
compiled in 1534 suggest that he was turning over in his mind much
more ambitious plans for making his royal master the richest ruler
in Christendom by expropriating ecclesiastical resources. One such
scheme proposed to suppress all monasteries with fewer than
thirteen inmates, and to transfer bishops' estates to the Crown,
along with half the incomes of cathedrals and collegiate churches.[7]

The schemes for mulcting the secular clergy were quickly dropped; perhaps they were so drastic as to be in danger of evoking too much opposition; and Cromwell may even have been in some doubt about getting rid of the monasteries. Probably neither he nor anyone else knew at this stage how far he could or would go. But whatever measures he might ultimately adopt, he would need, as an essential preliminary, as comprehensive and accurate a report on the property of the Church as he could get. So, at the beginning of 1535 he set in train all over England and Wales those commissions of enquiry that were to produce that extraordinary Domesday Book of the English Church—the *Valor Ecclesiasticus*.[8]

On 30th January, 1535, the Commissioners for the diocese of Llandaff were appointed. Headed by Bishop de Athequa and Sir William Morgan, they numbered nineteen in all and had two professional auditors associated with them.[9] The members were drawn from among the leading families of gentry of the diocese, and the Morgans, Herberts, Carnes, and Mathews were particularly well represented. In spite of the impressive list of commissioners, only one of them in fact did most of the work, and he was Sir William Morgan. He appears to have completed his task in the astonishingly short space of four months, between June and October 1535. How this came about was explained by him in letters written to Cromwell in August and October 1535.[10] Because the bishop was non-resident and the other commissioners lived 'forty or fifty miles asunder', he wrote, 'I could not have them together and many of them did little or nothing in executing the effects of the commission'. Though Morgan had often enquired after the two auditors, Thomas Brene and John Welldey, he 'could in no wise . . . have no knowledge of them'.[11] So he had to perform his task as best he could without their professional help, and he asked Cromwell 'whether it shall please your mastership to have the said books sent up so as they be after a rude fashion, or else to appoint some auditor to come to me for the engrossment of the said books after the auditor's fashion'.[12] No auditor came, and Morgan had to do the best he could with the help of Master Quarr, the archdeacon of Llandaff. Towards the end of his enquiry, Morgan had been pressed by Cromwell to complete it, and he may well have had to seek the archdeacon's assistance for the Glamorgan deaneries of the diocese. This could possibly account for the marked difference between the *Valor's* returns for the Monmouthshire deaneries and those for the Glamorgan deaneries. The former, presumably undertaken by Morgan himself, are much fuller and better organized than the latter; indeed, they are much the best returns we have for any part of Wales. Their author could, with some justification, write in pride to Cromwell on 27th October: 'I have sent a book unto your mastership . . . in as perfect a manner as I and my friends could devise possible; which book I do no doubt

but it shall amount above any "presidens" (= 'precedents'?) that
any bishop in the diocese of Llandaff could make, as Master Quarr,
archdeacon of Llandaff, can inform your mastership the very truth
of the same'.[13]

Cromwell had had to press for completion of the *Valor* because he
was anxious to put another set of commissioners at work visiting the
monasteries. He had had the machinery ready and waiting since
January 1535, but had not wished to prejudice the efforts of the
earlier commission by setting the later one in motion too soon.
The object of this second commission, it has often been assumed,
was to collect evidence of moral delinquencies on the part of the
monasteries so as to justify their suppression. It is not, in fact,
certain that this is what Cromwell had in mind at the outset—he
may have been toying with the idea of drastic reform. But, brilliant
improvisator as well as masterly long-term organizer that he was,
within a very short space of time, he had undoubtedly made up his
mind to dissolve the smaller monasteries at least. His commissioners
for Wales were Adam Becansaw and John Vaughan who, after
visiting north Wales in September and October, arrived at Llandaff
cathedral on 11th November, 1535. There they found plenty to
criticize: 'the bishop and his archdeacon guilty not only of great
ruin and decay of their mansions but of other great faults as you
will see by our registry of visitations'.[14] (Unfortunately, this register
no longer appears to be extant.) They were also distinctly critical of
the state of affairs they found at the monasteries of Brecon, Monmouth, and Tintern.[15] But no record of their comments on
Glamorgan houses, critical or otherwise, survives. They were in
south Wales until as late as 28th April, 1536, so they must surely have
had ample opportunity of visiting Glamorgan monasteries and those
of St. David's diocese.[16] In one sense, the absence of such a report
makes very little difference. The fate of these monasteries did not
depend on their moral or religious condition. The decision to
dissolve them was taken for financial and political reasons, not on
moral grounds.

Such a decision had indeed been taken before the visitors had
had time to wind up their duties. In March 1536 a bill to suppress
all monasteries worth less than £200 a year had been introduced
into the House of Commons. All three Glamorgan houses were
valued in the *Valor* as worth less than £200 a year: Margam (£181),
Neath (£120), and Ewenni (£59); and all were included in an official
list of houses falling within the scope of this Act.[17] But already, in
1536, there were men who saw that the distinction between houses
worth less than £200 and those worth more was an arbitrary one
and they foresaw that the greater ones must, in due course, go the
same way. 'These [lesser ones]', they argued, 'were as thorns, but the
great abbots were putrified old oaks, and they must needs follow'.[18]

The first Glamorgan house to go was Margam. It was visited on 20th June, 1536, by a commission presumably made up in the usual way of an auditor, receiver, and a clerk, together with two or three of the local gentry. For two months afterwards the abbey remained in a state of suspended animation until on 23rd-4th August the final blow fell. On 23rd August a pension of £10 was assigned to its abbot, Lewis Thomas; its nine monks (not three as is usually said)[19] were paid the *peculia* or pocket money due to them; and its fifteen yeomen and thirteen 'hinds' were paid the balance of their wages. A careful note was made of cash receipts from temporalities (£235 4s. 9½d.), of its 131½ oz of plate, of the lead from the roofs worth £372 5s. 6d., already melted and in Sir Rice Mansel's custody for the king's use, of six bells weighing 5,203 qr. 21 lb. and worth £52 18s. 9d., of corn in hand, and of £51 8s. 0d. for the rest of the goods and chattels, which were sold at a profit of £12 2s. 0d. An equally precise and detailed note was made of the abbey's debts, amounting to £32 7s. 11½d. The convent seal was broken, and possession taken of the abbey on the king's behalf by Sir Rice Mansel on 24th August.[20]

The smaller priory of Ewenni, being a daughter of the large and undissolved house of St. Peter's, Gloucester, remained in an anomalous position for some time. It was obviously not taken into the royal possession in 1536 along with Margam and other houses in the diocese of Llandaff.[21] But neither could it be said to have continued to enjoy an entirely independent existence. An unusual arrangement was arrived at on 28th February, 1537 (not 1536 as is often said!) whereby the distinguished lawyer and diplomat, Sir Edward Carne, leased the priory and its possessions for the long term of ninety-nine years from the abbot of St. Peter's, Gloucester, at the highly favourable rent of £20 10s. 0d. In return, he also agreed to provide board, lodging, and pocket money for the prior, Edmund Wotton, at the rate of £6 13s. 4d. and his two monks at £3 16s. 8d. apiece.[22] This arrangement lasted until St. Peter's was dissolved in 1539.

The remaining Glamorgan monastery, Neath, was worth considerably less than £200 and was appreciably poorer than Margam. Even so, in January 1537 it was exempted from suppression on payment of a fine of £150;[22A] a large sum but about what might have been expected since the amount normally paid for such a concession was a year's net income. The reason for sparing some of the smaller houses appears to have been to enable the government conveniently to transfer some of the monks from dissolved houses who wished to continue in the monastic life elsewhere;[23] and there is evidence of at least one proposed transfer of a monk to Neath.[24] Why Neath in particular should have been thus singled out as one of the three Welsh houses to be reprieved may perhaps have been because the house had a good name, and because its abbot, Leyshon

Thomas, was the most eminent Cistercian in Wales.[25] Yet this need
not have entered into the calculation at all, for some houses which
were spared had a poor reputation—Strata Florida in Wales,
for example—and others had actually been sharply criticized for
their shortcomings by the royal visitors. In any event, Neath's
escape was dearly bought and short-lived. To recoup himself for his
outlay, its abbot had to make a large number of leases to tenants
from which he could reap large entry fines, and out of seventy-one
of Neath's recorded leases at the time of its surrender, fifty-one
were known to be dated later than the end of 1535.[26] Despite these
efforts, the abbot was slow in raising the £150 he owed the
government. Finally, in February 1539, when Neath Abbey was on
the point of being surrendered, John Price wrote to Cromwell:
'My lord abbot of Neath is contented to surrender his house', but,
he added, 'He hath ever hitherto lived worshipfully and well, and
also hath of late dangered himself and his friends very far with the
redemption of his house. This should be considered in the modera-
tion of his bill.'[27] In fact, Abbot Leyshon Thomas did come off far
better than almost any others of his Welsh brethren, being given a
pension of £40, together with the rectory of Cadoxton, which he
was allowed to hold until he got preferment worth £48 a year.[28]
Five of the monks there with him received pensions of £4 each, and
the other two, pensions of £3 6s. 8d. apiece.[29]

In the meantime, in 1538, the only two Glamorgan friaries, the
Grey Friary and the Black Friary at Cardiff, had been extinguished.
In February of that year, Richard Ingworth, suffragan bishop of
Dover and himself a former friar, had received his commission as
visitor of the orders of friars. At first accused of being somewhat
lenient with the friars, Ingworth soon evolved a subtle and effective
technique for dealing with them. His practice was, in the presence of
the mayor and aldermen of the town in which a friary stood, to give
the friars an apparent freedom of choice. 'Think not', he was
reported to have said, 'that ye be suppressed, for I have no such
authority to suppress you, but only to reform you'.[30] Very obligingly,
however, he offered to accept any voluntary surrender. This formula
rarely failed to produce the desired result, for by 1538 the friars
were almost universally in a state of squalor and despair. This was
not brought about by the 'lack of a fixed income, for this they had
never had', but by the 'failure of their world to support them any
longer and the failure on their part to hold or recapture the favour
of their world'.[31]

Certainly, the two Cardiff friaries, by the time the visitor reached
them on 6th September, 1538, were in a hopelessly reduced condition.
A generation or more earlier, long before they had begun to
experience the disintegration caused by the uncertainties of the

Reformation changes of the 1530s, Cardiff friars had had a depressing tale to tell of inadequate support.[32] By 1538, left in no doubt of their imminent fate, they found themselves in dilapidated buildings, with many of their possessions in pledge and themselves deep in debt. The Dominicans owed a local victualler, Thomas Robert, £1 for provisions and were 7s. 6d. in arrears with their servants' wages. To meet these debts Ingworth sold some of the friary's meagre possessions and also took a chalice to defray his own expenses.[33] The friars' poverty was in part brought about by their attempts to capitalize on what little they had in the way of possessions before the houses were suppressed. At this Dominican friary vestments worth £7 were missing, and 'there is gone many other things of the which we can have no knowledge, for the prior . . be dead'.[34] Of those possessions still left—plate, vestments, furnishings, and utensils—the visitor made an inventory, and he delivered it and the friary to the bailiffs of the town to keep safely on the King's behalf. On the following day, 9th September, 1538, the same procedure was observed at the house of the Friars Minor in Cardiff. Here, too, the friars were in debt and had been forced to raise money by putting two of their chalices in pawn. In this friary, again, a careful record was made of what little there was that might be turned to the King's profit: alabaster, vestments, plate, candlesticks, organs and bells in the church; cooking utensils, platters, tables, and the like, in kitchen, hall, and chamber.[35] All told, it provided no more than a meagre and worn-out haul for the visitor and his royal master. The visitation completed and the inventories compiled, it only remained to sign the deed of surrender. At the Dominican Friary the number of friars signing was seven—until a week or two previously they had been ten, but death had intervened and carried off the prior, sub-prior, and one other. Over at the Franciscan house there were nine left to sign the surrender.[36] That done, all were free to make the best of it in a hard world without the cushion of any pensions such as some of the monks had been allowed.

Once the monasteries had been dissolved, measures had to be devised for dealing with their inmates, buildings, and possessions. As far as inmates were concerned, there cannot have been more than about thirty-five to forty religious in all the county of Glamorgan.[37] In terms of materially providing for them, there can hardly be said to have been a very big problem, and it seems very likely that the arrangements made for them kept both monks and their secular relatives reasonably contented. The heads of the monasteries suffered least hardship; Leyshon Thomas of Neath being handsomely treated, Lewis Thomas of Margam distinctly less well rewarded at £20, and Edward Wotton of Ewenni rather badly with no more than £6 13s. 4d. and his keep. The two latter had no more to live on than the incumbents of a medium and a poor parish respectively. Monks' pensions—two at Margam, two at Ewenni, and eight at Neath—were considerably smaller, averaging from £3 10s. 0d. to £4.[38] This was not lavish treatment; they were being paid no more than they would have received as stipendiary priests. But it was not entirely inadequate, and it provided subsistence for men who were, very often, too old easily to have been able to make a living in any other fashion. Moreover, in fairness to Tudor governments, it must be said that they honoured their pledges, apart from a temporary crisis in 1552–3.[39] Nearly twenty years after the Dissolution, seven of the Neath monks and two of the Margam ones were still included in Cardinal Pole's pensions list.[40] Other monks and friars who got no pension were probably able to acquire benefices or serve as stipendiary priests; but the disappearance of episcopal registers for Llandaff and St. David's prevents us from tracing these ex-religious. Nor can we tell whether any of them reverted to the secular life. As for the considerable number of servants and labourers employed by each house, it would be reasonable to assume that most, if not all, of them would be needed by the new occupiers or owners and would continue to be employed in much the same way as before. What little evidence there is does not suggest that Welsh houses were 'over-staffed' with servants.[41] It seems unlikely, therefore, that any serious material hardship was caused to inmates and their servants by the Dissolution. It may even be that some of the monks who had no very strong vocation welcomed the opportunity of turning their backs on the cloister. But what we have no way of measuring, or even discovering, is the mental or emotional distress which may have been created by turning out into a very different, if not unsympathetic, world men who had taken a vow to live all their lives according to the rule of religion.

Once a monastery had been dissolved, such of its contents as were movable or saleable were quickly disposed of. Jewels, plate, cash, and valuable manuscripts were despatched to the royal treasury. All other assets, such as glass, vestments, missals, candlesticks, organs, timber, and other furnishings, were auctioned on the spot. Lead, bells, and any other removable metal work were melted down into pigs. The official instructions were that the commissioners should then 'pull down to the ground all the walls of the churches, steeples, cloisters, fraters, dorters, chapter houses, etc.'[42] But demolition cost money, and very often the commissioners contented themselves simply with defacing the buildings and making them uninhabitable by removing the roofs and stairs. Once that stage had been reached, the work of destruction was completed or taken a good deal further by the eager pillaging hands of neighbouring inhabitants. Such activity at the Cardiff friaries and the disputes occasioned by it led to two lawsuits in the Court of Augmentations. In the one, the farmer of the Grey Friary, John White, complained that four local men had 'broken and pulled to the ground . . . and borne away the stones, timber, windows and tiles thereof'.[43] In the other, a Cardiff cleric, Lewis Johns, complained that a lease he had taken of a house belonging to the Black Friars was being ignored by the farmers of the friary who had hastened to break and pluck down 'the walls, windows and timber of the same house . . . and carried away the same and taken it to their own proper uses'.[44] Of the two Glamorgan friaries little was subsequently left. Only the foundations and some of the tiled floors of the Dominican Friary can now be seen, and of the Franciscan Friary not much more than the skeletal and ivy-grown fragments of the town house later built on the site by the Herbert family.[45]

The three abbeys fared a good deal better. The church at Ewenni, because it was a parish church, survived virtually intact, together with much of the priory's massive fortification walls. At Margam, too, the nave of the much-truncated abbey church was preserved for parochial worship. Margam, like Ewenni, was quickly taken over by its new owners and never remained derelict for any length of time. As a result, more of its buildings survive than is usual. Its most striking feature, of course, was its superb chapter house, a building of the utmost grace and delicacy which was, unfortunately, allowed to fall into ruin in the eighteenth century. At Neath, the church was never preserved for worship by parishioners and, from an early date, became a gaunt and roofless shell. Paradoxically enough, however, more remains of its conventual buildings than those of any other abbey in Glamorgan. Particularly is this true of the former abbot's house and adjoining buildings which were retained largely intact, though modified somewhat to meet new domestic demands placed upon them by the Hoby family who lived there in the sixteenth century.[46]

More important than the fate of the buildings, however, was that of the temporal and spiritual possessions of the monasteries. In the first instance all passed into the royal possession; and if they had remained in the royal hands the revenue from them would have more than doubled the king's annual income. It seems very probable that the original intention was thus to retain the greater part of the newly-acquired gains from this biggest piece of land nationalization in English history, and a new organization, the Court of Augmentations, was set up to cope with all the financial, administrative and legal problems likely to arise.[47] In the short run, immediately after the Dissolution, a large number of leases were entered into; but they were confined largely to vacant sites and to demesne not already leased by monks, and they almost never exceeded a term of twenty-one years. Thus, on 29th February, 1537, the site and demesne of Margam were leased for twenty-one years to Sir Rice Mansel, who had already acted as the royal commissioner there.[48] But, as soon as the process of dissolution had begun, the government found itself inundated with requests from the gentry for concessions in the form of gifts, leases, and purchases. Later on, heavy government expenditure, particularly on defence, forced the Crown increasingly to acquiesce in the outright sale of monastic lands. These sales began on a small scale from 1536–38 and, in December 1539, the first official statement of the terms, i.e. twenty years' purchase, was propounded.[49] The first such sale in Glamorgan took place in October 1540, when Sir Rice Mansel was allowed to buy the abbey church of Margam, a number of granges, a fishery, and some coal pits at twenty years' purchase for a total sum of £938 6s. 8d.[50] There was a temporary lull in 1541–42; but from 1543 onwards lavish expenditure on wars with France and Scotland led to further heavy sales during the last four years of Henry's reign. By the time of his death well over half of the monastic land of Glamorgan had been disposed of.

None of this land had been given away or sold at cheap rates. There was nothing in Glamorgan to compare with the virtual gift of Tintern Abbey and a large part of its Monmouthshire estates to the earl of Worcester.[51] Apart from the setting aside of former monastic tithe income to endow the new bishopric of Gloucester (see below), the only concession was that made in 1543 to Sir Rice Mansel, when out of a purchase price of £731 11s. 6d. made for some more Margam land the sum of £100 was remitted to him in recognition of faithful and acceptable services rendered by him to the king.[52] Otherwise, all the rest was paid for at the rate of twenty years' purchase at least, and sometimes more, as when Sir Edward Carne bought lands at Colwinston for twenty-three years' purchase,[53] or when Thomas Stradling bought the manor of Llantwit at twenty-five years' purchase.[54] But spiritual income— tithes and the like—could be bought more cheaply, normally at the rate of ten years' purchase.[55]

Very little of the land alienated by the king came back into the possession of the Church. It is true that the newly-created chapter at Gloucester benefited to some extent from former monastic posses- sions in Glamorgan. In August 1541 it was endowed with tithes at Tregough, Pennon, and Llancarfan which had formerly belonged to St. Peter's, Gloucester, and with the rectories of Llantwit, Llan- bleddian, Llantrisant, Penmark, and Cardiff, which Tewkesbury Abbey had for centuries possessed.[56] But it is noticeable that the whole of this endowment consisted of spiritual income, for which demand was far less brisk than for the temporalities; and Tewkes- bury's more valuable temporalities, the manors at Llandough and

Llantwit, were, in 1543, sold to two lay purchasers, Sir George Herbert and Edward Stradling respectively.[57] No former monastic property was in Glamorgan set aside for the foundation of schools.

Purchasers from outside the county were comparatively rare. A merchant like one John Smith of Bristol might take advantage of the opportunity to acquire one of Neath's former tenements in that city[58]; but, in general, merchant interest in Glamorgan monastic land was slight, and certainly no new Glamorgan landed family was founded on the basis of investing merchant wealth in monastic estates. It was in almost every instance existing landed families who acquired fresh interests. Some might have their main estates outside the county, even far distant from it, but nearly always they had a local connexion of some kind. Sir John St. John, for instance, had his chief seat in Bedfordshire, but he had important interests in Glamorgan at Fonmon and Barry. He took prompt advantage of monastic land when it came on the market in order to acquire holdings adjacent to his existing estates in Glamorgan. He was an early purchaser of former Margam lands when, in January 1541, he acquired the rectory and manor of Bonvilston and the grange of Greendown by exchanging other lands with the Crown.[59] A somewhat similiar case is that of Sir Richard Cromwell, alias Williams, who acquired the bulk of the Neath estates in March 1542.[60] His main seat lay in Huntingdonshire, but his family had originally come from Glamorgan. It is worth noting, however, that by October 1542 he had obtained a licence to sell the grange at Nash and other valuable estates to Thomas Stradling, and another licence in April 1543 to alienate Sker Grange to Christopher Turberville.[61] Similarly, Sir Thomas Heneage, a big-scale speculator in monastic land who had no special connexion with Glamorgan, having bought the former Margam lands at Cibwr and Cardiff and at Resolven and Court Colman on 17th August, 1548, just over a week later obtained a licence to alienate them to a pair of Monmouthshire brothers, James and William Gunter.[62] These two acted as agents for south Wales families in a number of ventures of this kind.[63] In this instance they were acting for Sir George Herbert of Swansea, into whose hands these Margam estates ultimately passed.[64] For the most part, however, those who wished to buy monastic land in Glamorgan did so directly and not through agents. Still less does there seem to have been any purchasing from big-scale speculators out to make large profits by re-selling locally at a high price.

The main beneficiaries from the sale of monastic lands in Glamorgan were a small group of leading local families: the Mansels, Carnes, Stradlings, Lewises, and Herberts. The most strikingly successful individual among them without doubt was Sir Rice Mansel,[65] who managed to acquire the lion's share of the estates of

Margam, the county's wealthiest abbey. The process by which he achieved this feat is sufficiently illuminating to merit being recapitulated in outline. First of all, he was involved as the chief royal commissioner at the time of Margam's dissolution. In a matter of months he had obtained a lease of the site and demesne in February 1537. His actual purchase of the land was a lengthy transaction, spread over seventeen years and carried out in four main stages. The first was undertaken on 22nd June, 1540, when he purchased the site and other possessions for £938 6s. 8d. Three other purchases followed in 1543, 1546, and 1557.[66] In all, in order to acquire these estates, Mansel raised the sum of £2,482 13s. 1d.—an enormous amount for a man of his status and background—and he had to pay the money in a number of instalments. In 1552, he turned part of the abbey into a dwelling house, making it his chief residence and leaving the old family home at Penrice and Oxwich in Gower as a secondary seat.[67] Finally, in 1557, he was given a royal grant of free warren and permission to make a park of 100 acres.[68]

Next to Mansel we must place Sir Edward Carne.[69] He, like Mansel, had acquired the lease of the site and lands of the monastery he was ultimately to buy—in his case, Ewenni. But before he acquired Ewenni outright, he made valuable pickings elsewhere in the county. He, too, had an interest in Margam's lands; indeed, he is sometimes reputed to have been Mansel's unsuccessful rival in trying to obtain the bulk of the Margam properties. In 1542, he succeeded in buying the Margam granges of Crwys Bychan and Llystalybont near Cardiff.[70] In 1543 he acquired an estate much nearer the main centre of his interests when, for twenty-three years' purchase, he bought the valuable manor of Colwinston, worth £21 2s. 5d. a year and formerly part of the possessions of the priory of Deptford in Kent.[71] In August 1546 he achieved a long-standing ambition when he paid £727 6s. 4d. for the site and lands of Ewenni, the advowsons of Colwinston, St. Bride's and Llandyfodwg, and '200 oaks being timber of 100 years' growth'.[72] In the following year he bought the Margam grange of Llanfeithyn in the Vale of Glamorgan.[73]

None of the other families did anything like as well from monastic lands as the Carnes and the Mansels. The Stradlings made only two main 'killings': the first was the acquisition of the grange and chapel of Nash, lands in St. Bride's, Wick and Marcross, together with the vicarage of St. Donat's, by sale from Richard Cromwell in 1542; and the other was the purchase of Tewkesbury's manor of Llantwit in 1543.[74] The Lewis family of Y Fan acquired Keynsham's former manor of Roath Keynsham in Henry VIII's reign, and later, in Mary's reign, the grange known as Moor Grange near Cardiff.[75] Another who acquired important interests in and near Cardiff was Sir George Herbert of Swansea, who acted with Sir Rice Mansel as commissioner for the dissolution of Neath. In 1543 he secured the Tewkesbury manor of Llandough via Lord Clinton.[76] Two years later he bought the site and lands of the Grey Friars and Black Friars at Cardiff, and it was here that his grandson, Sir William Herbert, who inherited his estates, built his town house.[77] In 1545, also, he got possession of Llangattock rectory which had formerly belonged to Neath, through the agency of the brothers, Richard and James Gunter.[78] Shortly afterwards he was able to lay hands on the manors of Cardiff and Roath which had formerly belonged to Tewkesbury.[79] At first sight it seems a little odd that Sir George Herbert was the only member of his family, one of the two most influential in Glamorgan, to benefit from the sale of monastic lands in the county. The explanation may lie in the fact that Sir William Herbert, the head of the clan and later earl of Pembroke, was busy acquiring monastic lands elsewhere and, in Glamorgan itself, appears to have been primarily interested in another even more valuable group of crown lands—the estate of Jasper Tudor, former duke of Bedford.[80] The other outstanding family in south-east Wales—the earls of Worcester—were likewise too preoccupied elsewhere to be able or, perhaps, to need to acquire monastic land in Glamorgan. Possibly, too, they hesitated to compete with the Herberts in the latter's sphere of influence in Glamorgan.

The dispersal of monastic lands in Glamorgan cannot, therefore, be said to have created a new class of gentry in the county. All those families which had shown most initiative and enterprise in acquiring them were already well established before the Dissolution. Indeed, it was only families who were already prospering and who could lay hands readily on large sums or whose credit was good enough to raise money who could benefit from the availability of monastic estates for purchase. Even then it imposed a very great strain on some of them to be able to find the money needed. But if the acquisition of these estates did not create new families, it did help to increase the gap between their new owners and the rest of the gentry. Especially as they were also the ones who were already most likely to be able to lease or purchase other crown lands—and there were some very substantial and valuable acquisitions of this kind to be made, particularly from the estates which had reverted to the royal possession after the death of the childless Jasper Tudor. These were, moreover, the families whose fingers were nearest to, and most readily entrusted with, the plums of office and responsibility by a Tudor régime rapidly extending the sphere of its activities in Wales. It is no coincidence that the two men who did best out of the Dissolution in Glamorgan, Rice Mansel and Edward Carne, had achieved more than local distinction in the royal service; the former in war and the latter in diplomacy.[81] In Tudor Glamorgan an 'upper crust' of some half a dozen families clearly emerged among the gentry; without exception they had benefited, to a greater or lesser extent, from the erstwhile monastic lands.

However, it should be pointed out that the very fact of acquiring monastic lands did not, by any means, automatically make these fortunate families Protestant or anti-papal in sympathy. The confident orthodoxy in these matters, which used to assert that the primary object of the Dissolution was the creation among the gentry of a vested interest in an anti-papal church, has long since tended to crumble away. Certainly, the history of the Glamorgan families lends it little support. Sir Edward Carne was devoted enough a papist to become Queen Mary's ambassador at Rome and chose not to return to England after Elizabeth's accession.[82] Thomas Stradling was imprisoned in the Tower for recusancy, and he and his relatives created a great stir by publicizing the 'miracle at St. Donat's' from which many Catholics derived much consolation.[83] Sir Rice Mansel and his wife were close friends of Queen Mary, well rewarded by her for their constancy.[84] The Turbervilles were the leading recusant family in Elizabethan Glamorgan.[85] It is true that in the end all these families conformed, but it can hardly be argued that it was monastic land that was chiefly responsible for inducing them to do so.

Before leaving this subject we should try to measure, however clumsily and crudely, what Glamorgan lost when its monasteries disappeared. No precise assessment is possible, nor is there one which will commend itself universally, irrespective of religious creed or sympathy. Yet on one score there need probably be no disagreement: the loss to architecture and art. In a county not over-endowed with fine ecclesiastical buildings, the monastic churches were the largest and, architecturally, the finest. Most of Ewenni survives to prove the point, and Neath and Margam in ruin still testify movingly to the splendour and dignity that once were theirs. Within their walls, too, were housed the best examples of medieval sculpture, woodwork, glass, plate and vestments,[86] of all of which little or nothing survives for posterity to admire. Their manuscripts and books probably suffered less. Edward Carne of Ewenni was himself a fine scholar who would surely not have been indifferent to the fate of the priory's library, though no record exists of any books or manuscripts having survived from it.[87] Only one of Neath's manuscripts, the *Digestum Novum*, now at Hereford Cathedral, can be traced;[88] but soon after the Dissolution, many of Neath's treasures, including the famous 'Register of Neath' undoubtedly found their way to the Stradlings' fine library at St. Donat's, so much admired by Archbishop Ussher.[89] Since then, however, to the loss and chagrin of Glamorgan historians they have all been dispersed and lost. A number of Margam's manuscripts are still extant. The

Annales of the monastery survive at Trinity College, Cambridge, and
the British Museum has an abbreviated copy of Domesday Book
and a composite volume containing an edition of William of
Malmesbury's *Gesta Regum* and *Novella Historia*, and a version of
Geoffrey of Monmouth's *Historia Regum Britanniae.*[90] Very recently,
Dr. F. G. Cowley has drawn attention to two other manuscripts
which may have a connection with Margam.[91] The one consists
mainly of a copy of miscellaneous writings by St. Bernard and is
now in the British Museum (Royal MS. 6 B XI), though its
provenance is also tentatively assigned to one of the daughter cells
of Tewkesbury Abbey, presumably Cardiff.[92] The other manuscript
contains concordances to St. Bernard's Song of Songs and was
compiled by an abbot of Margam. Once part of the library of the
Belgian abbey of Dunes, it has now passed to the municipal library
of Bruges.[93] After the dissolution of Margam, it would seem that its
new owners, the Mansels, though careful enough to preserve the
large collection of its deeds and records,[94] were markedly less
solicitous for its other books.

Economically and socially, the monasteries no longer had much
to commend them. They were not, and had not for centuries been,
the pioneers of estate management, stock-breeding, wool production,
mining, and metallurgy that once they had been. They had long
ceased directly to exploit their lands or their mills or their mineral
resources; they were content to lease them out to laymen and to live
on their rents. There is no sign that in Glamorgan early in the
sixteenth century they had begun to resume 'high farming' or the
more intensive exploitation of their estates as some large English
houses did. Nor is there any evidence to suggest that as landlords
they differed significantly in their methods or attitude from
surrounding laymen.[95] Conversely, there is little to point to the new
proprietors who succeeded them having been unduly harsh or
oppressive in their treatment of their tenants. The records of the
great law courts reveal no trace of such behaviour, nor do the
voluminous archives of the Margam collections.[96] In general, it
seems that many of the new owners, though not without an eye to
business, were more concerned with the prestige than the profits
accruing from their new estates. Besides, the Crown had leaned over
backwards when appropriating monastic land to confirm the sanctity
of tenants' contracts already entered into with their former landlords.

Nor could the monks be said to have been very conscientious
rectors of those parishes whose tithes they pocketed. They treated
the appropriated churches primarily as a source of profit and had a
poor reputation for fulfilling rectorial obligations such as maintaining chancels in good repair and paying adequate stipends to vicars
or chaplains.[97] Admittedly, the laymen into whose hands these

churches now passed were no better; but at least they could not be said to have fallen away from previously high standards. The major criticism should be reserved in this context for the State's failure to see that this appropriated tithe was returned to the parishes whence it came, to be applied to worthwhile religious or educational ends.

If the monks were not conspicuously good landlords or rectors, neither can they be said to have been fulfilling their social functions with much insight or vigour. It is only fair to acknowledge that they were still maintaining a handful of corrodians (i.e. people normally of advanced years, who were given board and lodge in return for gifts to the monastery). They were also continuing to dispense charity; Margam gave £2 in alms every year and maintained six almsmen, while Neath gave £3 in alms and 'Our Lady's loaf & half a bushel of wheat weekly'.[98] They probably maintained some hospitality, too; and Neath had a reputation for learning, though the wilder fables once current about its 'university' have had to be summarily dismissed.[99] Both Neath and Margam were generous and influential patrons of Welsh literature.[100] But in all these spheres much of the momentum had gone out of monastic life. Such charity as they ministered was perfunctory, haphazard, and not very closely related to need. Much of their hospitality had about it a secularism and a taste for luxury which bore little relation to the Rule of St. Benedict. Their patronage of literature often had a laïcized quality which betrayed a greater concern for the standards of the world than of the cloister; and their contribution to education and learning had become negligible.

But in the last resort it is as centres of religious and spiritual life that they must be judged. In this respect it must be recognized that they now fell a long way short, not simply of the original ideals of their founders, which were after all tremendously exacting and rarely achieved or maintained anywhere in all their fullness, but of their own earlier achievement. They were not, and for a long time had not been, able to exercise a positive influence as the creative minority within the Church. Reduced in numbers, zeal, and morale, they were but a shadow of their former selves, incapable of giving a lead or inspiring devotion. They were not even strong enough in number to maintain a full round of worship and prayer. Nevertheless, those who sympathize with the monastic ideal may argue that the life of the community was the poorer when this source of vicarious acts of worship and prayer, however attenuated, was lost from its midst for ever. That is an imponderable over which it would be profitless to dispute. But it can perhaps be added that contemporary laymen who were to prove among the most loyal sons of the Roman Church in Glamorgan did not seem to think that such loyalty ought to embrace the preservation of the monasteries. Sir Edward Carne was one of Tudor Glamorgan's most distinguished Roman Catholics; the Stradlings and Turbervilles were its foremost recusant families. Yet none of them had hesitated to participate in the Dissolution and to benefit from it. It would, indeed, have been difficult for them to have behaved otherwise towards institutions which, as they existed in 1536, seemed so largely to have outlived the essential religious or social functions they had once so notably performed.

NOTES

[1] The substance of this article was delivered as a lecture at Port Talbot in October 1965 in memory of my young colleague, William Greenway, who died at the tragically early age of 28. The last piece of research on which he was engaged was a history of the medieval church in Glamorgan, which we were to have written jointly. Some of the results of my share of that work, in which I was so sadly deprived of his collaboration, were embodied in the lecture.

[2] See Glanmor Williams, *Welsh Church*, pp. 393-4, 545-6.

[3] *Letters and Papers, Foreign and Domestic, of the Reign of Henry VIII*—hereinafter referred to as *L. and P.*—XIII, ii, 345.

[4] For details, see F. H. Pugh, 'Glamorgan Recusants, 1577-1611', *S. Wales and Mon. Rec. Soc.*, III (1954), 49-67.

[5] *Cal. Papal Letters*, VI, 282.

[6] Williams, *Welsh Church*, chs. III-V, X-XI, XIV.

[7] *L. and P.*, VII, 1355; cf. B.M., Cleopatra E. IV, 174.

[8] The returns for the Welsh dioceses are printed in *Valor Ecclesiasticus* (6 vols. Record Commission, 1810-34), vol. IV.

[9] *L. and P.*, VIII, 149 (69).

[10] Ibid., IX, 161, 695; cf. Public Record Office, S.P. 1/95, p. 168; 1/98, pp. 56-7. See also Lawrence Thomas, *The Reformation in the Old Diocese of Llandaff* (1930), pp. 21-8.

[11] P.R.O., S.P. 1/98, pp. 86-7.

[12] P.R.O., S.P. 1/95, pp. 167-8.

[13] P.R.O., S.P. 1/98, pp. 86-7.

[14] *L. and P.*, IX, 806; cf. P.R.O., S.P. 1/99, p. 35.

[15] *L. and P.*, X, 393; P.R.O., S.P. 1/102, p. 142.

[16] *L. and P.*, X, 746.

[17] Ibid., X, 1238; cf. B.M., Cleopatra E. IV, 290b.

[18] Quoted in David Knowles, *The Religious Orders in England: III. The Tudor Age* (1959), p. 292.

[19] This mistake seems to have arisen because only two Margam monks were awarded a pension.

[20] P.R.O., LR 6/151; cf. Williams, *Welsh Church*, p. 412.

[21] Ibid.

[22] G. T. Clark, *Cartae et Alia Munimenta quae ad Dominium de Glamorgancia Pertinent* (6 vols., 1910), V. 1927-29; cf. also J. P. Turbervill, *Ewenny Priory* (1901), pp. 49-51.

[22A] *L. and P.*, XII, i, 311 (43).

[23] G. W. O. Woodward, 'The exemption from suppression of certain Yorkshire priories', *Eng. Hist. Rev.*, LXXVI (1961), 385-401.

[24] *L. and P.*, XII, i, 706; *State Papers*, I, 451.

[25] Williams, *Welsh Church*, pp. 393-4, 398-9.

[26] Ibid., p. 362; based on P.R.O., SC6/Henry VIII/5156.

[27] P.R.O., S.P. 1/143, pp. 183-4; cf. *L. and P.*, XIV, i, 395.

[28] *L. and P.*, XIV, i, p. 602.

[29] Ibid.

[30] Quoted in Knowles, *Religious Orders*, III, 361.

[31] Ibid., III, 366.

[32] *Cal. Papal Letters*, XIV, 197; cf. Williams, *Welsh Church*, p. 356.

[33] P.R.O., E. 36/115/, f. 35; *L. and P.*, XIII, ii, 294; Clark, *Cartae*, V, 1872-74; cf. also Thomas, *Reformation in Llandaff*, pp. 66-8; William Rees, 'The Dissolution of the Friaries', *S. Wales and Mon. Record Society*, III (1954), 7-19.

[34] P.R.O., E. 36/115/f.35; cf. Clark, *Cartae*, V, 1873.

[35] P.R.O., E. 36/115/f. 83; Clark, *Cartae*, V, 1874-77.

[36] *L. and P.*, XIII, ii, 294, 295.

[37] Williams, *Welsh Church*, pp. 559-61 for details of monastic numbers in Wales.

[38] *L. and P.*, XIV, i, p. 602; XIII, i, 575, f.25b.

[39] A. G. Dickens, 'The Edwardian Arrears in Augmentations Payments and ·he Problems of the Ex-religious', *English Historical Review*, LV (1940), 384-418.

[40] P.R.O., E. 163, p. 75*v*.

[41] Williams, *Welsh Church*, p. 372.

[42] Quoted in Knowles, *Religious Orders*, III, 384.

[43] P.R.O., Augmentations Proceedings, E. 321/12/91; cf. also J. H. Matthews (ed.), *Records of the County Borough of Cardiff* (6 vols., 1898-1911), III, 32-4.

[44] P.R.O., E. 321/12/96; *Cardiff Records*, III, 35-7.

[45] The foundations and tiled floors of the Dominican friary can be seen in the grounds of Cardiff castle, now open to the public. What remains of the Herbert house, not very far away, seems in imminent danger of collapse if not of clearance.

[46] W. de G. Birch, *A History of Neath Abbey* (1902), pp. 117-8.

[47] G. R. Elton, *The Tudor Revolution in Government* (1953), pp. 203-19.

[48] *L. and P.*, XIII, p. 580; Clark, *Cartae*, V, 1903-04.

[49] Joyce Youings, 'The terms of the disposal of Devon monastic lands', *Eng. Hist. Rev.*, LXIX (1954), 18-38; idem., *Devon Monastic Lands: Calendar of Particulars for Grants* (Devon and Cornwall Rec. Soc., new series), I (1955), vii-xxxiii.

[50] W. de G. Birch, *A Descriptive Catalogue of the Penrice and Margam Abbey Manuscripts* (6 vols., 1893-1905), I, 140-2; Clark, *Cartae*, V, 1918-23 for full text. For Rice Mansel's career, see Glanmor Williams, 'Rhys Mansel of Penrice and Margam', *Morgannwg*, VI (1963), 33-51.

[51] *L. and P.*, XII, i, 795 (16).

[52] Clark, *Cartae*, V, 1941.

[53] P.R.O., Particulars for Grants, Henry VIII, nos. 243, 244.

[54] Ibid., no. 1067.

[55] Youings, *Eng. Hist. Rev.*, LXIX, 23.

[56] *L. and P.*, XVI, 1226 (5); cf. also for a grant to the dean and chapter of Bristol, ibid., XVII, 1154 (60).

[57] Ibid., XVIII, i, 623 (4), 802.

[58] Ibid., XVIII, i, 981 (54).

[59] P.R.O., Particulars for Grants, Henry VIII, no. 1058.

[60] Ibid., no. 329.

[61] *L. and P.*, XVII, 220 (95); 1012 (5); XVIII, i, 474 (11); cf. Clark, *Cartae*, V, 1932-33.

[62] P.R.O., Particulars for Grants, Henry VIII, no. 567; *Cal. Patent Rolls*, 1547-48, p. 278.

[63] N.L.W., Milborne MSS., nos. 2201, 2203, 2204, 4841, 4842, 4959.

[64] *Cal. Patent Rolls*, 1547-48, p. 2.

[65] For details, see Williams, *Morgannwg*, VI, 33-51.

[66] For the full text of these grants, Clark, *Cartae*, V, 1918-23, 1937-48, 1964-71.

[67] His eldest son, Edward, appears to have made the fortified mansion of Oxwich castle his home; see the present writer's 'The Affray at Oxwich Castle, 1557', *Gower*, II (1949), 6-11, based on P.R.O., St. Ch. 2/20/160; 2/24/365 and 4/1/26.

[68] Birch, *Catal. Penrice and Margam MSS.*, I, 143.

[69] No biographical study of Carne exists, but a valuable short article by A. H. Dodd is to be found in *The Dictionary of Welsh Biography* (London, 1959), pp. 67-8; cf. also Turbervill, *Ewenny Priory*, pp. 57-62.

[70] William Rees, *Cardiff: A History of the City* (1962), p. 48.

[71] P.R.O., Particulars for Grants, Henry VIII, no. 243.

[72] Ibid., no. 244.

[73] Ibid., no. 245.

[74] Clark, *Cartae*, V, 1932-33; *L. and P.*, XVIII, ii, 107 (62).

[75] *Cardiff Records*, II, 16-17; *Cal. Patent Rolls*, 1553-54, pp. 153-4.

[76] *L. and P.*, XVIII, i, 802 (72).

[77] Ibid., XX, i, 465 (101); XX, ii, 910 (82); cf. also N.L.W., Milborne MSS. 2204, 4841, 4842, 4959; and William Rees, *S. Wales and Mon. Record Society*, III, 14-15.

[78] *L. and P.*, XX, i, 465 (16) and (101).

[79] Ibid., XX, ii, 910 (82).

[80] Gareth E. Jones, 'The Glamorgan Gentry, 1536-1603' (M.A. Thesis, Wales, 1963), pp. 66-8, for an analysis of Pembroke's estates.

[81] Williams, *Morgannwg*, VI, 37-41; Dodd, *D.W.B.*, pp. 67-8.

[82] Ibid.

[83] David Williams, 'The Miracle at St. Donat's', *The Welsh Review*, VI (1947), 33-38.

[84] Williams, *Morgannwg*, VI, 46-7.

[85] F. H. Pugh, 'Glamorgan Recusants, 1577-1611', *S. Wales and Mon. Record Society*, III (1954), 51-52.

[86] Williams, *Welsh Church*, pp. 386-7.

[87] N. R. Ker (ed.), *Medieval Libraries of Great Britain* (2nd ed., Royal Hist. Soc., 1964), contains no entry relating to Ewenni. Nor are are there any likely survivals among the Carne MSS. in the Glamorgan County Record Office.

[88] Ibid., p. 133.

[89] G. J. Williams, *Traddodiad Llenyddol Morgannwg* (1948), pp. 194-200; cf. the present writer's 'The Stradlings of St. Donat's' in Stewart Williams (ed.), *The Vale of History* (1960), pp. 85-95.

[90] Ker, *Medieval Libraries*, p. 129.

[91] 'The Monastic Order in South Wales' (Ph.D. Thesis, Wales, 1965), pp. 335-7.

[92] Ker, *Medieval Libraries*, p. 48.

[93] Cowley, 'The Monastic Order', pp. 386-7.

[94] For the huge collection of Margam deeds and documents, see W. de G. Birch, *Descriptive Catalogue of the Penrice and Margam Abbey Manuscripts* (4 series, 6 vols., 1893-1905).

[95] For the condition of Welsh monasteries generally on the eve of the Reformation, see Williams, *Welsh Church*, chs. X and XI.

[96] See, for example, E. A. Lewis and J. Conway Davies (ed.), *Records of the Court of Augmentations relating to Wales and Monmouthshire* (1954), *passim*, or Birch, *Catalogue of Penrice and Margam MSS.*

[97] Williams, *Welsh Church*, pp. 348-52.

[98] *Valor Ecclesiasticus*, IV, 351.

[99] Birch, *Neath*, pp. 139-41; Williams, *Welsh Church*, pp. 393-4.

[100] G. J. Williams, *Traddodiad Llenyddol*, pp. 191-3.

V. THE PROTESTANT EXPERIMENT IN THE DIOCESE OF ST. DAVID'S, 1534-55

I. WILLIAM BARLOW AND THE DIOCESE OF ST. DAVID'S

William Barlow's connexion with the diocese of St. David's, first as prior of Haverfordwest, and later as bishop, has justly been regarded as one of the most interesting episodes in the history of the Welsh Church during the Reformation period. Barlow himself, fanatical, iconoclastic, rash, and often unscrupulous, but a courageous and not insincere innovator withal, commands attention if not respect. Moreover, he was the first whole-hearted Protestant to reach a position of authority in the Welsh Church, and only in St. David's during his episcopate and that of his successor was any determined attempt made to implant Protestant doctrine in Wales before the reign of Elizabeth. This early experiment has the advantage of being much less inadequately documented than most of the Welsh Church history of the Tudor period. It is therefore surprising to find that no detailed examination of Barlow's connexion with the see has been undertaken.[1] Such accounts as have been written present a somewhat bare and over-simplified description of an inevitable clash between an aggressive Protestant bishop and a stubborn conservative-minded clergy.[2] Closer scrutiny reveals, as students of the Reformation elsewhere might expect, a more complex state of affairs, with a much subtler intertwining of diverse motives, selfish and altruistic, spiritual and mundane; in fact, a not unrepresentative microcosm of the great conflict of the age.

The complexities of Barlow's career as an Augustinian canon and diplomat fortunately need not concern us here.[3] Suffice it for our purpose to say that his first contact with the diocese of St. David's appears to have been his election in 1534 to the small priory of Haverfordwest[4] within Anne Boleyn's lordship of Pembroke, preferment which on his own showing he owed to Anne's favour.[5] He seems to have arrived there in time to take the oath under the Act of Supremacy in July 1534.[6]

South Pembrokeshire was one of the very few parts of Wales where conditions were not entirely unpropitious for the reception of changes in religion. In and around its flourishing little seaports there existed a small but vigorous merchant-class in close contact with Bristol and other trading centres still further afield. The people of the area may have been to some small extent susceptible to anti-clericalism and heterodoxy. At all events, the only two cases of

heresy occurring in the pages of the medieval registers of St. David's
diocese both relate to south Pembrokeshire.[7] Still more important
perhaps, there existed here a sizeable community of English-
speaking people who could be influenced by the anti-papal and
Protestant literature of Henry VIII's reign, and by Barlow's fiery
preaching, to both of which propaganda media the rest of the
population of Wales, other than the inhabitants of market towns,[8]
was immune. As early as 1535, one of Barlow's servants in the town
of Tenby possessed a copy of the New Testament in English and
other similar books;[9] while Barlow, by virtue of his headship of
the priory of Haverfordwest, had control of three out of four
pulpits in the town,[10] and he seems to have taken full advantage
of this for delivering himself of anti-papal orations.

These advantages apart, Barlow found conditions in the diocese
most uncongenial to a zealot of his persuasion. The cathedral
church, not to mention many lesser shrines, was the most resorted-
to place of pilgrimage in the land and a hotbed of what he deemed
superstition and idolatry. The bishop, Richard Rawlins, and most
of his clergy were strongly conservative in their bent, while the
laity were 'miserably ordered under the clergy'.[11] The new and
heady doctrines imbibed by Barlow had no supporters other than
he, so to strengthen his endeavours 'against Antichrist and all his
confederate adherents', and to prosper family fortunes, of which
he was ever very tender, Barlow brought three of his brothers to
Pembrokeshire. John Barlow was, like William, a cleric-diplomat.
He was now a fire-eating anti-papist, but had not always been so.
He humbly confessed to having been 'sometime a fautor of the
papistical sect', hastening to add, however, that he had since seen the
light, and to make up for his earlier errors he was eager to suppress
all papists by every means he could devise.[12] Roger Barlow, a
layman, was a most interesting personality. Explorer, author, and
Bristol merchant, his shrewd businessman's eye soon discerned
some very promising investments in Pembrokeshire.[13] The third
brother, Thomas, also a cleric, was altogether less conspicuous
and more colourless than the others, and played little part in the
affairs of the diocese.

Even while newly arrived as prior of Haverfordwest, Barlow's
enthusiasm for innovation and his appetite for power led him to
meddle in the affairs of the bishopric in a way which was almost
bound to give offence to the bishop and his clergy. He opened his
campaign with a series of violently anti-papal sermons which won
him the enmity not only of the secular clergy but also of the Black
Friars of Haverfordwest. The latter may have felt their professional
status as preachers affronted by the eloquence as well as the heresy
of this interloper. Certainly it was one of their number who was
Barlow's chief antagonist in public, and who, at Rawlins's instigation,

presented a series of articles against him to the King's Council. Barlow himself stood too high in the favour of Cromwell and Anne Boleyn for his reputation to be damaged by these attacks, but his adversaries had been able to take vengeance on one of his servants by accusing him of heresy. They had ransacked this man's house at Tenby and seized a Testament in English and other books belonging to him, 'withholding them with vehement reproaches and clamorous exclamations against heretics, as if to have the Testament in English were horrible heresy'. They had then had him imprisoned by the mayor of Tenby.[14]

Barlow denounced in unmeasured terms the hostility of the clergy of whom 'is there not one that sincerely preacheth God's word, nor scarce any that heartily favoureth it, but all utter enemies there-against', and the backwardness of the diocese with its 'enormous vices, the fraudulent exactions, the misordered living and heathen idolatry'. He believed no diocese to be 'more corrupted, nor none so far out of frame, without hope of reformation except your master-ship shall see a redress'.[15] The redress which Barlow undoubtedly wanted Cromwell to see was his own appointment as suffragan bishop within the diocese, and he managed to obtain from Cromwell letters to that end. But on 19th March, 1535, he complained that these letters were being studiously ignored or opposed by the bishop and his officers.[16] A fortnight later, on 31st March, John Barlow, to reinforce his brother's appeal to Cromwell, sought Queen Anne's support by writing to her vice-chamberlain, Sir Edward Beynton. He claimed disarmingly that his brother was not seeking to become suffragan for his own worldly advancement (a disclaimer which almost automatically makes us suspect that he was!), but simply for the furtherance of God's word. He repeated the charges of the ill-handling by Rawlins's minions of his brother's servant, only because he was 'toward' William, 'whom of all men they most hate for his preaching'. Lest Anne should find herself unmoved by a mere tale of the petty persecution of God's servants in a distant corner of Wales, he was at great pains to point out that Rawlins was stirring up the opposition not only of the clergy but of the gentry and commons as well, and—a deft touch this—nowhere worse than in Queen Anne's own lordship of Pembroke.[17]

It may very well have been the brothers Barlow who, about this time, tried to discredit Rawlins still further by reporting to Cromwell the unsoundness of the bishop's beliefs concerning the nature of purgatory and the validity of prayers for the dead. Rawlins's reply to these accusations is undated and was placed among the documents for the year 1536 in the Record Office. But since Rawlins died in February 1536, his answer should almost certainly be ascribed to the previous year.[18] He was undoubtedly somewhat conservative in his views on purgatory, for he admitted to believing that it was

meet and expedient to pray for souls of the departed, without
determination of any special place or expressed assertion of any
name. But he firmly denied any intention of reviving the popish
purgatory, or any notion that any expiatory acts such as offering
candles, grants of pardons, or saying any paternosters before some
appointed altar, could release souls from purgatory.[19] What gives
added likelihood to the possibility that the Barlows were at the
bottom of these attacks on Rawlins is the fact that William Barlow
is known to have held advanced views concerning purgatory, for
which, among other things, he was himself to be denounced to the
government a year or two later.[20]

Soon afterwards, in the early summer of 1535 in all probability,[21]
William Barlow was removed from the diocese to become prior of
Bisham. Later in the same year he was sent on an important mission
to Scotland, the object of which was to induce James V to abandon
the Pope. Since the whole idea of this embassy was Cromwell's, it
suggests that his confidence in Barlow had increased. This was
further borne out by the appointment of Barlow, while he was still
engaged on the Scottish mission, as bishop of St. Asaph in January
1536.[22] News of his brother's impending promotion seems to have
impelled John Barlow to underline the importance of the appointment by drawing Cromwell's attention to the serious danger to be
apprehended from papists in Wales, especially those of the diocese
of St. David's. They were presumably more incorrigible than ever
now that their scourge had been removed from their midst. Writing
from his collegiate church of Westbury-on-Trym on 3rd January,
he spoke of the way in which papists in St. David's were supported
by the bishop and the higher clergy, who persuaded the gentry to
stick with them in their old *mumpsimus*. He alleged that they had
lately given assistance to the Irish rebels, and that they unashamedly
expressed their hope of seeing the world alter and change again.
The only way to deal with them, John Barlow thought, was to
summon before the council the chief offenders whom his brother
had named, and to reform the lesser fry by means of a local commission, on which he would be glad to serve.[23] In view of these warn-
ings and of the dangerous intrigues of the House of Dynevor,[24] it
was not surprising that Cromwell should pay close attention to the
Barlows' views concerning the diocese of St. David's. When the
see became vacant on 23rd February, 1536, by the death of Bishop
Rawlins, he wasted no time in translating William Barlow there
in April of the same year.

It was as well for the Barlows that they stood so high in Cromwell's
esteem, in view of the disgrace and execution of Anne Boleyn
during May 1536. The downfall of their powerful patroness had
undoubtedly made them very apprehensive at first. William was
still far away in Scotland during those fateful May days. Up there

in Edinburgh amid unregenerate Romanists on whom he had quite failed to make any favourable impression, he must have heard the bad news concerning Anne Boleyn with growing alarm, It may well have been nervousness about his future prospects, no less than the failure of his mission in Scotland, which made him declare in a letter dated from Edinburgh on 23rd May, 1536, that he would 'no more regret to depart than Lot did to pass out of Sodom'.[25] In Henry VIII's reign, when events moved so savagely and so swiftly, it was dangerous to be so far away without reliable news of what was happening at court. His brother John also seems to have been taken unawares by the bad news, and was busy in the diocese of St. Asaph at the time.[26] But he wasted no time in hurrying down to Pembrokeshire to safeguard their interests. Indeed, so precipitate was his advent that one of his enemies thought he intended to decamp from Milford Haven. But this man, Robert Colyns, vicar of Tenby, soon learned that John Barlow relieved his nerves at a time of crisis by laying about his enemies promptly and forcefully. Colyns, according to his own evidence, had been seized by Barlow and wrongfully imprisoned at Llawhaden Castle for not completely expunging the Pope's name from service-books, and for speaking certain words on first hearing of Anne Boleyn's treason. He had apparently said that he marvelled at the great speed with which Barlow had come to Pembrokeshire, and that as Barlow had always been a Boleyn man, had obtained his preferment through Anne's favour, and been an ambassador for her, he should be made sure of, in case he attempted to escape by sea from Milford.[27] All of these accusations of a treasonable Boleyn connexion could be equally well applied to Bishop Barlow, as Colyns must certainly have known. But, thanks to Cromwell's influence, both the brothers survived the crisis unscathed.

Bishop Barlow probably arrived back from Scotland about the end of June or the beginning of July.[28] His arrival in St. David's in the autumn soon shattered the uneasy peace which had prevailed since his departure in 1535. Any hopes his opponents may have had that Anne Boleyn's fall had weakened his position were quickly falsified. Before the end of the year, in an important letter to Cromwell,[29] he had already made plain his intentions with regard to the diocese. He struck again that note of denunciation of the inveterate superstition, 'with horrible blasphemy of God and his verity', which made St. David's to Wales what Bethel and Dan were to Israel.[30] He also put forward in this letter, and in an accompanying document described as 'instructions for the bishop of St. David's suits',[31] what might be described as the Barlow plan for the diocese. Its two most important features were a proposal to remove the see from St. David's, 'the most barren angle in the diocese', to St. Peter's, Carmarthen,[32] and another to endow grammar schools and Protestant preaching, mainly out of the proceeds of suppressed colleges or friaries.

What Barlow omitted to tell Cromwell in these missives was that he was also trying to force upon the cathedral chapter an unconstitutional extension of his authority over them. His attempt to do so seems to have precipitated an almost immediate trial of strength between himself and the canons. It is at this point that we can begin to see that this was not a simple clear-cut issue between a Protestant bishop and a recalcitrant clergy. For it quickly became plain that the canons were not merely resisting Barlow's proselytizing tendencies, but also his attempts to make himself head of the chapter. It was probably this latter issue which appeared most important to them and, possibly, to Barlow. For the episcopate of Barlow's successor, Ferrar, shows that a Protestant bishop could meet with even fiercer opposition from Protestant canons who believed that their established rights were being infringed.

Throughout the Middle Ages and indeed as late as the beginning of the nineteenth century, St. David's was in the unusual position of having no dean. In the absence of a dean, the precentor had established a prescriptive right to be regarded as the head of the chapter. But there was considerable uncertainty concerning the authority of the bishop over the chapter. He certainly had extraordinarily large and uncontested visitatorial authority, 'exercised by the bishop strictly as a bishop, and not by virtue of that vague and uncertain claim to the deanery'.[33] Barlow, however, was not content with the very wide powers the chapter normally accorded to the bishop, and was pressing to the utmost the 'vague and uncertain claim to the deanery'. His brother John later claimed that the canons had actually recognized the validity of the bishop's claims at the time of his installation, when they first of all gave him the bishop's stall in the choir and then the dean's.[34] If they had indeed installed him in this way, they could hardly have intended this act to alienate their much-cherished capitular independence.

When it became unmistakably Barlow's intention to go much further than any of his predecessors had done in subordinating the chapter to episcopal control, the canons naturally resisted with some spirit. If the bishop was seeking to get his own way by denouncing their shortcomings to Cromwell, they could reply in kind by exposing his unorthodoxy in the opposite direction. In January 1537 there were forwarded to Cromwell via Rowland Lee a series of charges of heretical beliefs held by Barlow, which were causing grave disquiet among the people of his diocese. The list, drawn up by Roger Lewis, LL.B.,[35] accused Barlow of having said that in earlier times no one had preached the word of God truly, that confession was inexpedient, reverence of the saints pure idolatry and

purgatory an invention of the bishop of Rome for lucre, for dead
souls had no need of prayer. He had also declared that where two
or three simple persons, such as cobblers and weavers, were ass-
embled in the name of God, there was the true church, and that
the king could make any learned layman a bishop.[36] Even making
allowance for a certain degree of exaggeration on the part of the
canons in the heat of their controversy with Barlow, we can well
understand the consternation the expression of such views must
have caused in a conservatively minded diocese.

A month or two later the conflict took a new and bitter turn,
when Thomas Lloyd, precentor of St. David's and founder of the
first grammar school at Carmarthen, was accused by Barlow of
complicity with pirates. He seized Lloyd's person, took possession of
his house, and distrained his goods, in most oppressive fashion.[37]
Since Lloyd was a much respected figure who shared some of
Barlow's opinions concerning the need for extending the 'New
Learning' and who had had professions of great affection and
favour from him,[38] this sudden and violent attack by the bishop
was most revealing. It seemed to suggest that Barlow was willing
to jump at any opportunity of disgracing the head of the chapter,
who was doubtless prominently associated with the resistance of
its other members. But in so doing he overreached himself. Lloyd
was a well-liked man ,'much esteemed at St. David's for his learning,
liberality, and kindness'.[39] He and his friends among the canons
were not disposed to submit without a struggle to this further act
of aggression by Barlow. Lloyd promptly brought a Star Chamber
suit against him.[40] Unfortunately the records of this suit are tant-
alizingly incomplete, and give information only of two orders taken
by the Council of the Marches. The first taken at Leominster on
4th March, 1537, called for the appearance of the bishop of St.
David's to answer to the complaint of Thomas Lloyd, and for the
restoration of Lloyd's goods until further deliberation of the matter.
The second, taken at Worcester on 15th March, required the
appearance of the bishop's attorney along with Thomas Lloyd to
determine the respective rights of the bishop and the precentor in
the lordship of Pebidiog. Neither the Star Chamber record nor
Lloyd's statement of grievances gives a precise indication of the
nature of the dispute between him and Barlow; but at least both
documents make it clear that the real issue was a clash of jurisdiction
between bishop and precentor, and not the latter's complicity with
pirates as Barlow alleged in a letter to Cromwell dated 5th March,
1537.[41] The documents also make it clear that Barlow had exceeded
his rights in acting so high-handedly.

Meantime, some of the most influential canons had been active
in Lloyd's behalf. They were accorded the powerful support of
Richard Devereux, deputy-justice of south Wales and son and

heir to Lord Ferrers. the most important layman in west Wales. Anticipating formidable opposition, Barlow, in his letter of 5th March, 1537, had tried to gain Cromwell's goodwill by offering to make him or his son steward of the lands of the bishopric of St. David's jointly with the earl of Worcester at a fee of twenty marks, to be increased on the earl's death. In the same letter, significantly enough, Barlow also appealed for the strengthening of his position as a marcher lord. On the very day after this letter was written Richard Devereux came to the bishop's house, and, according to Barlow, with 'brags and hault words' presumed to interfere with liberties granted to him by the king and contrary to Cromwell's directions, and prevented him from from sending the confessions of the pirates to Cromwell.[42]

Cromwell, however, was not as convinced of the righteousness of Barlow's cause as was Barlow himself. He seems to have upheld the order of the Council of the Marches calling for the restoration of Lloyd's goods, and we find Barlow very much on the defensive when writing to him next on 5th April.[43] He claimed that upon receipt of Cromwell's letters he had delivered up the remainder of the precentor's goods, though Lloyd, writing a month or more later, denied that he had done so.[44] He then proceeded to justify his earlier acts: he had not rifled the chanter's house and carried away his goods but had merely removed chests containing his plate and money because of the threatening attitude of Lloyd's friends, who were raising the countryside on his behalf. He complained bitterly of Lloyd's 'far abused demeanour and intolerable fashion', and of the intervention of Richard Devereux and two of the richest canons, Griffith ap Owen and John Lewis, to thwart the course of justice. Barlow made the most serious accusations against the canons, 'two valiant bearers' and 'sworn chaplains' to Lord Ferrers. Griffith ap Owen he accused of gross immorality, and John Lewis of having had in his possession letters from rebels against the Crown.[45] They opposed him only because of the sincerity and zeal of his attempts at reform; if they could justly convince him of any 'rash inordinate extremity', he would never again desire Cromwell's favour.

For all his fair words, it would seem that Barlow still continued for some time to try to bluster his way out of his difficulties. Lloyd accused him of ignoring the Council's order for the restoration of his goods, and of sending him to answer the Council mounted on a 'stumbling jade' and guarded by armed men 'to his great shame and slander'. The week after Low Sunday, which in 1537 fell on 8th April, Lloyd had been excommunicated at the college of Abergwili by the bishop's commissary without due citation. His kinsman, William Phillipps, apparitor-general for life to the bishop of St. David's, had been imprisoned and compelled to surrender his patent solely on account of his relationship to Lloyd. Another kinsman, David Powell, clerk, and David Cole, his household steward, had been indicted at St. David's. Lloyd's nominee for the sub-chantership had been refused by the bishop, who proposed, contrary to law and custom, to make his own nomination.[46]

Judging by the silence of the documents for nearly a year after this episode, there seems to have been a lull in the conflict, caused perhaps by Barlow's rebuff following his harrying of the unfortunate precentor. But the events of the following year, 1538, were again to show how dangerously near the surface bad feeling was. Not a little of it was due to the resentment felt at the way in which the Barlow brothers were pushing their secular interests within the diocese. Roger Barlow had already acquired a lease of some of the possessions of the preceptory of Slebech and of the possessions of the dissolved priory of Haverfordwest. This led to a sharp clash with the officers of the town of Pembroke, and to still more bad blood between the Barlows and the Devereux, for the Pembroke men chose as their next mayor, Sir James Baskerville. Baskerville was Ferrers's son-in-law and steward of the lordship of Pembroke, and, according to Roger Barlow, a powerful man who might 'do what he list, more by force than by justice'.[47] John Barlow's attempts to force the pace were also leading to trouble. It was at his provocation that William Barlow was claiming rights over the wild birds of the sea, gulls, mews, and divers other birds, on 'Perys Iland',[48] against another member of the chapter, Griffith Leyshon, LL.D., archdeacon of Carmarthen. In a Chancery suit brought against the bishop Leyshon claimed that these rights had always been a part of the profits of his archdeaconry. He was 'desirous of peace, and loath to strive with his ordinary', but John Barlow's attitude, his 'menacing words', and his threats to 'expel and put out' Leyshon, and his declared intention of getting his way willy-nilly, had been intolerable.[49] Another Chancery suit of the same period accused the bishop of extortion and sharp practice against one of his life-tenants.[50]

The attacks on superstition, launched in 1538, and the dissolution of the friaries, provided Barlow with an admirable pretext for renewing his attacks on the canons, and for pressing more vehemently than ever his programme of reform for the diocese. Writing from Carmarthen on 31st March, 1538,[51] he castigated the canons for setting forth 'feigned relics' 'for to allure the people to superstition on St. David's Day', and in this and several other letters in the course of the year reiterated his favourite projects for the removal of the see and the establishment of grammar schools.[52] In all fairness to Barlow, it must be admitted that Carmarthen, the largest town in Wales and the hub of many radiating roads, would have made a more convenient administrative centre for his vast, sprawling diocese than St. David's. Moreover, the cathedral was far too intimately associated with medieval religious traditions for Barlow's taste. It had always been 'esteemed a delicate daughter of Rome, naturally resembling her mother in shameless confusion, and like qualified with other perverse properties of execrable malignity, as ungodly image service, abominable idolatry, and licentious liberty of dishonest living, popish pilgrimages, deceitful pardons, and feigned indulgences'. These 'memorial monuments' of Rome's 'puppetry' could not be extirpated without translation of the see.[53] There is no doubt, also, that Barlow hoped that the translation of the see would make it possible for him to exert his authority over the canons far more vigorously.

The canons for their part were no less determined that the cathedral should remain at St. David's. They were, it was said, prepared to 'spend to their shirts in the quarrel'.[54] Apart from any feelings of affection for the associations of St. David's—and it would be foolish to discount the strength of such sentiments—they were probably reluctant to lose a valuable source of income which accrued to them through the offerings of the faithful.[55] Devotees thronged to St. David's and its chapels to do honour to those relics which Barlow so contemptuously dismissed as 'two heads of silver plate enclosing two rotten skulls stuffed with putrified clouts; item, two arm bones, and a worm-eaten book covered with silver plate'.[56] And we may be quite sure that the prospect of the bishop's being always in close proximity to the cathedral and its chapter did not hold the attraction for them that it did for Barlow. Distance could make their bishop more bearable; nothing could lend him enchantment. To show their hostility to his proposals, and as a visible sign of their hopes and affection for the old cathedral, they embarked on a quite extensive building programme, which seems to have overstrained their resources and got them into financial difficulties.[57] Nothing could have exasperated their worthy bishop more. He thought it quite intolerable that they should 'utterly consume the small residue of the church treasure remaining in their custody, without any profitable effect, saving to nourish clattering conventicles of barbarous and rural persons, the deformed habitations of the poor collegians in such beggarly ruin and so wretchedly that honesty will abhor to behold them'.[58] All his threats and protests were in vain. A last despairing appeal to Cromwell on 24th December, 1538, by John Barlow,[59] went unanswered. The canons had successfully defied their bishop.

Great events outside the diocese, involving fundamental changes in royal policy, now came to the aid of the chapter. The free rein which had earlier been given to the more radical critics of the papacy was now severely curtailed. The year 1539, and the years that followed, saw a marked reaction against the Protestant tendencies which had hitherto been winked at or encouraged. The Six Articles Act was passed; two extreme Protestants, Latimer and Shaxton, lost their sees; reformers like Barlow were no longer in favour. It may have been the changing religious climate which prompted John Barlow to play the part of informer against George Constantine in August 1539,[60] thinking it now necessary to show that a Barlow could be as good a heretic-hunter as the next. But as late as March 1540, William Barlow was still sufficiently in favour to be a royal preacher.[61] It was the execution of Cromwell in July of that year which was the most serious blow to him. He was deprived of his most powerful patron, and there are no longer to be found any appeals for the reorganization of the diocese such as those which had been pressed with such importunate urgency during the years 1535-8.[62]

All this did not mean the abandonment by Barlow of all hope of fulfilling some at least of his plans. In 1541, less than a year after Cromwell's execution, he obtained permission for the college at Abergwili to be transferred to Brecon.[63] There he established a new collegiate foundation and grammar school. Then again, he gradually weakened the resistance of the chapter by introducing his own nominees as opportunities presented themselves. He brought in hot gospellers like Friar Barnes[64] and George Constantine, both of them former Protestant book-agents. He gave preferment to young graduates of Protestant views like Thomas Young, Rowland Meyrick, and Stephen Green, who were later to play a leading part in the life of the diocese. Wherever possible, also, he gave valuable benefices to his brothers. John Barlow for a short time became archdeacon of Carmarthen; it would be instructive to know if he then took his brother's part over the profits of 'Perys Iland'! Thomas Barlow became prebendary of Mathry, and even the layman, Roger, was made prebendary of Llanarthne.

Barlow further strengthened his own position, at the expense of the best interests of the see, by making numerous grants of advowson rights to kinsmen and friends.[65] As a result of his grants of this kind and his dilapidations of episcopal palaces, Barlow has had an unpleasant reputation for impoverishing his bishopric. While the wilder tales of his stripping the lead from the roof of the palace at St. David's to provide dowries for his daughters have long been dismissed, it may nevertheless have been he who first allowed that magnificent building to fall into disrepair. In the light of his resolve to make Carmarthen the cathedral centre, and his indignation at the building undertaken by the canons at St. David's, he would have been most unlikely to prevent the decay of the palace, even if he took no active steps to bring it about.

It is his alienation of the manor of Lamphey that has provoked most criticism of him as an impoverisher of the see. The main stages in this transaction, briefly recapitulated, were: early in 1546 the

bishop of St. David's, at his own suit, received the royal permission
to grant, bargain, or give in fee simple, the lordship of Lamphey
to Richard Devereux.[66] On 14th August, with the consent of the
precentor and chapter, Barlow surrendered the lordship and manor
to the Crown.[67] On 16th October he received a grant of the advowson
of the rectory and vicarage of Carew in return for the surrender of
Lamphey,[68] which two days earlier had been granted to Richard
Devereux.[69] The motives which led Barlow to alienate this most
valuable manor, which had been one of the richest possessions of
the diocese for 500 years, in return for inadequate compensation,
have never been very satisfactorily explained; and indeed it is not inconceivable that they never can now be adequately accounted for. It
is true that this was an age when bishops were subject to the most
severe pressure from the Crown and the laity to part with their
temporal possessions. The year 1546 saw Henry VIII's finances
reach such a low ebb that he began to think seriously of another
immense raid on Church property, this time on the chantries. Yet
it was not the Crown, but the Devereux family, which gained from
the surrender of Lamphey. Barlow was not always a careful husband
of the resources of his diocese, but it is difficult to imagine his
consenting to enrich his old enemies except under very heavy
pressure. This pressure, according to one tradition, they could apply
because Barlow was discovered to be keeping a concubine.[70] It is
not out of the question that there was some scandal, the details of
which were never recorded and soon forgotten, which led Henry VIII,
always a great puller-out of motes from other men's eyes, to punish
Barlow, thus enabling the Devereux family to take a long-delayed
vengeance on their old enemy. This does not seem very probable.
What may have more significance is a marked change in the religious
allegiance of the Devereux during these years. Whereas in 1537-8 they
had been the allies and patrons of some of the most conservative
canons of St. David's, in 1546 the records of the Privy Council
reveal that Richard Devereux and one John Olde, Lord Ferrers's
chaplain, were brought before it on charges of heresy.[71] This, and
the rapid elevation of Ferrers and his son under the Somerset
régime, suggest that the family had moved quite some way to the
religious left. Had this change of front brought about a *rapproche-
ment* with Barlow? On the basis of the surviving evidence it is
impossible to tell. But an old tradition that Barlow alienated
Lamphey to his godson, Walter, Richard Devereux's young son
and later the earl of Essex, may have some significance. And it could
have been more than coincidence that in the very summer when
Barlow was yielding up Lamphey, his brothers, Roger and Thomas,
were acquiring by purchase from the Crown the Slebech estates, and
the possessions of Pill Priory, Haverfordwest Priory, and Haverfordwest Friary. The resentment felt earlier by the Devereux at
the intrusion of the Barlows into the area has already been noted.

Had they modified their attitude by 1546? Did both sides now regard each other as useful allies?[72] And was the acquisition of Lamphey regarded as adequate compensation for the undisputed acceptance of the Barlow claims to the Haverfordwest and Slebech estates? It is a not impossible explanation of what remains a most mysterious transaction.

With the coming of the new Protestant régime of Somerset, men of Barlow's views were quickly restored to favour. Within a year of Edward VI's accession he was translated from St. David's to the wealthier see of Bath and Wells. Before he went he took care to exert his influence in favour of the election to St. David's of a protégé and fellow Protestant, Robert Ferrar. Ferrar, an Augustinian canon like Barlow, had, at the latter's request, accompanied him on his mission to Scotland in 1535–6.

For all the upheavals he caused, Barlow was not without his qualities. The sincerity of his Protestantism, however unfortunate the forms in which it sometimes found expression, could hardly be held in question. The accusations made against him for being a waverer and a time-server do not square with the tenacity with which he clung to his opinions during the years 1540–7, and later, during Mary's reign. He honestly desired to effect the spread of Renaissance learning within his diocese, and no impartial observer would deny the need for better facilities for training the clergy of St. David's. Nor was he unsympathetic to the acute financial difficulties of the lower clergy, which he brought to Cromwell's attention as early as 1536.[73] His plans for the removal of the see to Carmarthen, however offensive to tradition and sentiment, would certainly have made for more effective administration of a vast and unwieldy diocese; and his attacks on some of the religious practices of the clergy and laity were a not unhealthy reaction against the grosser forms of superstition which had crept into the religion of the later Middle Ages.

His weaknesses were more readily apparent. He was greedy, impetuous, and frequently unprincipled. For a man with long experience as a diplomat, he had a most overbearing and tactless manner, and a remarkable propensity for making enemies. Like many revolutionaries, he had an arrogant contempt for traditional views, which only succeeded in stiffening resistance to him. Even the sincerity of his Protestantism was not unalloyed by curious contradictions. It never seems to have occurred to him that his personal ambitions and the advancement of his family were often incompatible with the best interests of religion, or that his opponents were as a result likely to impute the worst motives of self-aggrandizement to even his best-meant schemes for reform. The worst blind spot of all was his apparently complete failure to realize how unintelligible Protestantism must be for most of the Welsh clergy and laity until it could be presented to them in Welsh. In all his letters there is not a single indication that he had ever seized upon this cardinal point. His failure to do so was not caused, as has been suggested,[74] by contempt for the Welsh as such, for Barlow referred just as slightingly to the 'superstition' and 'idolatry' of the people of the north of England and the Scots. Whatever occasioned the omission, whether it was personal vanity which refused to allow him to believe that his efforts were unlikely to touch most of his flock, whether it was lack of experience of conditions outside the towns and the English-speaking areas, whether it was sheer lack of perspicacity, or a combination of all or some of these things, it constituted a paralysing handicap to all his attempts to protestantize his diocese. Nor was this defect ever appreciated, much less overcome, until the election as bishop in Elizabeth's reign of a thoroughgoing Protestant who was no less ardent a Welshman.

II. THE EPISCOPATE OF ROBERT FERRAR, 1548–55

When Bishop Barlow was translated from St. David's to Bath and Wells in 1548, he was at pains to secure the appointment of a Protestant as his successor. He strongly recommended Robert Ferrar, a former Augustinian canon like himself. Since Ferrar was also a protégé and chaplain of the all-powerful Protector, Somerset, Barlow's recommendation was favourably received. Ferrar was made bishop of St. David's in July 1548, the first bishop to be appointed by royal letters-patent instead of being elected by the canons. His consecration in September 1548 was the first to be celebrated according to the rites of the new English ordinal.

Ferrar was born in the parish of Halifax, Yorkshire, some time during the first decade of the sixteenth century in all probability. Having begun his career at the University of Cambridge, he later transferred to Oxford, where he joined the order of Augustinian canons. As an undergraduate he was strongly attracted by Protestant doctrines, and was one of a group of students caught peddling Lutheran literature in 1528 and obliged to recant. In 1535, at Barlow's own request, Ferrar had accompanied him on the luckless diplomatic mission to Scotland.[75] A few years later he became prior of Nostell in Yorkshire, just in time to hand it over to the king, receiving in return a pension of £80. His first connexion with the diocese of St. David's would appear to have been his appointment in 1547 as one of the royal visitors for the Welsh and border dioceses.

Ferrar came in 1549 to a diocese that had long been sharply divided by conflict between bishop and chapter. Nor were the circumstances of his own appointment propitious for bringing about a reconciliation. He was not the canons' choice, but was imposed on them by Somerset at the instance of the detested Barlow. Their initial resentment could only be deepened by the realization that Ferrar proposed to live among them in the diocese. He, like Barlow, was a bishop of the new style; not a lawyer and absentee civil-servant but a theologian and resident pastor, who considered that the direct exercise of his spiritual authority over his clergy should be his chief concern. Although one or two of the leading figures within the diocese, like his registrar, George Constantine, were at first willing to co-operate with him, most of the canons were suspicious and unforthcoming from the start. Their ablest and most influential leaders were Thomas Young, precentor of St. David's, and Rowland Meyrick, prebendary of Treflodyn. Both were astute clerical lawyers who were destined eventually to reach the episcopal bench, the former as bishop of St. David's, 1560–1, and archbishop of York, 1561–8, and the latter as bishop of Bangor, 1559–66. Convinced Protestants, they had been introduced into the diocese by Barlow during the latter years of his episcopate, but had identified themselves with the interests of the chapter. They were to be the most alert and vocal watch-dogs of its rights against any trespass by the bishop. This had not, however, prevented them from shame-fully pillaging the cathedral of some of its treasures during the years 1547–8[76]

The very first encounter between Ferrar's representative and the chapter, in April 1549, led to a serious quarrel.[77] The bishop had given his chancellor, Edmund Farley, letters of commission to visit the cathedral clergy. When Farley came to St. David's for that purpose, it was only after a great deal of discussion that the canons would agree that the bishop had the right to visit the chapter at all. Reluctantly they allowed Farley to read his commission. No sooner had he done so than Rowland Meyrick was on his feet to protest that the commission was invalid since it bore the bishop's own name and authority only and made no mention of the royal supre-macy. It was 'plain a romish commission; it groundeth his authority not from the King, but of himself, according to the accustomed popish manner.'[78] George Constantine, who had accompanied Farley, at once saw that the quick-witted Meyrick had him by the hip. 'By the mass, we be all shamed and the bishop undone', he told Thomas Huet. 'That fool his chancellor hath brought with him a commission wherein the chancellor's authority is not derived from the King.'[79] Despite this humiliating experience, however, Constantine was sufficiently well-disposed towards Ferrar to try to act as a peacemaker between him and the canons. He and Huet at once set out for Haverfordwest to impress upon Ferrar the seriousness of the offence that had been committed in his name. Having heard of it, Ferrar protested that he was no papist and had not intended to 'derogate anything of the King's authority'. He urged Constantine and Huet to make amends to the canons on his behalf: 'You two be my two hands. Do what you will. Kindle the fire or quench it.'[80]

Constantine and Huet made peace, but on terms very favourable to Young and Meyrick. Young became chancellor of the diocese and Meyrick Ferrar's commissary.[81] Peace patched up on these conditions was very short lived. Elated by their quick and easy victory, Young and Meyrick may well have abused their new powers. Ferrar, for his part, grudged them their triumph, suspected Constantine's motives, and turned in search of more reliable allies. During the next year or two relations between the bishop and canons were very bitter. But it is almost impossible to trace clearly the sequence of their disagreements. Dates rarely occur in the articles presented against Ferrar in 1551, or in the depositions of witnesses, or in Ferrar's answers. When they do occur, they may be quite erroneous.[82] In the absence of a reliable chronology, only a very tentative reconstruction of the course of the quarrels can be attempted.

Both sides took advantage of every opportunity to thwart and annoy each other. But Ferrar, as bishop and as favourite of the Lord Protector, was in the stronger position. When Young collated John Gough to the rectory of Hasguard, Ferrar replaced him with his own nominee, Henry Goddard, and forced Gough to appear before his consistory court, first at Carew, then at St. David's, and finally at Carmarthen.[83] Ferrar's chief lieutenant, Stephen Green, with his master's support, made it virtually impossible for Young to get a curate to serve his church at Spittall. Green either scared the curates away with threats[84] or else forced them to appear repeatedly in ecclesiastical courts.[85] Another of Young's curates, Geoffrey Lloyd, who ministered at Nash and Hodgeston, was excommunicated by Green for pluralism.[86] Like Young, Rowland Meyrick also came under pressure. His jurisdiction as commissary was bypassed and his protégés discouraged.[87] Even George Constantine, whom Ferrar at first regarded as his 'old faithful brother',[88] fared no better. He and Ferrar bickered over the position of the altar in St. Peter's Church, Carmarthen, and over sermons preached by Ferrar there.[89] When Young married Constantine's daughter, Ferrar refused, understandably perhaps, to preach or to minister communion at the service.[90] At length, relations between him and Constantine got so bad that Constantine refused 'to attend either himself or by his sufficient deputy, for writing of records and other instruments'.[91] Ferrar tried to deprive Constantine of his registrarship and to act as registrar in his own name. For eighteen months the diocese was virtually without a registrar, until in the end the Council of the Marches obliged Ferrar to restore Constantine to his office.[92]

The chapter as a whole felt the force of the bishop's discontent. He disputed their advowson rights,[93] quarried millstones on their lands,[94] excommunicated one of their officers,[95] and farmed the

Isle of Ramsey, one of their traditional perquisites for the maintenance of hospitality, to his crony, Stephen Green.[96] According to one uncorroborated testimony, he even took away some of their property by force, removing 'two fine wainscot doors with the two spring locks, with all the ironwork of the same, and also all the seats and desks with the sealing of the same'.[97]

During all this time Ferrar was not only at loggerheads with his canons but with some of the prominent laymen of his diocese as well. Part of the blame for this unmistakably lay with him. His loyalty to friends and servants, whose morality was to say the least questionable, did him more credit as a friend than as a bishop.[98] In matters of business he was undoubtedly a shrewd, hard-headed Yorkshireman with an eye alert for a good investment; but his enemies went further and accused him of covetousness, sharp practice, and even oppression. Certainly, in his anxiety to capitalize the resources of his diocese he appears to have overstepped the bounds of episcopal decency and decorum. A number of witnesses agreed in testifying that when he was ostensibly engaged on an episcopal visitation of his diocese, he in fact spent most of his time surveying its mineral resources, agricultural potentialities, and other 'commodities'.[99] There was considerable criticism of his alleged oppression of tenants near Abergwili,[100] and his alleged attempts to enclose the highway near Carmarthen.[101] But the most serious instance of his bringing improper pressure on a tenant was the quarrel between him and Robert Birt of Llandygwy(dd), Cards., in 1549. Here the accusations against Ferrar seem much better attested and more convincing than in most other instances. Birt was the farmer of the episcopal manor of Llandygwydd, and had enjoyed uninterrupted possession since 1544. But, about Corpus Christi Day (20th June, 1549), according to Birt, Ferrar came to Llandygwydd on a court day with a large retinue. He had intended to take possession by force but, happily, was prevailed upon to allow the king's servant, John Powell, to hold the court that day. After that incident Ferrar had seen that he had no rightful claim to the possession of the manor and had troubled Birt no further.[102] Birt's evidence was strikingly confirmed not only by Ferrar's avowed enemies but also by John Powell and by Richard Vaughan, who had been one of Ferrar's retinue on that occasion.[103] At the same time as he was trying to get possession of the manor, Ferrar had also indicted Birt at Cardiganshire Quarter Sessions for trespass in the episcopal forest at Atpar. During the hearing at Cardigan Ferrar, it was alleged, had violated all justice and propriety in vehemently urging the justices to find a verdict favourable to him. He had even gone so far as to try to corrupt the jury, according to one of their number.[104]

In fairness to Ferrar, nevertheless, it should be recognized that his quarrels with the laity sprang chiefly from his attempts to

repair some of the damage inflicted upon the see by Barlow. His
efforts against Birt, however misguided, may well have arisen out
of his reluctance to maintain agreements entered into by his predecessor to the detriment of the see. This was certainly true of
Ferrar's quarrels with Roger Barlow and Lady Devereux. He was
clearly unwilling to accept the disastrous consequences of the
Barlow-Devereux *entente*.[105] He strongly challenged Roger Barlow's
claims to the farm of the prebend of Brawdy and his lease of
Monkton, and also charged him with withholding tithes which
ought to have accrued to the bishop from Carew, which had come
to the diocese in exchange for Lamphey.[106] As for Lamphey itself,
he did his best, early in his episcopate, to recover possession of it
from Lady Devereux, who had held it since the death of her
husband in 1547.[107] The attempt failed, but it made powerful
enemies for Ferrar. Closely associated with Lady Devereux, and
apparently acting as her attorney,[108] was Griffith Donne, one of
the most influential landowners in south Carmarthenshire,
and mayor of Carmarthen and a leading figure in the town. He was
an intimate of George Constantine, and he and some of his friends
among the Carmarthen merchants, notably Humphrey Toy and
Alexander Farmer, were to be some of Ferrar's bitterest opponents.
Other powerful laymen in the diocese who had profited by William
Barlow's reckless alienation of advowson rights, and who found
their claims ignored or challenged by Ferrar, included Arnold
Butler, William Owen of Henllys, and William Philips of Picton.[109]
They, too, became members of the powerful coalition of clergy
and laity which Ferrar was raising against himself.

During the later months of 1549 and the spring of 1550 there may
well have been a lull in the conflict. If we may accept the testimony
of the canons, they believed themselves to have been on much better
terms with their bishop during the early summer of 1550 than they
had been for some time, and his renewed attacks upon them at that
point took them by surprise.[110] This may not be as incredible as it at
first sounds. Ferrar's patron, Somerset, had been deposed in October
1549 and lay in prison until February 1550. During these months
Ferrar may have thought it prudent not to stir up too much trouble
with his enemies. However, by midsummer 1550, with the marriage
of Anne Seymour to John Dudley, Viscount Lisle, Somerset seemed
well on the high road to power again. It may have been this favourable turn in Somerset's fortunes which emboldened Ferrar to take
the initiative against his enemies, lay and cleric alike.

About the month of June 1550 Ferrar sought a definitive verdict
from the Court of King's Bench on the rights of the bishop over the
chapter of St. David's.[111] Weary of what he considered to be the neglect of their duty by chantor and canons, their resistance to his lawful authority over them as *decanus et quasi decanus*, and their refusal

to show him the book of cathedral statutes 'for the better knowledge of his and their duties', he obtained a writ of *quo warranto* to force them to answer his claims.[112] Significantly, Ferrar said he could not remember how long it had taken to deliver this writ. The canons alleged that he had treacherously held it back from them for three months, revealing its existence only ten days before they were to appear in court. Since the journey to London would take them at least seven days, they were left with only three days in which to prepare their defence. They also accused Ferrar of having withheld from them the key to the chapter records so as to prevent their gaining access to documents essential for their defence. They were left with no option but to force the locks and remove the documents they needed.[113] This took place about the end of September. In the following month, because some of the canons were behindhand with the payment of their subsidies, Ferrar took the drastic step of declaring recusant the whole chapter, including Young and Meyrick, who claimed that they had paid all their dues.[114]

About the same time some of Ferrar's friends seem to have been responsible for initiating a most injurious lawsuit against Meyrick in the Court of Augmentations. Information was lodged with the court that Meyrick's church of Llanddewibrefi was a concealed college which ought to have passed into the royal possession. The most hostile and damaging witness against Meyrick was Ferrar's right-hand man, Stephen Green, who came very near to perjury in his anxiety to testify against Meyrick. In view of the importance to the diocese of the church and its associated prebends[115] the suit reveals how bitter the quarrel between the factions had become, and how reckless it was making them of the best interests of the see.

A dispute over the prebend of Llanbister at this time provided Ferrar with a further opportunity for striking at a number of opponents simultaneously. The prebendary, John Whitmay, was a friend of the canons. He was declared recusant for the nonpayment of subsidy and his benefice deemed to be void. The advowson was held by Roger Barlow on the strength of a grant from his brother William. Ferrar ignored Barlow's claims and collated Stephen Green. Green, in turn, refused to recognize Lady Devereux as a farmer of the prebend and leased it to a neighbouring squire. There ensued a fracas which led to the appearance of the contending parties before the Council of the Marches. The Council was said to have upheld the claims of Whitmay and Lady Devereux.[116]

It has generally been supposed that the canons did not dare launch a counter-attack until after the second imprisonment of Somerset in October 1551.[117] However, judging by the contents of the fifty-six articles against Ferrar presented by Hugh Rawlins and

Thomas Lee on behalf of the canons, and by the references to them in the records of the Privy Council,[118] they must have been drawn up in the spring or early summer of 1551. Meantime, Roger Barlow had brought Ferrar before the Great Sessions in a suit involving a charge of *praemunire*. Ferrar, on his side, was still capable of spirited action in his own defence. He laid objections—though in vain—with the Privy Coucil against his accuser, Hugh Rawlins.[119] He also removed the suit between himself and Roger Barlow to the Court of Star Chamber on the grounds of the 'scarcity of learned men in these parts of Wales, and thinking it meet that so weighty a matter should not there be determined'.[120]

But Somerset's second downfall made an enormous difference to Ferrar's position. For if serious charges had been preferred against the bishop before his patron's eclipse, it was not until after Somerset's execution in January 1552 that they were prosecuted. Thereafter, Ferrar's own downfall was not long in being encompassed. In February four leading witnesses against him, Meyrick, Young, Griffith Goch, and Constantine, were examined. On 9th March a commission was granted to Sir Thomas Jones, Sir John Wogan, David Vaughan, and Owen ap Owen, to examine and take depositions of witnesses on behalf of Ferrar's accusers. Early in May these commissioners examined more than 120 witnesses.

The fifty-six articles[121] concerning which these witnesses gave evidence had ostensibly been presented by Thomas Lee, a Carmarthen merchant and brother-in-law to George Constantine, and Hugh Rawlins, vicar of Tenby and fellow visitor with Ferrar of the Welsh dioceses in 1547. Neither Ferrar nor anyone else had any illusions concerning the real instigators. In his objections to the accusations made by Lee and Rawlins, Ferrar protested with great bitterness that these two were merely the tools of the chapter, and in particular of Young, Meyrick, and Constantine, his 'mortal enemies, and the very devisers and procurers of the informations and bolsterers and bearers of the promoters in the suit thereof'.[122]

The accusations were grouped under the five headings of abuse of authority, maintenance of superstition, covetousness, wilful negligence, and folly. Ferrar's answers to some of them are rather lame and we have no depositions of witnesses for his defence. Even so, he can be seen to have emerged from the welter of indictment and denial with considerable credit. The charges included under the heading of folly were absurdly trivial,[123] and they suggest that the canons were sadly deficient in a sense of humour. The charges of covetousness no doubt had a certain degree of justification, though they read very strangely as a protest from a clique of acquisitive clerical lawyers to the duke of Northumberland, himself the most grasping man in the realm. Equally incongruous are the charges that Ferrar was unduly sympathetic to the 'maintenance of superstition in religion' when we remember that the arch-protestant, Hooper, thought that Ferrar was one of the few bishops whose doctrines were sound. There seems no reason to doubt Ferrar's own explanation that he was inclined to compromise or to soft-pedal over traditional practices such as the use of rosaries or the beating of breasts at communion simply in order to avoid provoking rebellion or tumult.[124] Nor is it easy to believe that it was papist sympathies which led him to condone or overlook the deficiencies in the wording of Farley's commission, and so to lay himself open to the main charge of *praemunire*. That he was guilty of a technical offence is undeniable. But it seems quite certain that it was caused by an unthinking reliance on the legal skill of Farley, who, for all the recommendations with which he came to Ferrar,[125] proved himself a most inexpert notary. His bungling had the most unfortunate consequences for Ferrar. Technically it made him guilty of a very grave offence at a time when his judges and his accusers wanted him removed for other reasons; his judges on account of his connexion with Somerset, his accusers because of his attempts to extend his authority over them. For although the dispute concerning the authority of the bishop over the chapter was not once mentioned in the fifty-six articles, it was nevertheless the real grievance that lay at the bottom of the quarrel. Ferrar, prompted perhaps by his predecessor, honestly believed that he was the canons' '*decanus et quasi decanus*; having also their dean's stall in the choir, with a prebend thereunto annexed, and the chief place in the chapter-house, with a key of their chapter-seal'.[126] He was convinced that the cathedral statutes proved this and that they were being withheld from him by the chapter deliberately to prevent the truth from being known. In justice to him it must be recognized that he had to put up with a great deal of prevarication from the canons. Yet they, on the other hand, though now predominantly Protestant in sympathy, were in no mood to relinquish their ancient privileges. They were no more prepared to admit the bishop's claims than their more conservatively minded predecessors in Barlow's time. Young doubtless spoke for them all when he averred that to have allowed Ferrar to become head of the chapter 'would have made void as well the premises as all the grants passed this three hundred years'.[127]

Many of the articles, and much of the content of the depositions of witnesses, consist of attacks on Ferrar's servants and friends rather than on himself. He certainly seems to have been unfortunate in his choice of servants. This may well have been because his choice was so limited by circumstances. He began his episcopate under the great handicap of being well known as a friend of Barlow. His Protestantism made him suspect among the traditionalists; his determination to be master of the chapter alienated the leading

Protestants. The men to whom he was therefore obliged to turn did little to enhance his reputation. His chief ally among the clergy, Stephen Green, was in no small measure responsible for his master's troubles. Green, the former master of St. Mary's College at St. David's, was a pushing, headstrong, and unscrupulous fellow, of whom, it was suggested, Ferrar himself had held no great opinion, describing him as a 'common adulterer, contentious and drunken man'.[128] Two Cardiganshire clerks, Thomas ap Richard and David ap Rhydderch, whom Ferrar employed a good deal, were hardly fit confidants for a bishop in view of the grave circumstantial evidence brought against their moral character.[129] Nor were some of his lay associates any better. Very serious charges of moral laxity were brought against Thomas Brine and his son, and against Lewis Thomas John Boole, with whom the bishop was very friendly.[130] Two of his household servants, William Chambers and Meredith Thomas, were also involved in unsavoury scandals.[131] Too much store should not be set by charges of this kind. Accusations of sexual immorality, incest, and adultery were so freely bandied about in the sixteenth century as to be almost common form in altercations of this kind. Nevertheless, it is clear that these men were of more than questionable reputation whose company was unlikely to have brought Ferrar any credit.

Whatever the truth or falsehood of the articles presented against Ferrar, he was, by the early months of 1552, too far out of favour to be able to refute them successfully. He was not allowed to call witnesses in his defence. Two letters which he wrote to the Lord Chancellor, Bishop Goodrich of Ely, brought him no assistance.[132] He was detained in London through the influence of his enemies, who also did their utmost to prevent his tenants from fulfilling their obligations to him. In July 1552, and again in October, he appeared before the Court of Great Sessions at Carmarthen to answer to a charge of *praemunire*.[133] The verdict very probably went against him, for before the end of the year he was put in prison. In captivity he remained for the rest of his life.

St. David's was only one of many dioceses which had been convulsed by religious bitterness and dissension during the turbulent years of Edward VI's reign. But whereas in the other dioceses the conflict was, in part at least, one of religious principle, St. David's was vouchsafed only the demoralizing spectacle of a Protestant bishop quarrelling furiously with a Protestant chapter. It could only have served to confirm the suspicions of those who disliked religious innovation that the Protestants, for all their talk of reform, were nothing better than wrangling self-seekers. On Protestantism in the diocese the conflict had a most debilitating effect. Its few adherents could not agree among themselves over the position of the new communion table in the church. In St. Peter's, Carmarthen, where the table was moved a dozen times within a very short space, the position would have been farcical had it not been for its dangerous implications. They quarrelled, too, over clerical marriage. Some accused Ferrar of preaching nothing but clerical marriage until they were 'wearied with the one lay';[134] others accused him of harbouring prejudice against honest married priests and encouraging 'naughty livers and such as kept openly concubines'.[135] Even the supply of Bibles and *Paraphrases* to the churches of the diocese became a weapon in the conflict. Ferrar alleged that Constantine had 'cornered' the supply and was holding all copies back,[136] while Constantine retorted that Ferrar and 'his' clergy were not making any efforts to obtain them.[137] Each faction so victimized and discouraged the other's preachers that Griffith Donne went so far as to declare that 'if reformation be not had, and such means found that God's word may be sown among the people, and that shortly, they will think that there is no God. For how shall men think there is such a one, as is not worthy to be talked of.'[138]

The consequences of Ferrar's episcopate were, therefore, in many ways more unfortunate than those of Barlow's. Yet Ferrar, though not without his faults, had shown himself to be a better bishop than Barlow. He was neither as violent nor as overbearing. He was more willing to compromise intelligently, and more content to hasten slowly in a backward-looking diocese at a time of rebellion and upheaval. He was nothing like as nepotistic as Barlow, nor as reckless of the best interests of the see. It is true that he has long been castigated as a 'miserable dilapidator',[139] but there is no surviving evidence of this, while there is a good deal of evidence of his attempts to regain lost rights. In his attitude towards the Welsh he was vastly more sympathetic than Barlow. Indeed, one of the most serious charges brought against him was that he was too favourably disposed towards them. The accusation is so remarkable as to be worth quoting at length:

> Robert the bishop of St. David's that now is, the 19th day of April last past or thereabouts, in the town of Carmarthen, in the diocese aforesaid, perceiving himself to be evil beloved in that country, and utterly out of credence with the people there . . . yet thinking to get the favour of the people again with flattery, spoke and said these words following openly in the pulpit, saying that Welshmen were more gentle than the Englishmen were, for the Welshmen would salute gently the one the other, and that the English be more cruel, and more sturdy, rushing one at another without salutation or greeting. 'But you Welshmen are more gentle, and no marvel, for sometime ye were Britons, and had this realm in governance, and if the prophecy of Merlin be true, ye shall so have it again'.[139]

Ferrar's answer to this was that in his sermon he had exhorted the people to be friendly to strangers,

affirming that it seemed well by the diligent observing of that precept in the
country of Wales that these people as Britons, of whom this realm was first
called Britain, (and if Merlin's saying be true it should be called Britain
again) that they had received that lesson of loving kindness towards
strangers originally from God's people, and that they were worthy of much
commendation for that they kept the same more diligently than other
parts of the realm even to this day.[140]

It may have been Ferrar's known sympathy with the Welsh which
later inspired some anonymous Welsh poet to pen some verses in
memory of the Yorkshireman.[142]

But it was Ferrar's death, not his life, which was best remembered
in Wales. Following his imprisonment in 1552, he returned to his
diocese only once, in 1555, to stand his final trial for heresy and to
be executed. Unwilling to recant, or even admit he had been in error,
he went to his death at the stake with exemplary courage. His fortitude in this last hour of crisis made his name a legend in Carmarthen
and the surrounding countryside.[143] Even the bitterest of his old
opponents, with the exception of Meyrick, were reputed to have
made their peace with him before his death. The smoke of his
burning, even if it could not entirely conceal the extent of his earlier
failures, did much to blot out the memory of them.

The Protestant experiment, then, had met with little success in
the diocese of St. David's by the eve of the Marian reaction. This
was hardly surprising when the main weight of responsibility for
implanting the new doctrines fell on the bishops. Both Barlow and
Ferrar realized this, and were anxious to assume the role of resident,
evangelizing bishops of the new Protestant kind. But, ardent Protestants though they were, both were grievously handicapped by having
been chosen more on account of their political connexions than
their reforming zeal. This dependence on powerful patrons, helpful
enough at first, in the long run accounted for the failure of each to
impose completely his authority on the chapter. Such uncontested
mastery over his clergy each regarded as an indispensable step
towards destroying 'superstition' and inculcating reforming doctrines
among the lower clergy and laity, who, largely unprepared for the
Reformation, were apathetic or openly hostile. Yet even if the
bishops had been unaffected by the vicissitudes of their patrons,
and even if the chapter had for some reason capitulated, it may be
doubted whether Barlow and Ferrar themselves would have got
beyond the fringes of their task. There still remained the formidable
barrier of language. Barlow gave no appearance of having known it
existed. Even Ferrar, for all his gracious words about the Welsh,
could not really reach them. When he preached at Abergwili,
'a mile or two from the English town of Carmarthen', he found
'scarce three or four who understood him'.[144] Small wonder that
most of his flock remained unmoved by his Protestant zeal. For in

Wales, as elsewhere, the trigger which alone could release the dynamic forces of Protestantism was the appeal in the vernacular. Without it, the new doctrines were doomed to remain as *ffydd sayson* ('faith of Saxons') for most Welshmen, while the mass appeared as *hen fraint y saint* ('the old privilege of the saints'). Yet even the impact of the Welsh Bible and the Welsh book of Common Prayer was a slow and almost imperceptible process. Late in Elizabeth's reign, accounts of the persistence of medieval practices and beliefs bear a striking resemblance to those of Ferrar and his critics.[145] Habit was still the most powerful force in the religious life of the *gwerin*.

NOTES

[1] This is true even of T. H. Lewis's valuable 'Carmarthenshire and the Reformation Movement', *Trans. Carms. Antiq. Soc.* xiv (1919-21), 33-37, 48-50.

[2] The best short accounts will be found in James Phillips, *History of Pembrokeshire* (London, 1909), pp. 415-20, and J. W. James, *A Welsh Church History* (Ilfracombe, 1945), pp. 105-7.

[3] The most recent and best discussion of the early career of this cleric of much 'motion and promotion' will be found in E. G. Rupp, *The English Protestant Tradition* (Camb., 1949), ch. iv.

[4] Founded in the twelfth century, it had in 1534 only five canons and was rated at £133. 11s. 1d. in *Valor Ecclesiasticus.*

[5] *Letters and Papers of Henry VIII's Reign*, ix. 1091; cf. T. Wright, *Suppression of the Monasteries*, p. 77, for the full text of the letter.

[6] *L. and P.* vii. 1024 (19).

[7] In the one instance, an Irish priest, Sir Roger Burley, had spoken heretical words concerning the mass in 1486, while in the other, a layman, Stephen Hall, of Pembroke, had expressed heretical opinions concerning the Trinity. For further details see R. A. Roberts, *The Episcopal Registers of St. David's*, 1397-1518 (Cymmr. Rec. Ser., 1920), iii, 102-4.

[8] It is John Penry who tells us that they spoke English, but his evidence should be regarded with some reserve, for his whole object was to emphasise how widely English was spoken. *The Aequity of an Humble Supplication* (1587), p. 52.   [9] See p. 113.

[10] Phillips, *Pembrokeshire*, p. 416. The only pulpit not under his control was that of the Dominican Friars, by whom he was to be strongly opposed.

[11] Wright, *Suppression*, p. 77.   [12] In a letter to Cromwell, January 1536, *L. and P.* x. 19.

[13] For an excellent summary of Roger's history, and indeed the Pembrokeshire Barlows in general, see B. G. Charles, 'The Records of Slebech', *National Library of Wales Journal*, v (1948), 179-98.

[14] All this information is derived from a letter written by Barlow to Cromwell. It is undated, but its contents are so similar to those of two other letters, the one written by Barlow and the other by his brother John, in the month of March 1535, that this undated letter must almost certainly be ascribed to this period also. The original letter is in B. M. Cotton MS., Cleop. E. iv f. 107, but is printed in full in Wright, *Suppression*, pp. 77-80, cf. also *L. and P.* ix. 1091.

[15] Wright, *Suppression*, p. 79.   [16] *L. and P.* viii. 412.   [17] Ibid., viii. 466.

[18] *L. and P.* x. 225 note.   [19] Ibid.   [20] Ibid., XII. i, 93; cf. p. 116-7.

[21] On 27th April, 1535, Sir Nicholas Carew wrote to Cromwell to thank him for having written on behalf of Barlow's appointment as prior of Bisham. *L. and P.* viii. 596.

[22] For the controversies concerning the validity of Barlow's consecration see Claude Jenkins, *Bishop Barlow's Consecration*, &c. (Church Hist. Soc. Publications, No. 17, S.P.C.K., 1935).

[23] *L. and P.* x. 19.

[24] See W. Ll. Williams, 'A Welsh Insurrection', *Y Cymmrodor* xvi (1902), 1-93.

[25] *L. and P.* x. 944.   [26]Ibid. XIV. ii. 400.

[27] Robert Colyns to Master Leche, 22nd June, 1536, ibid. X. 1182.

[28] His letters of credence to James V were drawn up on 3rd October 1535, and he himself said in an undated letter of 1536 (ibid. xi. 1427) that he spent about ten months altogether in Scotland and in travelling to and from there.

[29] Ibid. xi. 1427.   [30] Ibid.   [31] Ibid. xi. 1428.

[32] Similar proposals were being made at this time for the removal of the cathedral from St. Asaph to Wrexham: D. R. Thomas, *History of the Diocese of St. Asaph* (3 vols., Oswestry, 1908-13), i. 78.

[33] W. B. Jones and E. A. Freeman, *History and Antiquities of St. David's* (London, 1856), p. 347.

[34] *L. and P.* XIII. ii. 1132.

[35] It is tempting to suppose, though I have no conclusive proof, that he was related to the treasurer John Lewis, who was one of Barlow's chief opponents.   [36] Ibid. XII. i. 93.

[37] In a statement of his grievances, described as 'wrongs done by the bishop of St. David's to the chaunter of the same', Lloyd gives his own account of Barlow's actions. He claimed he was summoned all unsuspecting to the episcopal palace, and there, the bishop, 'uttering his malicious and devilish purpose towards the said chaunter of long time conceived and to then by dissimulation cloaked', imprisoned him and would suffer none to speak with him except in the presence of his jailers. He refused to release him on sureties, and broke into, and took possession of, his house. *L. and P., Addenda*, I. i. 1225. Undated, but probably drawn up about the end of May 1537.

[38] Ibid.   [39] *L. and P.* XII. i. 1251.   [40] P.R.O., Star Chamber, Henry VIII, 23/177,

[41] *L. and P.* XII. i. 575.

[42] *L. and P.* XII. i. 597.

[43] Ibid. XII. i. 830. The text of the letter may be seen in full in Wright, *Suppression*, pp. 187-9, where the date is, however, given by implication as 5th April, 1538. This dating is upheld in *L. and P., Add.* I. i. 1225. But as the letter refers to events which are known to have taken place in the spring of 1537, as there is no chronological contradiction between Barlow's account and that of Lloyd, and as there is not a single mention of this episode in any of Barlow's many letters of 1538, I see no reason to date it other than 1537.   [44] *L. and P., Add.* I. i. 1225.

[45] In passing, it is of interest to note that Barlow was one of those singled out by the northern rebels as being especially obnoxious to them: *L. and P.* xi. 705, 828*v*, 1319; XII. i, pp. 405, 409.

[46] *L. and P., Add.* I. i. 1225.

[47] *L. and P.* XIII. i. 320.

[48] I identify this, very tentatively, as Pirus's Island, that is, Caldey Island, Welsh, *Ynys Bir*.

[49] P.R.O., Early Chancery Procs., 1533-8, bdle. 884, No. 36; cf. E. A. Lewis, *Early Chancery Proceedings* (Cardiff, 1937), p. 65.

[50] P.R.O., E.C.P., 1533-8, bdle. 884, No. 66; cf. Lewis, op. cit., p. 67.

[51] *L. and P.* XIII. i. 634; cf. Wright, *Suppression*, pp. 183-6.

[52] *L. and P.* XIII. ii. 111; 614, 1072-3; cf. Wright, pp. 206-10.

[53] *L. and P.* XIII. i. 634; Wright, pp. 208-9.   [54] *L. and P.* XIII. ii. 1132.

[55] Jones and Freeman, *St. David's*, p. 230, for the large sums brought in from the outlying chapels on Saturdays, and reputedly divided out 'in dishfuls' among the canons.

[56] Wright, *Suppression*, p. 184.

[57] Thomas Stradling, executor of William Stradling, a former chancellor, sued the precentor and chapter for £90 6s. 8d. advanced by William when master of works for the fabric of the cathedral. P.R.O., Early Chanc. Procs., bdle. 1071, Nos. 55-8; cf. Lewis, *E.C.P.*, p. 70.

[58] Wright, *Suppression*, pp. 184-5.   [59] *L. and P.* XIII. ii. 1132.

[60] Ibid. XIV. ii. 400; cf. *Archaeologia*, xxiii (1831), 50-78.   [61] *L. and P.* XVI. 380, f. 119.

[62] The death of Cromwell marks the end of a period when governmental control of ecclesiastical life in the dioceses generally was more complete and intimate than it had ever been. There is an astonishing falling off in the number of communications passing between royal officials and the dioceses after 1540.

[63] *L. and P.* XVI. 468, 503 (30); cf. Dugdale, *Monasticon*, VI. iii. 1497.

[64] Cromwell allowed Barnes to become prebendary of Llanboidy in 1539 at Barlow's request, *L. and P.* XIV. ii. 688; but it was a short-lived appointment, for in the following year Barnes was executed.

[65] Some indication of the nature and number of these grants will be gained from the registers of his successors, an abstract of which was published in *B.B.C.S.* xiv. 45-53, 125-38.

[66] *L. and P.* XXI. i. 650 (1).   [67] Ibid. XXI. i. 1455.

[68] Ibid. XXI. ii. 332 (85).   [69] Ibid. XXI. ii. 332 (86).

[70] Yardley, *Menevia Sacra*, p. 88.   [71] *Acts of the Privy Council*, i (1542-7), 401, 479.

[72] They were certainly banded together in opposition to the next bishop's attempts to upset Barlow's arrangements.

[73] *L. and P.* XI. 1427.   [74] T. H. Lewis, *Trans. Carms. Antiq. Soc.* xiv. 35-36.

[75] See above, p. 114-5.

[76] John Foxe, *Acts and Monuments* (edit. S. R. Cattley and G. Townsend, 1837-41), vii. 9; hereafter referred to as *A. and M.*

[77] The evidence for this quarrel, and indeed for most of what follows, is derived from the voluminous records of the accusations brought against Ferrar in 1551-2. They are preserved in one of John Foxe's manuscripts in the British Museum. This manuscript volume, now Harleian MS. 420, contains the depositions in full of no fewer than 127 witnesses called on behalf of Ferrar's accusers. The text of the 56 articles drawn up against him and other relevant documents may be seen in *A. and M.* vii. 4-28.

[78] Harl. 420, f. 80.   [79] Ibid., f. 141.

[80] Ibid.   [81] *A. and M.* vii. 10.

[82] For example, the canons declared that Ferrar was elected in 1547 and that he came down to his diocese in 1548. In his answer Ferrar did not draw attention to the error.

[83] Harl. 420, ff. 95-96, 100, 146, 158, 171-2.

[84] As in the case of Hugh Says and James Esmund, who said he 'durst not serve there one day more for Mr. Green's threatenings'. Harl. 420, f. 161.

[85] As he did with John Dobbins, William Davies, James Jones, and Morris Jones, ibid., f. 162.

[86] Ibid., f. 162.   [87] Ibid., ff. 80, 81, 82-83.

[88] *A. and M.* vii. 27.   [89] Harl. 420, ff. 97-98, 112-14.

[90] Ibid., f. 175.   [91] *A. and M.* vii. 11.

[92] Harl. 420, ff. 98, 103, 163.   [93] Ibid., ff. 82-83, 163.

[94] Ibid., ff. 103, 163.   [95] Ibid., f. 81.

[96] Ibid., ff. 102, 165-6.

[97] Deposition of Thomas Wogan, Archdeacon of Brecon, ibid., f. 163.

[98] See below, p. 132.

[99] Harl. 420, ff. 82, 86-87, 102.   [100] Ibid., ff. 82, 102, 153-4.

[101] Ibid., ff. 113, 116, 145.   [102] Ibid., ff. 125-6.

[103] Ibid., ff. 177, 129.   [104] Ibid., ff. 140-1.

[105] See above, p. 122.

[106] Harl. 420, ff. 102, 170; cf. Star Chamber Procs., Edw. VI, 3/3/73.

[107] Harl. 420, ff. 82, 112, 173.

[108] Harl., 420, f. 112.   [109] Ibid., ff. 159, 160, 176.

[110] Ibid., ff. 82, 87, 103.

[111] It is extremely difficult to tell when Ferrar embarked on this course. But the canons declared—and Ferrar did not deny it— that the writ was held up for three months and that they had to break into the Chapter House to get records for their defence. This forcing of the Chapter House, according to Stephen Green's evidence in a suit in the Court of Augmentations (P.R.O., E. 321/37/31), took place at the end of September 1550. That suggests that Ferrar obtained the writ about the end of June.

[112] A. and M. vii. 14.

[113] Harl. 420, ff. 163-4; cf. Aug. Procs., P.R.O., E. 321/37/31.

[114] A. and M. vii. 6.   [115] See Trans. Cymm., 1948, pp. 162-3.

[116] Harl. 420, ff. 82-83, 114.

[117] E. Yardley, Menevia Sacra, p. 93, misreading Foxe's account, was the first to suggest this, I think. Though Yardley seems to have thought that the canons attacked immediately after Somerset's first downfall.

[118] Acts of the Privy Council, 1550-2, pp. 202, 313, 318.   [119] Ibid., p. 313.

[120] Star Chamber Procs., Edw. VI, 3/73.

[121] Text in A. and M. vii. 4-9.   [122] Ibid., vii. 17.

[123] For example, he was charged with having whistled 'by the hour' to a seal in Milford Haven.

[124] A. and M. vii. 13.   [125] Ibid., vii. 9.

[126] A. and M. vii. 14.   [127] Harl. 420, f. 103.

[128] Ibid., f. 101.   [129] Ibid., ff. 81, 135, 136-7, 140, 148.

[130] Ibid., ff. 81, 86, 101, 127, 128,-9 144 (Brine); 82, 113-14, 115-16, 119, 123, 145-6, 156-7 (Boole).

[131] Ibid., ff. 119, 145-6, 151-2 (Chambers); 96, 111, 115, 121, 142, 145-6, 151 (Thomas).

[132] Text in A. and M. vii. 26-8. The first letter is undated, the second is dated 9th March, (1552).

[133] A and M. vii. 20-21.   [134] Harl. 420, ff. 98-99, 111, 114, 117, 121-2.

[135] Ibid., f. 86.   [136] A. and M. vii. 15.

[137] Harl. 420, f. 99.   [138] Ibid., f. 115.

[139] Yardley, *Menevia Sacra*, p. 92.

[140] Harl. 420, f. 90.   [141] Ibid., f. 94.

[142] Peniarth MS. 60, f. 77; cf. Evans, *Report on MSS. in Welsh Language*, I. ii. 439.

[143] As the present writer discovered when lecturing in Carmarthen. But how much of this springs from a subsequent knowledge of Foxe's account it is difficult to tell.

[144] Harl. 420, f. 134.   [145] See below, pp. 175-7.

VI. THE ELIZABETHAN SETTLEMENT OF RELIGION IN WALES AND THE MARCHES, 1559-60

When Elizabeth succeeded to the throne she faced a situation demanding the utmost caution on her part. A disastrous foreign war, an exhausted treasury, and an insecure title, all forced her to move warily. Nothing was more urgent than the satisfactory solution of the very awkward religious problem bequeathed her by her sister. It would have to be such as would not offend national suscepti-bilities and yet not offer foreign powers any excuse for intervention. For a ruler in a position as uncertain as Elizabeth's, it was dangerous to delay, but it might be fatal to act too quickly. During the early months of 1559, then, the Queen was trying to move carefully and unhurriedly towards a settlement dictated by expediency rather than dogma. She hoped to win over the majority, who, though alienated by Mary's policy, were by no means convinced Protestants.

It was a minority only who adhered rigidly to either Catholic or Protestant principles. The backbone of conservative resistance came from the bishops, who refused to budge an inch from the position they had taken up during Mary's reign. Even those who had acquiesced in Henry VIII's assumption of the supreme headship, refused utterly to accord his daughter the title of Supreme Governor. Proof against threats and cajolery alike, their constancy was the marvel of Catholic observers.[1]

The strength of their enemies lay in the returned exiles, the 'wolves from Germany'. Though these were by no means all Calvinists, they had all returned to England expecting the undelayed establishment of a thoroughly reformed church. They were dismayed by the Queen's caution in religious matters and her undisguised dislike of the Calvinists among them.[2] Yet, though they found the process of waiting 'very tiresome' they did not doubt that all would soon be well, for they had a 'wise and religious' queen, 'favourably and propitiously disposed' towards them.[3] Recent work has strikingly revealed how strongly they were supported by the great majority of the members of the House of Commons, and even by a number of influential privy councillors. As a result of their skilful and determined tactics they were able to push the Queen much further and faster in the direction of religious change than she probably wished to go.[4] Yet even when the new religious settlement was formulated in the Acts of Supremacy and Uniformity, they regarded it as a beginning only.

After the new arrangements had been made known by the Acts of Parliament, a royal visitation was planned in the summer of 1559. The visitors were to administer the oath to the clergy under the Act of Supremacy, to enforce the use of the Prayer Book, and to promulgate the royal injunctions.[5] To make their work easier, episcopal authority was inhibited, and the dioceses grouped into circuits.[6] The Welsh bishoprics, together with those of Hereford and Worcester, formed the western circuit. On 18th July a royal commission was issued to the visitors for these dioceses. Cecil's list of western visitors ran as follows:

Richard Davies	Wigorn.
Rycharde Pates	Herf.
Thomas Yonge	Assaven
D. Rowland Merick	Bangor.
	Meneven.
George Constantine	Landaven.

John, Lord Williams	Sir Thomas Russell
Sir Hugh Paulet	William Sheldon
John Throgmorton	Thomas Hoby
Sir Nicholas Arnold	William Gerard
Sir John Perrott	
Sir James Baskerville	

Despite this imposing list of names, the real work of the visitation fell to the lot of the five clerics and lawyers whose names come first. The nobility and the gentry were only to be called upon if the authority of the divines was resisted. As the Queen put it in her instructions, 'It is not meant by her majesty that any of the said noble men shall be molested with the execution of any part of the said commission but as occasion shall arise when . . . the visitors . . . shall have need to require the aid of the said noble men'.[7]

The divines and lawyers were all 'reliable' men, of firm reforming sympathies but not Calvinists. Their leader was Richard Davies, a returned exile and soon to become bishop of St. Asaph and later of St. David's (see below, pp. 163-4). Richard Pates was a well-known Tudor lawyer. Born at Minsterworth, Gloucestershire, in 1516, he was admitted to Corpus Christi College, Oxford in 1532. He later acted as a commissioner to Henry VIII and Edward VI for the suppression of religious foundations in the south-west. Founder of Cheltenham Grammar School, he was for many years recorder of Gloucester and was buried in the cathedral there in 1588. Thomas Young was born at Hodgeston in Pembrokeshire in 1507. He was educated at Broadgates Hall, Oxford, of which he was subsequently principal from 1542 to 1546. He proceeded B.A. in 1529, B.C.L. in 1538 and D.C.L. in 1566. Made precentor of St. David's, he took up residence there in 1547. In the first Convocation of Mary's reign he was one of six reformers who publicly avowed their allegiance. He was deprived and fled to the continent, where he remained for the rest of Mary's reign. He was made bishop of St. David's in January 1560 and was translated to York in 1561. Rowland Meyrick was another clerical lawyer. Born at Bodorgan, and the scion of a well-known Anglesey family, he was also an Oxford man, having graduated B.C.L. at St. Edward's Hall in 1531. He became principal of New Inn Hall from 1534 to 1536, proceeded D.C.L. in 1537-8, and later became chancellor of St. David's. Deprived of his position during Mary's reign, he did not go into exile. He was consecrated bishop of Bangor in December 1559 and held it until his death in 1566. He is best known as the father of Sir Gelly Meyrick, lieutenant and confidant of the second earl of Essex. The last of the five visitors, George Constantine, was also connected with the diocese of St. David's. In his younger days he had been an ardent reformer and a close but unreliable associate of William Tyndale. Father-in-law of Thomas Young, Constantine was registrar of the diocese of St. David's during the episcopate of Barlow, Ferrar and Henry Morgan. In Ferrar's time he, Young and Meyrick had been among the most formidable of that unfortunate bishop's enemies. Constantine was made archdeacon of Brecon in 1559, but he seems to have played little or no part in the few surviving documents recording their activities. Of the four active visitors on the western circuit, the three divines, Davies, Young and Meyrick were soon to be raised to the bench of bishops. They may have been chosen for the visitation in order to impress upon them the salient features of the new régime, to give them some indication of the state of affairs prevailing in the various dioceses, and possibly even, in some cases, to supervise their own elections as bishops.

The visitation was not one to be undertaken lightly. Formidable opposition could certainly be expected. The Marian bishops, with the exception of the trimmer, Kitchen,[8] were intractable. The mass of the clergy was watching events in uneasy or resentful silence. The reformers feared the most stubborn resistance from them: 'the whole body remains unmoved', wrote Cox; and Grindal gave it as the general opinion that 'almost all the bishops and also many other beneficed persons would renounce their bishoprics and functions'.[9] The Protestant leaders, alarmed by the inflexibility of the bishops and the effect it was having on the morale of the lower clergy, struck a consistently pessimistic note in their letters during the summer of 1559. Nevertheless, the visitation confounded their gloomy prophecies, and exposed the hollowness of Catholic hopes of resistance. By November, Jewel, so lugubrious earlier in the year, could proclaim jubilantly that the 'ranks of the papists had fallen almost of their own accord'.[10] The completeness of the débacle surprised the reformers no less than it disappointed their antagonists at home and abroad.

Unfortunately, there is less information to be gleaned about the activities of the western visitors than any of the others. All of them were instructed to send Cecil a sealed account of their doings, but if the visitors for the western circuit ever returned such a report it has long since been lost or destroyed. The only traces of their work which have survived are three sets of visitation articles, for the cathedrals of Worcester (incomplete), Hereford and Llandaff,[11] and a few other miscellaneous scraps of information. Their comission was issued to them on 18th July, 1559. They seem to have begun their work at Llandaff cathedral, where they issued injunctions dated 9th August, 1559. From there they went on to the diocese of Hereford and later to Worcester. In addition to visiting the cathedrals they also held sessions at convenient centres like Wrexham on 2nd October, 1559, where they gave judgment over the rectory of Trefriw in favour of Thomas Davies, later bishop of St. Asaph.[12] But for some unknown reason they retraced their steps to the west Midlands by 31st October, when they met at Stratford-on-Avon. On that day they deprived John Blaxton, archdeacon of Brecon, and Thomas Harvard, prebendary of Llangamarch, of their livings. Three days later, they were still at Stratford, and on this occasion they deprived John Lloyd, dean of St. Asaph.[13] By 28th November they were back again at St. Asaph, where they presented David Edwards to the vicarage of Ruabon, vacant by the death of the previous incumbent.[14] They were probably still at St. Asaph on 4th December when Richard Davies was elected bishop. It may well be that the visitors also supervised the election of another of their number, Rowland Meyrick, as bishop of Bangor in December 1559. By 10th January, 1560 they were down at St. David's when the election of Thomas Young as bishop took place. On that occasion the chapter of St. David's had to borrow the visitors' seal to seal the letter to the Queen announcing their election of Young, because their own seal could not be found.[15]

The filling of vacant bishoprics must have been one of the visitors' most important tasks. The dioceses seem to have been deliberately kept vacant as long as possible by the Queen for her own enrichment. As Jewel wrote, 'The new bishops are yet only marked (for promotion) and their estates are in the meantime gloriously swelling the Exchequer'.[16] Cecil had already drawn up lists of suitable candidates earlier in the year,[17] and it seems very probable that the new bishops knew in advance – perhaps as early as August 1559 – of their impending promotion.[18] In Wales, Bishop Kitchen of Llandaff alone was prepared to take the oath. Of the other sees, Bangor had been vacant since the death of William Glyn in 1558. Morris Clynnog had been nominated by Queen Mary to succeed him, but she died before he could be elected and consecrated. An Oxford graduate, who had also studied at Padua for a time, Clynnog had become chaplain and domestic to Cardinal Pole during Mary's reign. He was not a man who could look for Elizabeth's favour, nor indeed would he attempt to seek it. He had fled abroad in 1559 and remained the stormy petrel of Welsh Catholic exiles during Elizabeth's reign. The incumbent of St. Asaph diocese, Thomas Goldwell, was the staunchest and most formidable of the Marian bishops of Wales. Another Oxford graduate, he had resisted Henry VIII's religious changes and attached himself to Cardinal Pole's household in Italy at an early date. He did not return from the Continent until Mary's reign, when he shared the triumph of his eminent master. He was Pole's trusted lieutenant and was made bishop of St. Asaph in 1555. In the last year of her reign Queen Mary had decided to translate Goldwell to the diocese of Oxford. The temporalities of his new diocese had actually been granted to him on 5th November, 1558;[19] but a letter written by him to Cecil a month later seems to suggest that there was still some confusion as to his exact status.[20] In this letter he had expressed surprise at not having received a summons to attend Parliament as he still considered himself bishop of St. Asaph. By the summer of 1559 Goldwell had concluded there was no future for him in England under the new régime. As early as 26th June, 1559, he had written to his brother, Stephen, expressing his intention of going abroad and requesting Stephen to go into Wales to settle up his affairs there on his behalf. On 29th June this letter was sent to Cecil, and orders were given to stop Goldwell from leaving the country.[21] But the bird had already flown. Once more in exile, Goldwell became one of the most active of English Catholic exiles. He died in 1585, the last survivor of the ancient Catholic hierarchy of England. As Goldwell's successor at St. Asaph, Mary had, just before her death, nominated one of her chaplains, Thomas Wood. But once Elizabeth had come to the throne, as might be expected, nothing was heard of Wood's elevation to the see. It was not until 4th December,1559, that the chapter of St. Asaph, *per viam compromissi*, elected Richard Davies as its new bishop.[22] It is interesting to observe that although Davies had been singled out for promotion by Cecil, he was not the first and undisputed choice of the canons. It may perhaps not be too much to suggest that they reached their decision as a result of official pressure and that that pressure was applied by the visitors of 1559, particularly when we know that the same sort of thing happened at Salisbury when Jewel was elected bishop.[23] Davies was consecrated by Parker in the archbishop's chapel at Lambeth on 21st July, 1560.[24] Meantime, in the fourth Welsh diocese, that of St. David's, Henry Morgan, bishop there since 1554, was also steadfast in his refusal to accept the new settlement and was deprived in the summer of 1559. He was replaced by Thomas Young, who was consecrated bishop on 25th January, 1560.[25] All three of the new Welsh bishops had promptly to be given licences to hold livings *in commendam* on account of the impoverishment of their sees. Meyrick and Young enjoyed much of their Edwardian preferment in the diocese of St. David's, the former to the value of £80 a year, and the latter to the value of £67.[26] Davies held his two Edwardian livings of Burnham and Maidsmorton in Buckinghamshire together with a prebend and rectory in St. Asaph.[27] These measures offered no bright augury that any serious attempt was likely to be made to reform the long-standing abuses of pluralism and non-residence in Wales.

The way in which the new bishops had, as visitors, dealt with those whom they found to be incalcitrant was later described by one of those whom they deprived. Edmund Daniel,[28] dean of Hereford, in his testimony at the papal court during the process for the deprivation of Queen Elizabeth, deposed that, when he was dean, 'four delegates [presumably Davies, Young, Meyrick and Pates] came, sent by the Queen to visit that church; and I heard that commission read. And in that commission, authority was given to them over ecclesiastics, to deprive them and to imprison them; in particular, such as should refuse to subscribe to certain heretical and schismatical articles; which articles were of this kind: that it had ever been the prerogative of the English prince to decide ecclesiastical causes apart from any other potentates, as it was contained in the oath; and that everyone should acknowledge to be good and pious the forms which parliament had ratified for keeping the hours and ministering the sacraments. The articles were exhibited to me before the oath, that I should put my name to them; in my presence they were presented to all the priests of my church in which I was a dean, and to the whole chapter before my eyes. And I saw them, and I saw on them the Queen's great seal'.[29] Daniel's account makes it plain that the visitors were insisting upon two things to which the clergy had to subscribe: the royal headship as embodied in the Act of Supremacy; and worship according to the Prayer Book as prescribed by the Act of Uniformity.

The visitation articles which they issued are undistinguished by any individual characteristics. Like those for the south-western circuit, with which they have marked affinities, they stick closely to the injunctions issued by the Queen. The wary course that the visitors were to steer between the Scylla of Rome and the Charybdis of Geneva had been carefully charted for them beforehand. The tone of the articles is mild and conciliatory. Apart from the assertion of royal supremacy, there was little in them that even the adherents of the old church could view with distaste. Their careful phrasing attests the general belief that Elizabeth and her advisers were moving slowly and cautiously, unwilling to offend Catholic susceptibilities unnecessarily. Judging by the very small numbers of the clergy who refused to accept the oath,[30] they seem to have been largely successful in attaining their object, even though the new Prayer Book was, to all intents and purposes, the markedly Protestant book of 1552,[31] which must have been most distasteful to the conservatively minded.

How far this comparatively brief tour enabled the future bishops to acquaint themselves with the state of religion in the dioceses, it is difficult to say. Not only was it of short duration, but it was hardly concerned with the laity at all. In any case, it seems that most laymen were too confused by the bewildering vicissitudes of the previous twenty or thirty years to have any well-defined opinions about religion. The same was probably true of the majority of the clergy as well. This indecision is the more easily understood when we remember that the whole aim of the government was to discourage men from thinking of the settlement in terms of a clear-cut choice between Catholicism and Protestantism. Doubtless, the visitors viewed with mixed feeling the general acceptance of the oath and the articles by the clergy. While it was gratifying to note the readiness with which papal allegiance was abandoned by almost all except the bishops and some of the cathedral dignitaries, they must have had misgivings as to the fitness of some to minister in a reformed church. Still, the visitation enabled them to take note of their most intransigent opponents, to gain some insight into prevailing conditions and to form an impression of the agents upon whom they would have to depend.

Before they had been in their bishoprics very long, the new bishops were required to send a certificate of their clergy to Archbishop Parker, 'for certain considerations conducent to the general reformation of the clergy of the province of Canterbury'. Returns for three of the dioceses are available, and are of considerable value and interest.[32] They are careful and comprehensive reports, giving details of the pluralists and absentees, the preachers and graduates, the clergy who maintained hospitality, and of those who were in orders and those who were not. They reveal the existence of serious abuses; but, generally speaking, these were at least no worse in Wales than elsewhere. Absenteeism and pluralism tended to be common among the members of the cathedral chapters, and not a few of the canons were laymen. At St. Asaph, out of a chapter of fourteen, four (including the archdeacon) were absentees, and two more were boys ('de eruditione et habitatione nobis non constat'). Six out of fifteen of the Bangor chapter (including two out of three archdeacons) were non-resident, six others were resident on livings within the diocese, while one divided his time between Bangor and Oxford. Out of thirteen at Llandaff, six (the archdeacon was one of them) were non-resident, and six more resided in their livings. The treasurer alone was resident at the cathedral. Only one of the Bangor chapter was not in orders. There were four laymen among the Llandaff canons, and five at St. Asaph, where the archdeacon, too, was only in deacon's orders. Absenteeism among the diocesan clergy, too, was disturbingly prevalent, though it seems to have been less of a problem in St. Asaph than in the other two dioceses. Out of about a hundred mentioned in the St. Asaph return, some eighteen were absentees, but these included seven pluralists living in other parishes within the diocese. There were twenty-three absentees (five of them resident in other livings) out of about seventy in Bangor and thirty-six (eleven of them pluralists) at Llandaff. On the other hand, far more of the clergy of Bangor and Llandaff maintained hospitality. There were forty-six at Bangor, sixty-five at Llandaff, and only twenty-four at St. Asaph. Of course, it should be remembered that there is no means of checking the accuracy of the bishops' figures, nor can we be sure whether the standards they adopted were uniform. One of the most serious obstacles in the path of Protestant bishops was the shortage of preachers. Llandaff and St. Asaph could muster only five apiece. In Bangor, there were only two; but the sanguine Meyrick appended a list of some thirty names of 'such as be able to preach, and may do good.'[33]

Unfortunately, these returns tell us nothing of the reaction of either the clergy or the laity to the church settlement. However, it is difficult to avoid concluding that if Elizabeth's arrangements were not cordially received, they were at least not resisted. No doubt the hesitancy of the pope, restrained by Philip of Spain, helped many to accept. Many others must have accepted with all kinds of mental reservations. Above all, it is certain that the majority were as pliable as they had been throughout all religious changes of the age. Martyrs for conscience were as rare then as now.

APPENDIX
DEPRIVATIONS CARRIED OUT BY THE VISITORS, 1559

It should be clearly understood that the list which follows does not purport to be exhaustive, but it did seem worth while noting the names of those who were probably deprived by Davies and his colleagues during the visitation of 1559. The most striking features are the fewness of the clergy who can be shown to have been deprived, and the fact that almost all those who were removed were drawn from among the higher clergy instituted during Mary's reign.

Diocese of Bangor
Gruffydd Robert, archdeacon of Anglesey.[34]

The Edwardian archdeacon was John Salesbury, who was ejected in 1554 on account of his marriage.[35] It is known that he was reinstated, but not who restored him nor who deprived Gruffydd Robert. But it seems very probable that the latter's unshakable Catholic loyalties prevented him from taking the oath required by the visitors. While it is unlikely that he actually fled to the continent with Bishop Goldwell it is probable that he went about the same time.

Diocese of Hereford
Edmund Daniel, dean of Hereford

Daniel himself gave an account of the proceedings of the visitors.[36] After his refusal to take the oath, he was committed to the custody of the marquis of Winchester.[37]

William Leveson, treasurer and prebendary of Hereford, and archdeacon of Carmarthen.

Leveson (or Luson) was a wealthy man of an apparently more than doubtful morality and lack of scruple. He was not deprived by the visitors though he was presented by the parish of Withington. He seems to have escaped punishment entirely 'to the evil example of other like offenders'.[38] He was later denounced by the bishop of Hereford as one of the chief patrons of deprived Catholic priests in that diocese.[39] He must have been a man of considerable influence, for he retained his preferments in Hereford and St. David's until his death.

John Perfaye, precentor of Hereford Cathedral.

An entry in the patent rolls, dated 25th November, 1559, records the presentation of Walter Jones, LL.B., to the precentorship, then void by the deprivation of John Perfaye.[40] Since this is followed by another entry for 28th November giving the presentation of John Elize, M.A. to the deanery of Hereford,[41] voided by Daniel, who was unquestionably deprived by the visitors, it seems very likely that Perfaye also had incurred punishment at their hands.

? . . . . . . , rector of Kingsland, Herefordshire.

The unnamed incumbent was deprived about the same time as Perfaye, and was succeeded by Thomas Taylor.[42]

Diocese of Llandaff

As far as can be ascertained, there were no deprivations at this time in the diocese of Llandaff. It may be that the clergy were content to follow the lead of their bishop, Kitchen, whose ready acceptance of the new order led to the suggestion by Catholics that he was not really a bishop at all.[43]

Diocese of St. Asaph
Morris Clynnog, rector of Corwen, and prebendary of Blaenporth (St. David's)

Like Gruffydd Robert, Morris Clynnog was an ardent Catholic, and fled abroad in 1559. It seems very probable that the visitors deprived him also, though there is no record of their having done so.

John Lloyd, dean of St. Asaph

Lloyd was deprived of his deanery at Stratford-on-Avon on 3rd November, 1559, for 'contumacy', which in this context no doubt can be construed as a refusal to take the oath. Undeterred by this setback to his ecclesiastical career, Lloyd became an advocate, and subsequently attained the dignity of an Admiralty judge. He was also one of the first fellows of Jesus College, Oxford.[44]

Thomas Griffiths, rector of Trefriw.

Griffith was deprived by the visitors of the rectory and its annexed chapels of Llanrhychwyn and Betws at Wrexham on 2nd October, 1559.[45] This is a curious case. Thomas Davies, LL.D., had been presented to the rectory on 14th August, 1548. He resigned on 30th June, 1557 and was succeeded by Thomas Griffith. Yet, many years later, on 17th July, 1591, the death of a Thomas Griffith, rector of Trefriw, was recorded in the Bangor registers.[46]

? . . . . . . , canon and prebendary of Llanyvyth (Llannefydd).

The patent rolls recorded the deprivation of an anonymous incumbent, and the presentation of a new canon on 22nd November, 1559.[47]

Diocese of St. Davids

Morgan Phillips, precentor of St. David's

Phillips succeeded Thomas Young on the latter's deprivation in 1554.[48] On 22nd December, 1559, Young was allowed to hold the precentorship *in commendam*.[49] That points to Phillips' having been deprived during the summer or autumn of 1559. The visitors are not definitely known to have ejected him, but they would have had a double motive for doing so: he was a sincere Catholic; and Young was doubtless anxious to recover the valuable preferment he had lost in 1554.

John Blaxton (or Blakiston), archdeacon of Brecon.

Blaxton, instituted to the archdeaconry by Henry Morgan on 1st July, 1554,[50] was deprived at Stratford on 31st October.[51]

Thomas Harvard, prebendary of Llangamarch, and vicar of Llandeilo Fawr.

Also instituted by Morgan – on 12th August, 1554[52] – Harvard was deprived at the same session as Blaxton.[53]

Nicholas Morgan, vicar of Tref Eglwys.[54]

Morgan (or Morton) was collated to the living of Kylkennyn, alias Llanbadarne trefegloes, on 5th February, 1558–9.[55] Thomas Huet should have taken his place; but Morgan somehow managed to get himself reinstated.[56]

Robert ap Howell, prebendary of Hewyd (Dihewyd, Cards).

William Leech was admitted to his prebend in January 1560, it being then void by the deprivation of the last incumbent.[57]

Diocese of Worcester

Seth Holland, dean of Worcester

Deprived by the visitors,[58] he was succeeded by John Pedder on 4th December 1559.[59]

Henry Jolyffe, canon and prebendary of Worcester Cathedral.

The entry in the patent rolls[60] concerning Jolyffe comes among a number, of others relating to men who were certainly deprived by the visitors, and so suggests that Jolyffe, too, was deprived by them.

NOTES

[1] *Calendar of State Papers, Venetian* (9 vols., London, 1864-98), vii, 94, 104-5; cf. *Calendar of State Papers, Spanish* (4 vols., London, 1882-9), i, 86.

[2] She refused to allow the Calvinists, Knox and Gilby, whom she detested, to enter the realm. See also Jewel's letters, *Zurich Letters* (2 vols., Parker Soc., 1842-5), i, 10, 17, 33.

[3] *Zurich Letters*, i, 33.

[4] See a most important article by J. E. Neale, 'The Elizabethan Acts of Supremacy and Uniformity', *English Historical Review*, lxv (July, 1950), 304-332.

[5] The text of the royal injunctions is printed in W. H. Frère and W. P. M. Kennedy, *Visitation Articles and Injunctions* (3 vols., Alcuin Club, 1910), iii, 8-29.

[6] A full list of the circuits, and the visitors for each, is given in an excellent study by G. G. Bayne, 'The visitation of the province of Canterbury, 1559', *Eng. Hist. Rev.*, XXVIII, (1913), 636-77; and also in J. Strype, *Annals of the Reformation*, I, i, 135,

[7] Bayne, *Eng. Hist. Rev.*, XXVIII, 660.

[8] In July 1559 the Spanish ambassador had his doubts about Kitchen's loyalty. He described him as a "greedy old man, with but little learning", *Spanish Cal.*, I, 86.

[9] *Zurich Letters*, I, 27; II, 19.

[10] *Zurich Letters*, I, 45.

[11] The text of the articles for Worcester and Hereford in Frère and Kennedy, *Visitation Articles*, III, 44-6, 47-8; the Llandaff articles in G. Williams, 'The royal visitation of the diocese of Llandaff, 1559', *N.L.W. Journal*, IV (1946), 189-97.

[12] N.L.W., Bodewryd MS. 335.   [13] See below, p. 149.

[14] N.L.W. St. Asaph Miscellaneous Book 14 (SA/M/14), f. 8b.

[15] W. H. Frère (ed.), *Register of Mathew Parker* (Canterbury and York Soc. 1907), p. 83.

[16] *Zurich Letters*, I, 55.

[17] P.R.O., S.P.12, vol. 4, nos. 38, 39. The names of the appropriate candidates were placed alongside the names of the sees. It did not follow that they were actually elected to those dioceses, e.g. Richard Davies was designated as bishop of Worcester but in fact became bishop of St. Asaph.

[18] See letters by Jewel, *Zurich Letters*, I, 9, 16,

[19] P.R.O., S.P. 11, vol. 14, dated 5 November, 1588.

[20] P.R.O., S.P. 12, vol. 1, no. 52.

[21] Ibid., vol. 4, nos. 70, 71(i).

[22] *Parker's Register*, p. 85.

[23] John Jewel, *Works* (4 vols. Parker Soc., 1845-50), IV, xv.

[24] *Parker's Register*, pp. 84-5.

[25] *D.N.B. s.n.* Young.

[26] *Cal. Patent Rolls, Elizabeth,* 1558-60, pp. 324, 326.

[27] Ibid., p. 326.   [28] See below, p. 149.

[29] Quoted in R. W. Dixon, *History of the English Church* (6 vols. London, 1878-99), V, 168-9.

[30] See below, pp. 148-50.

[31] The Queen was averse to the use of the second Edwardian Prayer Book and seems to have been forced to accept it by the Protestant pressure group of the House of Commons and returned exiles.

[32] They are printed in Browne Willis, *St. Asaph,* p. 257 *et seq; Survey of the Cathedral Church of Bangor* (London, 1721), pp. 262-71; *Survey of the Cathedral Church of Llandaff* (London, 1717), pp. 194-211.

[33] Browne Willis, *Bangor,* p. 269.

[34] See G. J. Williams, *Gramadeg Gruffydd Robert* (Cardiff, 1939), p. xvii.

[35] A. I. Pryce, *The Diocese of Bangor in the* 16th *Century,* p. 13.

[36] See above, p. 146.

[37] Bayne, op. cit., p. 654.

[38] Ibid., p. 676.   [39] *Camden Miscellany,* ix, 11-23.

[40] *Calendar of Patent Rolls,* p. 257.   [41] Ibid.   [42] Ibid.

[43] 'Neque tamen sacer ille choris episcoporum per ejus defectionem qui episcopus legitimus nunquam fuit contaminatur'. Nicholas Sanders to Cardinal Morone, 1559, *Catholic Record Society Miscellany,* ix, 17.

[44] D. R. Thomas, *Life of Davies and Salesbury,* p. 14.

[45] N.L.W. Bodewryd MS. 335.   [46] A. I. Pryce, *Bangor,* p. 27.

[47] *Cal. Patent. Rolls,* p. 259. In 1561 Richard Davies described the new prebendary, Robert Whettells, as 'adhuc puer'.

[48] E. Yardley, *Menevia Sacra (Arch. Camb.* Supplement, 1927), pp. 130-1.

[49] *Cal. Patent Rolls.* p. 324.

[50] St. David's Episcopal Registers, 1554-65, f. 5.

[51] Bayne, *op. cit.,* p. 667.   [52] St. David's Register, f. 5.

[53] There are two certificates, dated 20th February, 1561, from the bishop of St. David's among the Exchequer plea-rolls, showing that both Blaxton and Havard were deprived 'per commissarios . . . Reginae ad vistandum clerum et populum diocesis Menevn. apud Stratforde super Abona ultimo die Octobris 1559', Bayne, *op. cit.,* p. 667.

[54] See a note by Professor R. T. Jenkins, *B.B.C.S.,* ix (1937-9), 274.

[55] The entry in the register seems to prove the accuracy of Professor Jenkins's identification of the parish. St. David's Register, f. 30.

[56] Bayne, *op. cit.*, p. 668.

[57] Parker, *Register*, p. 172.

[58] 'Sethus Hollandus, Wigorniensis Decanus, qui in schismate sub Edouardo VI Romae fuerat, eandemque iterum nunc visitare cupiebat, in ipso fugae apparatu captus, in carcarem conjectus, patriam quidem reliquit sed Roman non venit, quia coelum utrique praetulit'. Sanders to Morone, *Catholic Record Society Miscellany*, ix, 14.

[59] *Calendar of Patent Rolls*, p. 258.

[60] *Ibid.*

VII.   BISHOP RICHARD DAVIES (?1501-1581)

Richard Davies is best known as William Salesbury's colleague in that triumph of the early Welsh humanism and reform, the translation into Welsh for the first time of the New Testament and the Book of Common Prayer. His share in that great enterprise is still his chief claim to fame and veneration. Nevertheless, his exile on the Continent for some years during Mary's reign, and his tenure of the largest and most important of the Welsh sees during Elizabeth's reign, form significant episodes in the history of the Reformation in Wales. It is with these aspects of Davies's life that this essay is primarily concerned. Of necessity, his work as a translator cannot rightly be divorced from his experiences as an exile or his pastoral activities, still less subordinated to them, so that if less attention is paid to it in what follows this is not due to any attempt to discount its significance, but because it has already received the careful study it deserves.[1]

Davies was born the son of a parish priest, Dafydd ap Gronw, curate of Gyffin, near Conway. His father and his mother were both of gentle blood, sprung from the stock of Welsh *uchelwyr* who could proudly trace their lineage back over many generations.[2] The details of Davies's early life, like those of many of his contemporaries, some of them much more famous than he, are obscure. The date of his birth can be given with no greater precision than some time during the first decade of the sixteenth century. The source of his early education we can only guess at: possibly he went to school at the abbey of Aberconway (to which belonged the patronage of his father's living), if indeed there was one; or he may have gone to a seminary nearby, originally founded by Edward I, and perhaps still in existence; or, like many another Welsh priest's son in the Middle Ages, he aquired the rudiments of clerical education from his father. At all events, he learned enough to be able to enter the University of Oxford. Here he resided at New Inn Hall, a hall which has long since been merged in Balliol College but which at this time was much frequented by Welshmen. He took the degree of M.A. in 1530 and that of B.D. in 1536. No record of his doings between 1536 and 1549 has as yet been uncovered. In 1549 he received his first living. In that year he was made rector of Maidsmorton, Buckinghamshire, and in the following year he was presented to the vicarage of Burnham in the same county. His presentation to both on the nomination of the crown suggests that he was a convinced reformer.

The accession of Queen Mary in 1553 affected his fortunes sharply. It has usually been asserted that he lost his livings in the first few months of her reign on the grounds of marriage. This hardly tallies with the facts, however, for priests were not deprived for marriage alone until 1554.[3] But action was being taken against some on other grounds. During the summer of 1553 the Privy Council was summoning uncompromising Protestants to apear before it. Some were well-known bishops like Latimer and Hooper, others were humble country parsons like John Fisher of Amersham and his neighbour, Richard Davies of Burnham.[4] The records of the Privy Council tell us only that Davies was summoned to appear. They give no indication of the nature of his offence, or indeed whether he had committed any, or even whether he actually appeared before the Council. Yet on the analogy of so many other contemporary citations of the same kind there can be little doubt that it was overboldness in advocating sentiments and opinions repugnant to the Marian government that led to his being ordered to make his 'undelayed repair to the court'.

He may have been able to placate the authorities by recanting, or to escape their wrath by retiring into hiding; but whatever his course of action, he had lost his vicarage of Burnham before the year 1553 was out. By December, a certain Richard Edon had been presented to the living without any reason being given for the vacancy.[5] Deprivation as early as this was almost certainly due to something more serious than marriage. Coming so soon after the summons from the Privy Council, it was in all likelihood a punishment for active opposition to the new régime, by word rather than deed, presumably.

In the absence of any concrete evidence, his movements during the next two years can only be guessed at. Wherever he was, and whatever he was doing, there can be no doubt that this was a difficult and trying time for him. He was under suspicion from above; he had lost some, possibly all, his sources of income; and he had a wife and, perhaps, a family to support. The current was flowing strongly against the reformers, and it took courage to swim against it. The writings of the Protestant leaders were full of gloomy apprehension about the future, of laments for the pliability of some of the weaker brethren, and of exhortations to the remainder to hold fast. It says much for the integrity of Davies's convictions that he appears to have held them without wavering.

Meantime, many of his fellow Protestants had been leaving England for the Continent. The exodus had started as early as January 1554, many months before the ferocious policy of religious persecution had begun. Not all the Protestant clergy who had been deprived sought to make their way abroad, even though they were not imprisoned nor in any way hindered by the government. Indeed, exile as a corollary to deprivation seems to have been the exception rather than the rule. It is even possible that the Marian government connived at the scheme, and that Gardiner and Cecil were unwitting collaborators in the same enterprise.[6] Therefore, there now seem to be good reasons for believing that the movement was a deliberate withdrawal, a migration, not a flight.

So it was that the 'left wing' of English Protestants, a small minority within a minority – there were only about eight hundred of them all told, including children and servants – found it necessary to leave England in order to avoid being swamped by an over-whelming Catholic majority. The persistent tradition that they were persecuted martyrs hounded from their homeland by a cruel queen and ferocious bishops has arisen out of the statements of the exiles themselves. They had to assume the role of martyrs for conscience' sake or else they would never have been given asylum by the magistrates of the German cities, who were exceedingly loth to admit any who might be guilty of sedition.[7]

These exiles of the sixteenth century had to endure all the hard-ships and discomforts of the lot of the refugee with which events of the twentieth century have made us all so familiar. They were dependent to a large extent on the financial backing accorded by Protestant merchants; but although these contributions were maintained right up to the end of Queen Mary's reign, they were far from adequate to meet all the needs of the fugitives. They were compelled to resort to various expedients to augment their slender resources: some took up literary work; others opened schools; a few went into printing houses; and some were even compelled to return to England because they were so poor.[8] Housing was a problem of the first order in the congested cities of the Continent. The exiles were herded together 'sometimes five families to a house, in quarters far too small for them, and they experienced all the evils of overcrowding from exacerbated tempers to the plague'.[9]

Hitherto it has been generally supposed that Richard Davies spent his years of exile in the city of Geneva. His biographers have been content to follow the lead given by Sir John Wynn, who wrote that 'in Queen Mary's time he (i.e. Richard Davies) was fain to flee with his wife to Geneva, where being an exceeding poor man, and living on the contributions and alms of the fugitives there, he was so industrious that in three years or somewhat more he attained the country language spoken in Geneva; which I think to be French. He served a cure there and preached and in the latter end lived well thereby'.[10] However, since the Frankfort archives show quite conclusively that Davies spent at least the greater part of his time at that city, while the surviving Genevan records have no mention of his name, it seems impossible not to qualify Sir John's account, and even to repudiate parts of it.

In the first place it must be remembered that Sir John wrote his *History of the Gwydir Family* many years after the bishop's death and nowhere does he claim any acquaintance with him. Still he does say that he knew Davies's sons at Oxford, 'both born at Geneva', and it might be supposed that they, at least, would have known where they were born. On the other hand, the city of Geneva, as the adopted home of Calvin, enjoyed far greater fame than the comparatively unknown city of Frankfort, so the name of Geneva may have sprung far more readily to Sir John's mind even though Davies's sons told him that they were born in Frankfort.

The accuracy of his account of Davies's activities in exile is also open to question. It is very doubtful whether Davies ever learned a foreign language, and still more doubtful whether he ever served a cure. The English refugees rarely understood foreign languages, and still more rarely ever learned to speak any tongue but their own.[11] It is true that Grindal, the future archbishop, began to learn German, but that was only towards the end of the period of exile when he was despairing of ever being able to return home.[12] Normally, the Englishmen clung together in little homogeneous congregations. They made no attempt to obtain livings or pastorates abroad nor is it likely that such attempts would have been welcomed by the natives of the cities of refuge. The single instance of an Englishman officiating in this way occurred when Miles Coverdale was sent for by 'Wolfgang, Duke of Bypont, to take pastoral charge at Bargzaber, one of his towns in Germany'.[13]

The strongest argument against accepting Sir John's statements *in toto* is the lack of contemporary evidence in Genevan records. A list of the members of the English church at Geneva has survived,[14] but Davies's name is not on it, nor are the names of his children to be found among those of infants baptized there. Nor is his name found in the contemporary *Registre des Habitants* which contains twenty-six names not included in the *Livre des Anglais*.[15] Powerful as this argument is, it cannot be regarded as conclusive when it is recalled that the name of so famous and venerated an English Protestant as Miles Coverdale is not to be found in either the *Livre des Anglais* or the *Registre des Habitants*, though he is known certainly to have spent some time in the city.

It is possible, of course, that Davies spent some time in Geneva as well as in Frankfort. The personnel of the exile congregations was anything but static; the churches seem to have been in a constant state of flux, with the exiles moving from one to another at will. A group of them, whose views Davies shared, left Frankfort for Geneva in 1557, and, since his name is not found in the Frankfort records after the summer of that year, he may have left with them. Nevertheless, it seems quite certain that he spent most of his sojourn abroad at Frankfort, and he may well have spent the whole of it there.

The English church in that city had been founded in June 1554 with the arrival of William Whittingham and three companions. During the spring of 1555 a violent quarrel between two opposing groups within the church had flared up. The one party, led by Richard Cox, had insisted upon worshipping according to the Edwardian Prayer Book. They claimed, with justice, that to overthrow the authority of the Prayer Books would be to betray their brethren in England, many of whom were suffering imprisonment, torture, and even death, on their behalf. Their opponents, headed by John Knox, held that the Prayer Books had not gone far enough in the direction of reform, and that it would be a grievous sin not to proceed further. 'Among many sins that moved God to plague England', thundered Knox, 'I affirmed that slackness to reform religion, when time and place was granted, was one, and therefore that it did become us to be circumspect how we did lay our foundations and how we went forward'.[16] It was not a mere struggle for mastery between two fiery and domineering personalities who sought to disguise their true aims in a welter of high-sounding but meaningless arguments. It was the outcome of a fatal divergence of belief on fundamental issues; widened and deepened by passions born of years of violent controversy, it eventually rent the English church asunder.

However in the summer of 1555, it seemed as though the upholders of the Prayer Book had won a clear-cut victory when Knox was asked by the Frankfort magistrates to leave their city. Though the defeated party by no means relished the prospect, schism appeared inevitable. They refused to stay and worship according to the Prayer Book with what Knox called 'its things superstitious, impure, unclean, and imperfect'. Rather than betray their principles they betook themselves to Geneva, and there founded an independent church of their own.

Davies might well have come into contact with Richard Cox towards the end of his Oxford career, at which time Cox was one of the most prominent reformers at the university. It might be tempting to suggest that it was with Cox and his group that Davies first came to Frankfort, were it not that the latter's name is first mentioned in the Frankfort records late in the year 1555. This makes it unlikely that he retired there before the autumn of that year.[17] In these circumstances it seems very probable that the great dispute had subsided before he got to the city. But since he chose to go to Frankfort, he must have sympathized with the more conservative group. Had he sided with their antagonists he would surely have gone on to join them at Geneva.

On his first arrival in the city, he was described in the records as a 'student'. This need not imply that he was not a fully-ordained priest, for John Matchet, a deprived priest of the diocese of Norwich,[18] was listed in the same way. If the future bishop did pursue his studies further, he may have done so at a college established by Cox after the departure of the vanquished Calvinist party.[19] He is again mentioned in the Frankfort records in January 1557, when he was described as 'Pradikant, hat sonst kein narung' ('Preacher, has no other means of livelihood'). In June of the same year he was described as living with John Matchet and his family in a house near the 'prediger closter'.[20] Also in January 1557 he was one of those appealed to by John Hales;[21] but his name was later among those appended to the objections to the 'new discipline'.[22]

To appreciate the significance of the last reference, it is necessary to recount briefly the circumstances of the fresh quarrel which racked the unfortunate church again in 1557. It was in essence a revival of the controversy that had raged so fiercely in 1555, though it was complicated by disagreement over the handling of the church finances, and by various personal factors. Not the least of these was the personality of Horne, the minister of the church, a man of domineering character, fond of power, and anxious to display it. Even so, the original altercation between him and Ashley need not necessarily have become the occasion of an ideological conflict. It might have been amicably settled but for the action of the elders, who, feeling that due reverence had not been paid to Horne's sacred calling, summoned Ashley to appear before them. He denied their right to sit in judgment upon him, and appealed to the whole congregation. Very soon, the whole question of sacerdotal privilege, so hotly contested two years earlier, was brought to the forefront again.

The man who now emerged to challenge Horne in asserting the claims of the congregation was John Hales, a gentleman of Kent.[23] Led by him, the majority of the congregation refused to be browbeaten by Horne's barely-veiled threats[24] or intimidated by the financial pressure exerted by his ally, Chambers.[25] They were not content merely to judge Ashley, but also insisted on drawing up a 'new discipline' for the church. The new proposals sought to define the rights of the congregation in the most ample terms, and to bring the minister under its control. The nominal recognition of the validity of the Edwardian Prayer Book was deprived of most of its force by the saving clause to the effect that in the 'respect of time and places, and other circumstances, certain rites and ceremonies, appointed in this book as things indifferent may be left out, as we at this present do.'[26] Horne and Chambers could not accept the new discipline on principle, though they did not make themselves any better-liked by their complete unwillingness to submit to arbitration.

The quarrel was not long protracted. The congregation, having tasted the fruits of victory, was not likely to relinquish them easily. For the defeated minority, too small in number to found a separate church yet unwilling to remain and eat the broken crust of humiliation, nothing remained but to leave the field clear for the victors. So Horne, Chambers, and a number of their satellites left for Strasbourg.

If it is improbable that Davies was even living in Frankfort at the time of the struggle between Cox and Knox, there is no doubt as to which cause he committed himself in 1557. In January he was evidently considered sufficiently influential or prudent to be one of those specially appealed to by Hales. As his signature appeared later among those of the objectors to the new discipline it is plain that he upheld the views of the conservatives. It seems impossible to tell whether he withdrew with them to the city of Geneva, though perhaps it is significant that he was still living in Frankfort, as late as June 1557.

It has been deemed worthwhile dealing with this period of exile at some length not only because new facts have come to light concerning Davies and the exiles in general, but also because it is believed that these years spent abroad have a much greater significance for a study of his life than has usually been attributed to them. The very fact that he went abroad at all testifies to the strength of his Protestant beliefs. It was the 'marked' men, the men who feared imprisonment or death, or, more important still, the men who feared spiritual death, who fled to the cities of Europe. Nothing seemed to them to be of greater moment than that the tiny oases of English Protestantism should not be overwhelmed and desiccated by the arid sandstorm of Marian reaction. It may be doubted whether reformed religion could have survived in England but for their action. Certainly, the Elizabethan Church owed them an incalculable debt; in 1576, Archbishop Grindal declared that the reason why England had so many bishops and 'other ministers of God's word, which at that day preached the pure doctrine of the Gospel, was owing to Strasbourg, Zurich, Basel, but above all the rest to Frankfort.'[27]

Though the exiles represented all shades of reforming opinion, broadly speaking, it is possible to discern two main trends of opinion among them. The gulf which later divided anglicans and puritans had already been opened before the exiles returned to their homeland. For the more advanced reformers, the Prayer Books represented a step forward; but they must be regarded as a temporary expedient to be superseded by a more godly form of worship in the freer air of exile. They would tolerate nothing in their worship which could not find explicit authorization in the Bible, were it never so ancient a custom or revered a tradition.

Again, they argued that if a man was saved from sin by the action of divine grace through faith in the redemptive sacrifice of Jesus Christ, then there was no need for a priesthood with all the privileges of a sacerdotal class. But, for the more conservative in tendency, as for Luther, there was much that was praiseworthy and meritorious in the old faith once it had been purified of the dross that had accumulated as a result of the false claims of papal supremacy. This evil canker once removed, there was much that was good and wholesome, and worthy of preservation, in the old doctrine and organization. It also seemed to them to be both desirable and necessary that the apostolic succession among bishops and priests should be handed on unimpaired, though of course the bishop of Rome must be relegated to his rightful position. It was to this latter group that Davies belonged.

For him, as for many of the other exiles, these years must have witnessed an extension of mental horizons and of religious experience. He was one of a number taken from the isolated atmosphere of a country living, and brought into daily contact with many of the leaders of English Protestantism. It must have been a fruitful experience, for although the tares of selfish ambition and petty intrigue flourished in the ceaseless disputes of the exiles they were not unmixed with the wheat of genuine belief. Nor was it only the stimulating effect of contact with English leaders, because one of the most striking features of English Protestantism of this period is the extent to which it was influenced by the great continental reformers. At this time Calvin bestrode the Protestant world like a Colossus; his fame reverberated through all the reforming circles, and the prestige he enjoyed was immense. Though of lesser stature there were other giants who were frequently referred to for guidance and advice. The voluminous *Zurich Letters* give an indication of the innumerable letters that passed between them and the English leaders. Bullinger was regarded as a veritable fount of piety and learning; the great reputation of Peter Martyr, founded during his stay in England, suffered no eclipse when he retired to Strasbourg; other names that may just be mentioned are those of John à Lasco, Beza, Farel, Musculus, and Vyret. By this time, Melanchthon and the Lutherans had lost a good deal of their influence.

Last, but not least, Davies came into contact with men who were to be of considerable influence in ecclesiastical affairs during the early years of Elizabeth's reign. It may not be too much to suggest that without their influence he might never have gained the position which enabled him to render great services to his native land. He had left England an obscure parish priest in his fifties; a man who had made very little headway and who had not shown much sign of being a likely candidate for the episcopal bench. Yet, soon after his return to England, he figured on a list, drawn up by

Cecil, of divines suitable for promotion. This, and his appointment to head the royal visitation of the western group of dioceses in 1559, suggests that he was regarded by Archbishop Parker and Cecil as one of their eminently trustworthy lieutenants. It is not impossible that he was brought to the notice of the authorities by the leaders of the exiles who enjoyed their confidence. It will be remembered that he was a member of the minority group which supported Horne and Chambers, and the latter was probably Cecil's most trusted agent on the Continent. What could be more natural than that Cecil, seeking 'sound' men to put into effect the new ecclesiastical policy, should turn to his aide for his opinion of the fitness of those whom he had observed at close quarters.[28] It would have been more than unnatural if Chambers were not biased in favour of men who had shared his views, especially when they were those of an unpopular minority. And so, but for these years of exile, Richard Davies might never have emerged from obscurity to find the honourable place he later attained in the annals of his nation's history.

* * *

Within a very short time of Davies's return from exile at the time of Queen Elizabeth's accession, it soon became apparent that he was held in considerable esteem by the responsible authorities in Church and State. He was made a royal visitor for the Welsh and western dioceses in 1559 and played a considerable part in establishing the Elizabethan settlement of religion there (see above, pp. 142-7). Early in 1560 he was consecrated bishop of St. Asaph. Though he was to stay there for less than two years, it may have been an episode of vital importance, for it seems very probable that it was during this time he came into close and fruitful contact with William Salesbury, whose home at Llansannan would have made him a near neighbour to the bishop. On 15th March, 1561 Davies was elected bishop of St. David's but he does not appear to have taken up residence there until September of that year.

When Davies was translated to his new see, it was no sinecure to which he was called. The diocese was an enormous one, covering the whole counties of Pembroke, Carmarthen, Cardigan and Brecon, large parts of Radnor and west Glamorgan, and a few parishes in Monmouthshire, Herefordshire and Montgomeryshire. Despite its vast extent, it was sparsely populated: Davies, in 1563, reported the number of householders in his diocese as 24,161, so that an estimate of 4-5 persons per household would give a total diocesan population of some 100-120,000 people.[29] Many of these were scattered in inaccessible parishes, tucked away in remote valleys and spread over bare moorland. The diocese, as Bishop Barlow had rightly insisted, lacked a natural centre from which the bishop might administer it easily, while the wretched state of communications within its boundaries served only to aggravate the problem. Poverty, too, greatly handicapped the efforts of bishops and clergy. The *Valor Ecclesiasticus* of 1535 showed that many of the livings had been unusually poor even before the Reformation changes. Only a handful of livings were worth more than £30 a year; the average value of a benefice was worth no more than £10, and 94 of the livings, or 27.5 per cent of them, were rated at less than £5.[30] By Elizabeth's reign some benefices were, relatively speaking, even poorer; such had been the rapacity of laymen that no incumbents could be found to take such impoverished livings. But Davies's most important and difficult responsibility would be to implement Elizabeth's church settlement. His Protestant predecessors, Barlow and Ferrar, had done more to sow the seeds of discord among the clergy than to promote the success of reform. Their Elizabethan successor, Thomas Young, had been at St. David's far too short a time to achieve anything of note. It was to Richard Davies's lot that the brunt of the burden was to fall.

He was well qualified to assume such responsibility. Though he was not a young man, his subsequent activities showed that he possessed almost unimpaired up to the time of his death the abounding energy of mind and body which characterized the age. He had given signal proof of his integrity and ability during his long and varied apprenticeship as student, parish priest, exile and royal visitor. His brief stay at St. Asaph had begun his schooling in those hard lessons which every conscientious Elizabethan bishop had to learn. Nor was his new diocese entirely strange to him. The royal visitation of 1559 had given him a glimpse of conditions prevailing there and had provided an opportunity to begin the work of weeding out the most hostile Catholic priests. There was still much to be done – so much that, conscientious though Davies was, when he died twenty years later conditions had changed surprisingly little.

In considering Davies's activity as a bishop it may be useful to divide the discussion up under the four heads of I) his relations with authority in Church and State; II) the bishop and his clergy; III) the bishop and the laity; and IV) scholarly and literary pursuits.

I. RELATIONS WITH AUTHORITY

Although, in the sixteenth century, laymen were playing an increasing part in the government of the realm, at the expense of the former ecclesiastical monopoly of office, the services of the clergy did not immediately become redundant. There were still instances of illiteracy among influential laymen – neither Sir Rhys ap Thomas nor William Herbert, earl of Pembroke, for example, could read or write.[31] Moreover, the fusion of temporal and spiritual authority in the sovereign's person tended to make officials of state of all the clergy. The duties they were now called upon to perform were, generally speaking, much less exalted than those of the Middle Ages. They no longer shared to any great extent in the shaping of policy; they merely carried out the orders of the government. Even so, the increasing intrusion of the State into all walks of everyday life imposed upon the Elizabethan bishops a host of administrative duties which made serious inroads upon their time and energy. They might naturally be expected to have taken an important share in the fulfilment of the statutes against recusancy and other ordinances of a similar kind. What is perhaps more surprising is to find them engaged in a hundred and one other ways which do not seem to have had much connection with their spiritual functions.

Richard Davies does not seem to have taken a leading part in the ecclesiastical affairs of the realm as a whole. He attended the sessions of Convocation regularly but without appearing to take a decisive share in its deliberations.[32] He seems to have preserved his advanced reforming views and to have shared the aspirations of those bishops with a background of exile similar to his own who were not unsympathetic to some of the Puritan demands. For instance, Davies was one of those who supported Grindal's refusal to ban the Puritan 'prophesyings' which so exasperated the Queen.[33] He was also a member of the same humanist/reforming circle as Grindal, which was commemorated in Spenser's *Shepherd's Calendar* (see below, pp. 182-3).

Within Wales itself he has been described as the 'trusted adviser' of Parker and Cecil.[34] This description rests mainly on the strength of letters which passed between them in 1566.[35] The first of these was written by Davies to Parker and was forwarded to Cecil by the archbishop. It contained Davies's views on the filling of vacancies caused in the diocese of Llandaff and Bangor by the deaths of Bishops Kitchen and Meyrick. The other three letters, all written by Parker to Cecil, give the former's opinions on the matter. There is very little in the text of these letters to justify describing Davies as a trusted adviser. He was not the only one to be consulted; his advice was not accepted; and there is no evidence to suggest that either Parker or Cecil took the initiative in seeking his views. One of his main objects seems to have been to secure promotion for his friend, Thomas Huet, precentor of St. David's, and such a practice of eliciting favours from the influential was common enough in the sixteenth century. At the same time, however, there is no mistaking the sincerity of Davies's desire to find the 'chiefest means' of furthering 'Christ's Church in these places', nor the genuineness of his plea for the appointment of bishops who, 'by preaching the word of God and living according to the same', might 'set forth the glory of God and show light in these places of extreme darkness'.[36]

In the sphere of secular administration, Davies's duties were many and varied, ranging from his elevated position as a member of the House of Lords to his humdrum duties as a resident justice of the peace in Carmarthenshire. During the six sessions of the Lords between 1563 and 1581 Davies took his seat with marked regularity.[37] Apart from missing a number of sittings during the session of 1571, whether on account of illness or some other cause cannot be determined, he was always dutifully present in the upper chamber. The sittings which almost certainly interested him most were those of 1563, in the course of which an act was passed for the translation into Welsh of the Bible and the Book of Common Prayer. Davies was the only one of the Welsh bishops who was present at all three hearings of the act.[38] It is not known who was the prime mover in getting this extremely important act passed. It has been suggested that William Salesbury had been able to influence his brother-in-law, Ellis Price (the 'Red Doctor'), who was high in the favour of the earl of Leicester, to interest himself in the measure. But Richard Davies's own position in the House of Lords, together with the influence that he may have had with his fellow-exiles and with Cecil and Parker, makes him the most likely candidate for the honour of bringing this act to fruition. He may also have had the invaluable help of Humphrey Llwyd as the measure went through the Commons.[39]

Davies was also, like some other Welsh and border bishops, a member of the Council of the Marches. Membership of this body may well have been a stimulating and valuable experience for him. At its meetings he came into contact with the leading gentry of Wales; and at Ludlow he must have learnt much of what was going on in governmental circles in London. He may have been able to enlist the support of the council when his own spiritual or temporal authority was lacking. Certainly, he would be kept in touch with almost every aspect of Tudor administration, for there were very few matters of local or area government which did not fall within the scope of the council's jurisdiction. The Council of the Marches, like the Privy Council, placed a bewildering variety of responsibilities on the broad shoulders of its officers of local government. Richard Davies had to perform a miscellany of administrative duties, ranging from supervising the general musters in the county of Denbigh to promulgating orders concerning the recovery of stolen cattle. Some of his other responsibilities included enquiring into the misappropriation of victuals for the army in Ireland, supervising the activities of tanners, renewing parish overseers, and holding an enquiry – barren of results – into the exactions and bribery of sheriffs and other officers.[40]

Apart from these special duties Daveis shared in the routine business of local administration in his capacity as a justice of the peace. In a list of 1575 he was described as a resident justice in the hundred of Elfed in Carmarthenshire, the area in which his own palace at Abergwili lay, and as a non-resident justice for the hundred of Derllys in the same county.[41] In a careful return for Pembrokeshire prepared in the same year Sir John Perrott showed that there were no resident justices in the episcopal lands of Dewsland and Kemes; but he added that the bishop of St. David's came down 'perhaps once a year, or once in two years'. He added, however, that the bishop rarely 'meddled' in any 'case of commission'.[42]

The Privy Council also employed Davies directly, referring various matters to him from time to time. The most important, and the one with which he was called upon to grapple most frequently, was piracy, which was particularly serious in west Wales.[43] So deeply were most of the local squires themselves involved in the activities of pirates that Davies may have been called upon in the hope that a bishop, at least, might render disinterested service. The number of commissions of this nature assigned to him speaks highly of the esteem in which he was held by the Privy Council. In 1565, 1572 and 1578 he was one of the Council's special commissioners for piracy. These assignments meant exhausting and tiresome labours for him, and often came at most inopportune moments. In 1565 he had his hands full with the translation of the New Testament into Welsh; and in 1578, though he was busy with the harvest and the Great Sessions, he had to betake himself to Pembrokeshire 'with all convenient speed'.[44] It was not easy to obtain all the detailed information which the Privy Council demanded, especially in the short time it usually allowed for the purpose. The Commission of 1565, for instance, had to provide full information about creeks and harbours, and to compile a census of sailors, as well as having to check the licensing of all vessels and guard against the landing of unlicensed cargo and the sale of stolen merchandise ashore.[45] The most important witnesses were very often extremely elusive; as Davies ruefully explained to the Council in 1578, some men might be away on lawful errands, but there were many who 'wilfully absented themseves', while 'other very expedient and necessary witnesses' could not be apprehended 'by any means'.[46] Reliable deputies were equally hard to come by, as the Council itself acknowledged, when it admitted the scarcity of honest men who would do their duty unmoved by considerations of 'profession, manner of living . . . for hope of gain, fear of discovering their own misdemeanours or any other particular respect or affection.'[47]

The greatest obstacle, however, was the complicity of most of the prominent gentry of the south-west. Even Sir John Perrott and Richard Vaughan, the two chief royal agents for the suppression of piracy, were implicated. Nor did their intense dislike of one another help matters. Indeed, it seems very probable that Bishop

Davies and his colleagues were in 1578 called in by the Privy Council to hold the balance between Perrott and Vaughan. It would be instructive to know more about the relations between Davies and these two enemies. It could not have been easy to avoid falling foul of one or other, or both, of them. There may, therefore, be a substratum of truth underlying the accusation later brought against Perrott of having worried the bishop to death for his share in the enquiry of 1578. Perrott was a man of masterful temperament – inherited perhaps from his reputed royal sire, Henry VIII – 'by nature very choleric' and unable to 'brook any crosses, nor dissemble the least injuries, although offered by the greatest personages.'[48] Davies, on his side, was a courageous and spirited man, and Sir John Wynn said of him that he had 'stoutly confronted' Perrott, though without giving any details of the encounter.[49] It is possible that they had first crossed swords in 1574, when Davies may well have been drawn into the 'private quarrels' and 'public contentions' between his friend and patron, the earl of Essex, and Sir John Perrott.[50] In that event, anger and bitterness between them might all the more easily have been rekindled in 1578.

Another matter in which Davies received instructions direct from the Privy Council was the bill of complaint presented against Sir John Throgmorton by one Hugh ap David, alias Park.[51] Davies and his fellow commissioners were, in July 1570, empowered to summon both parties before them, to take depositions of witnesses, and to make a report to the council. Unfortunately there is nothing further to shed light on this mysterious bill of complaint, nor on the findings of the judges. Throgmorton had a known predilection for the Roman faith, and his devotion to it had won him favour with Queen Mary who had made him chief justice of the Chester Circuit. But it was not his religious sympathies so much as his actions as a justice which were giving rise to a number of complaints about him at this time.[52]

Davies's intimate connection with the secular administration awoke in him no enthusiasm for it. He was full of indignation at those public officials whose fawning on the great stood in such unhappy contrast to their oppression of the poor. Though there were a few who walked uprightly he held that many would do well to consider the day of reckoning, when it would plainly appear that 'commonly all that they did in their office was in respect of persons, to pleasure the great man lest he should find a hole in their coats'. They were 'void of all religion and fear of God', did not know the meaning of justice, and used their authority to 'pill and poll the country and to beggar their neighbours'.[53] Elsewhere Davies complained that it was they who often gave sanctuary to criminals: 'Often in Wales, though the law takes no note of it, the hall of the gentleman is the refuge of thieves . . . So I say that were it not for the arm and the wing of the gentleman there would be but little theft in Wales'.[54] Strong words; yet they are to some extent corroborated by the testimony of other contemporary observers like the lawyers, William Gerard and David Lewis.[55]

For all Davies's censoriousness, however, there are indications that his own 'coat' was not without its 'holes'. On one occasion the sharp practice in which Davies and his archdeacons had been indulging in shifting the burden of their responsibilities for finding and equipping troops had to be checked by the Privy Council acting on information provided in a petition from the lower clergy of St. David's diocese.[56] Much more serious, in view of Davies's position as a member of the Council of the Marches and a justice of the peace, were the accusations brought against him by Fabian Phillips, a fellow member of the Council of the Marches. Phillips was a man about whose character and ability opinions varied a good deal. Sir Henry Sidney dismissed him contemptuously as a 'common solicitor', 'more presumptuous and affectionate than wise', and William Gerard had no very high opinion of this 'utter barrister of small experience'.[57] Bishop Whitgift, however, was more complimentary; he knew of no cause of complaint against him and thought him 'stout and upright in judgment'.[58] In his attacks on Davies, Phillips bore out Sidney's view of him rather than that of Whitgift. In a fierce and intemperate attack on the bishop he accused him of failing to maintain justice and order, protecting his turbulent and unruly son-in-law, William Penry, and wilfully injuring a poor man who had committed no crime.[59] There seems no doubt that Penry was a hotheaded and quarrelsome fellow and that his father-in-law had attempted to soften the punishment imposed upon him. On the other hand, Fabian Phillips's foster brothers, Morgan David Deio and David David Deio, the other party to the dispute, were by no means poor innocents hardly done by. Whatever the rights and wrongs of the matter – and it seems a case of the pot calling the kettle black – Davies was much more conciliatory than Phillips. The bishop's letter to the Privy Council is altogether more restrained and courteous than Phillips's strident tones. The latter's attitude and behaviour had been offensive and provocative. He had forgotten 'common humanity and modesty', Davies complained, in order to make a public attack on the bishop in Carmarthen. He went on, 'He therefore purposely fell to choleric speeches of me; and after he had painted me out as a notorious wrongdoer to poor men (which I hope in God he shall never be able to justify whilst he liveth), he added threats, saying, "I will make the bishop answer", and still iterated, "I will make him, I will make him".[60] In spite of all this, Davies was reluctant to enter into a public controversy with him, fearing that such a course would only be to the 'great encouragement' of those who were inclined to papistry. Underlying Davies's laboured

avowals of his innocence and good intentions can be detected the unhappy dilemma in which he found himself. He reacted almost
instinctively to the need for upholding his son-in-law; but he shrank
from weakening his authority by publicly quarrelling with a prominent Protestant layman. Throughout we can sense his heartfelt
longing that his son-in-law and the Deios had found it possible
to live in peace without ever having dragged him into their
wretched bickerings.

II. THE BISHOP AND HIS CLERGY

During the years from 1559 to 1565 the Elizabethan church
settlement was put through with amazing smoothness in the dioceses
of England and Wales. St. David's was no exception. The registers of
its first two Elizabethan bishops, Thomas Young and Richard
Davies,[61] give no indication of any widespread resistance to the new
arrangements on the part of the clergy. Though Davies's surviving
register does not go beyond the first four years of his episcopate,
those years were in some ways the most decisive because they covered
the crucial period for the acceptance by the clergy of Elizabeth's
brand of reformed religion.[62] It is true that, after this date, there
were priests who felt that they had erred in accepting in the first
place. But there were very few who felt bound to give up their
livings after 1565. By this time the Queen's intentions, the nature
of her settlement, and the issues involved, were all defined fairly
clearly. Inevitably, the longer the waverers clung to their livings the
less likely they were to resist.

Davies's register records a total of 73 presentations over the period
between 16th September, 1561 and 23rd December, 1565. This figure
is so low as to suggest that some folios have been lost from the register;
a suggestion which gains added plausibility from the present confused
arrangement of the contents. The most usual cause of vacancies
was the death of the incumbent, which accounted for 43 out of
the 73. Only six priests were deprived by Davies, and of these, three ,
seem to have had no marked papist sympathies – two of them were
simply moved from one living to another. The other three
are obscure, but they may have been papists. Closer scrutiny of some
of the other entries suggests that there may have been other priests
who were turned out of their livings, or obliged to resign, because of
their beliefs. There are 14 resignations and one cession recorded
in the register. Of these, four may have been occasioned by religious
scruples, but the others who resigned were either known Protestants
or had been placed in their livings by Protestant bishops. There are
a further seven vacancies described as being lawfully (*de iure*) caused.
Four of these seem very unlikely to have been brought about by
the removal of papist incumbents, with the rest remaining doubtful.
There are two other livings where no reason at all was given for the

vacancy. Both may have been voided by papists.[63] However, even if all these doubtful cases, or a large proportion of them, could be proved beyond all question to have been the result of devotion to Rome, it would hardly change the general picture of a docile clergy. It is plain that there was no upheaval comparable with the wholesale displacement of the married clergy during the Marian episcopate of Bishop Henry Morgan, when there were about four times the usual number of entries in the register between April 1554 and April 1555.[64] The smallness of the total number of presentations between 1560 and 1565 alone proves that there was no large-scale eviction. This, it might be objected, was accounted for by the loss of a number of folios from the register, which, if they had been preserved, would reveal more priests as having been deprived. But it cannot safely be assumed that there are many of them missing, and it would be even more unwarranted to suppose that the register had been tampered with in order to conceal the highly undesirable fact (from the reformers' point of view) that there was a large number of non-juring priests. The defects of the St. David's registers for this period appear to confirm very clearly the view of a scholar who had examined more sixteenth-century registers than almost anyone else that they were marred as a result of 'carelessness in binding and registering them rather than deliberate tampering with them.'[65] So we must conclude that nearly all the clergy of the diocese accepted, with or without mental reservations, the Church by law established. Such ready complaisance on their part was received with mixed feelings by Davies and the other bishops. Bishop Jewel of Salisbury doubtless epitomized the feelings of many of his *confrères* when he pointed out that it would be no 'easy matter to drag the chariot without horses, especially up hill.'[66]

The bishops' sense of frustration was further intensified by the lack of suitable candidates for ordination. They complained that the supply of graduates had been gravely reduced. During Mary's reign the tide had flowed so strongly in favour of Romanism at Oxford and Cambridge that there were 'scarcely two individuals there with Protestant sympathies; and they were so dejected and broken in spirit that they could do nothing.'[67] So desperate was the shortage and so urgent the need that some of the bishops were driven to ordain 'mechanics' and other unfit persons, for which they were rapped over the knuckles by the Queen. The difficulties encountered by Davies are reflected in the ordinations celebrated by him between 1561 and 1565. At first they were a mere trickle. From November 1561 to March 1562 there were only 3, and from March 1562 to March 1563 there were 12. But from March 1563 to March 1564 there were 24, and in the year ending March 1565 there were 36. Numbers fell again during the next year 1565–66 to 15. As the register goes no further than March 1566 it is impossible to tell whether this drop in numbers during 1565 represented a temporary decline or whether it meant that the most urgent needs of the diocese had been met by then. All these ordinands included in the totals already given were from St. David's diocese itself, but during the same years Davies ordained candidates from other dioceses. It is noticeable, however, that very few graduates were ordained by Davies from his own diocese. There were only two of them, though another was described as a *scholaris* and two more as *literati*. Only one of the graduates ordained by him was later listed as a preacher within the diocese.[68]

Remembering the fewness of the evictions and the rather in-different quality of the ordinands, we need not wonder that down to Davies's death in 1581, and beyond, many of the diocesan clergy were content to jog along without changing their ways very much. One of Davies's archdeacons, William Luson, archdeacon of Carmarthen, was reputed to be a staunch Catholic and probably remained so until his death. He was described by the bishop of Hereford in 1564 as one of the 'chief and principal receivers and maintainers' of a band of deprived Marian priests; yet this did not prevent him from taking the oath of supremacy nor from holding in addition to his archdeaconry the treasurership of Hereford Cathedral and one of its prebends.[69] If so prominent a figure in the diocese could equivocate in this way without being removed, then there must have been a host of lesser men who did the same. Twenty years later in 1583, two years after Davies's death, his successor, Bishop Marmaduke Middleton, issued visitation articles and injunctions which shed light on conditions which had prevailed in the diocese for some time previously.[70] They showed that some of the clergy had continued to cherish all kinds of traditional rites and beliefs. It was necessary to forbid a 'sort of blind, ignorant priests and ministers' from elevating the host and practising other customs which retained a memory 'of the idolatrous mass'.[71] They were to desist from practices 'after the use of the popish superstition' which were still observed at baptisms, burials and the churching of women.[72] The images, pictures, roodlofts, and 'other monuments of feigned miracles', which still held pride of place in many churches, were to be pulled down and 'utterly defaced'. The old holy days, still so dear to them, were not to be observed under any pretext.[73]

Middleton's sweeping indictment of the state of affairs in the diocese was one of the severest denunciations of papist survivals ever to come from an Elizabethan bishop. Indirectly, of course, he laid the blame for the 'infinite number of papist ceremonies', 'erroneous opinions, idolatrous amity, and wicked superstition' at his predecessor's door. His criticisms would have more weight, however, if Davies himself had not so often deplored this attach-ment to the past, if it were not so usual for an Elizabethan bishop to seek to establish his own reputation by comparing his own tire-lessness with his predecessor's ineffectuality,[74] and if the reputation of Middleton himself, who was deprived of his diocese for grave offences, had been less tarnished. Davies tolerated many short-comings not because he wanted to but because he had to. His vigilance may possibly have become dulled as he grew older; but it has already been pointed out how, during the first four years of his episcopate, at least, he had very little real choice in the matter.

The suggestion that impotence rather than negligence accounted for Davies's apparent slackness is strengthened by examination of his attitude towards the poverty of clerical livings and stipends. In this matter he cannot justly be accused of either apathy or coward-ice. In a report on the state of his diocese sent to the Privy Council in 1570 he forcefully attacked those lay patrons into whose hands the livings formerly appropriated to the monasteries had come. They numbered among them some of the wealthiest and most powerful of the lay landowners, but Davies gave scant regard to the danger of provoking the wrath of such adversaries. He claimed that in most instances they were squeezing the clergy into dire poverty, were allowing them only the most inadequate stipends or even in some instances denying any responsibility to provide a stipend at all. As a result a number of vicarages and curacies, some of them in important centres like Carmarthen or Llanstephan, were either inadequately served or had no incumbent at all. Conscious of his own powerlessness, he urged the Queen to give him authority to compel the gentry to fulfil their obligations.[75] Nothing further was heard of his proposals for reform, however. The chances are that they were ignored, for Middleton was no less gloomy about the impropriated churches.[76]

The impoverishment of the Church was a taproot from which sprang many other evil growths. It accounted for many of the gravest abuses of the Elizabethan Church, though, of course, simony, pluralism and non-residence had been common enough in the Middle Ages. But it was the lack of preachers which most worried Elizabethan bishops, especially those with advanced reform-ing opinions like Richard Davies. At no point was their armour more vulnerable to Puritan barbs. Throughout the realm there was a 'great and alarming scarcity' of preachers, 'especially those who had any ability'.[77] In Wales, they were still more scarce because of the lack of a Welsh Bible and of apologetic literature in Welsh, and also because of the greater poverty of the livings. Davies ended his report of 1570, in which he had so roundly attacked the lay patrons for their responsibility for keeping the clergy poor, with the plea that his efforts were directed primarily to improving the supply of preachers: 'that the small patrimony of the Church which is yet remaining to the maintenance of God's service, may still continue to the sustentation (as I trust) of preachers and teachers, after that the incumbents now being no preachers, shall happen to depart'.[78] The only way in which Davies could get preachers was to tempt them with two or three of the better benefices. Even then, in 1570, there were only 10 (if we include the bishop) within the diocese. By 1583 there were 14 of them, still far too few to meet the need.[79]

The twin evils of pluralism and non-residence were not confined to the preachers and graduates; they were rife among the clergy from the highest to the most humble. Davies had to admit that Hugh Price, the treasurer of the diocese, 'who by his office should always be resident', was allowed to dwell elsewhere 'by dispensation under the great seal'.[80] Hardly any of the four archdeacons were ever resident; in 1563 all four were absentees, and in 1570 only one was resident.[81] The medieval tradition of handsomely providing the higher clerical dignitaries with a number of preferments in order to maintain them in circumstances proper to their station still continued. Davies can hardly be held entirely responsible, but it must be admitted that he did not act very wisely or scrupulously at times. He was apt to place youths of incomplete education in stalls at his cathedral and at the collegiate church of Brecon.[82] Nor did he hesitate to provide for his own sons out of the patronage of the see. His son Peregrine was made archdeacon of Cardigan in 1563 when he was still a child. When his youngest son, Gerson, was about 17 years of age he was given the prebend of Clydai (£30 *p.a.*) and the vicarage of Penbryn (£40). He had also acquired the rich prebend of Llanbister (£40) before his father's death

While the greater luminaries collected benefices to keep themselves in luxury, the lesser lights did so in order to keep alive. Davies referred anxiously to the sore straits in which some of the poorer parsons found themselves and to those churches which had not 'whole service once a year, but upon Sundays and Holy days the epistle and gospel or suffrage only'.[83] Middleton's return, too, brings out clearly the widespread pluralism among the lower clergy and the meagreness of the stipends which drove them to it. On the other hand, it would seem that it was greed, as much as or even more than poverty, which led some of them to grab livings unrestrainedly. Davies reported that as a result of corrupt bargainings with the gentry and the sheriffs some clergy defied his attempts to discipline them: 'some against all injunctions to the contrary taking upon them to serve three or four, yea sometimes five, cures: but never one aright; being supported by gentlemen, farmers of the said churches and cures, who do procure the favour of the sheriff, so as they neither regard any interdiction nor can be brought to observe any good order'.[84]

Information about the morals and behaviour of the clergy is very scanty. Generalization is therefore palpably dangerous; but it seems incontestable that the sixteenth-century clergyman was as much more turbulent and undisciplined than his modern counterpart as his lay brother was more violent and disorderly than the average citizen of today. Particularly wild and insubordinate were the vicars choral at the cathedral of St. David's itself. Their misdeeds found their way into the chapter records on more than one occasion during Davies's episcopate.[85] They seem to have found drinking and gaming and madcap pranks much more to their liking than pursuing their studies. Their unseemly behaviour often had to be reprimanded by the precentor and chapter; but they listened with scant respect and were disconcertingly frank in their rejoinders. When the chancellor, David Powel, had lectured one vicar-choral, Thomas Lloyd, for keeping a tavern, the latter promptly rounded on him and charged him with acting 'more of malice than any good reformation', and then proceeded to denounce him for keeping a woman of ill fame in his house. Davies himself recognized that many of his clergy were leading scandalous lives for which he wanted to discipline them. But as the sheriffs, on whom responsibility for executing the writ of excommunication fell, were open to bribery, the delinquents could snap their fingers in their bishop's face.[86]

III. Davies and the Laity

Many of the Elizabethan bishops, forced to contend with both Puritans and recusants, needed a Cerberus to keep an eye on the laity in their sees. At St. David's, however, Richard Davies had only the conservative element with which to deal. This was not a militant opposition like that which made Bishop Pilkington of Durham compare himself to St. Paul struggling with wild beasts at Ephesus, but a stubborn adherence to the past, bred from ignorance and dislike of change rather than conviction. No open recusancy was discovered during his episcopate, but there was widespread sympathy for the old ways in religion and general lukewarmness towards the new.

In matters ecclesiastical the queen looked for docility and obedience, not militancy or enthusiasm, on the part of the officials of government, since the delicate balance of her settlement with its prime concern for national unity might all too easily be wrecked by zealots of any complexion. The bishops, especially those with experience of exile in Mary's reign, were naturally inclined to think and speak differently. They were apt to classify all those who were not strongly for reform as being against it. Davies lashed out fiercely at the gentry of his diocese for applying 'all their power to further and continue the kingdom of Antichrist' and defending 'papistry, superstition, and idolatry'. He found it most lamentable that in a 'blessed time of light and knowledge of the Gospel' they would 'neither enter themselves into the kingdom of heaven, nor suffer them that would'.[87] It was because he did not wish to give this opposition, already formidable enough, any further encouragement that he deplored Fabian Phillips's attempts to provoke a quarrel. But the attachment to old loyalties and the slowness to accept change survived Davies in the diocese. In 1583 Middleton complained, as Davies had done, of the slackness of lay officials. They would not apprehend obstinate papists and he could not.[88]

Nevertheless, on both the occasions when Davies was called upon to give information about the number of recusants within the diocese, he had none to report. During the troubled times of 1569-70, when the Rising of the Northern Earls was making the Privy Council very nervous, Guerau de Spes, the Spanish ambassador and an irrepressible optimist, was raising the hopes of his master by confident reports that the people of Wales were 'for the great part Catholic', 'with many attached to the Queen of Scotland'.[89] Yet, 'after diligent enquiry', the bishop and his officers could allay the fears of the Council by reporting no one of note 'within contempt of religion established in the realm'.[90] They found a 'great number', however, who were 'slow and cold in the true service of God', 'some careless for any religion,' and others wishing the return of the 'romanish' faith. On the second occasion, in 1577, Davies had only one man – and he a very poor one – who refused to come to church; but he had his doubts about a good many others whom he suspected of being 'infected with papistry'.[91] The other Welsh bishops, except Bleddyn of Llandaff, had much the same story to tell at this time.[92] Without impugning their sincerity, it may be doubted whether their returns accurately reflected the religious condition of the country in 1577. Walsingham allowed them only a week to draw up their lists. That meant they had to rely very largely on such information as they had gleaned in the course of their visitations. But as Davies himself pointed out, churchwardens were subjected to a great deal of pressure on these occasions and their mouths effectively stopped.[93] In any case, the fact that recusants were almost unknown was no guarantee of the eradication of Catholic sympathy or of the progress of Protestantism. Loyalty to the state, and to their own interests, led some of the gentry to conform outwardly, though inwardly they clung to their old beliefs, or had little interest in religion at all.[94] They could, for the most part, count on remaining undetected as long as they were not too blatant in their opposition. Episcopal visitations were as a rule few and far between, while in the event of a sudden danger, like a proposal to make a secret search of their houses, they were very often warned in advance by friends and relatives.[95]

With many of the squires conservative or indifferent, and many of the clergy little better, medieval beliefs and practices appear to have persisted strongly among the ordinary people. In 1571, under the very noses of the bishop and chapter, the sexton of St. David's, one Ellis ap Howell, was discovered to have hidden certain 'ungodly popish books; as mass books, hymnals, grails, and such like (as it were looking for a day)'.[96] Yet, such was the tolerance, possibly even sympathy, of the time, that the offending sexton not only regained his position, but was actually promoted verger.[97] Davies made it plain that the people still reposed much of their trust in the miraculous powers of Catholic saints and shrines. In his report of 1570, and in the *Funeral Sermon*, he commented sharply on the 'pilgrimages to wells, and watchings in chapels and desert places' still observed by the 'supporters and bearers of superstition'. Reference has already been made to the fulminations of Middleton against Catholic survivals two years after Davies's death.[98] Broadly speaking, outward conformity was all that had been achieved during his episcopate; complete conversion to Protestant ideals was still a long way off.

In the absence of consistory court records, only a cursory glimpse can be obtained of the morals of laymen. We learn, however, from Davies himself that there were more than two hundred 'vicious livers' within his diocese in 1570.[99] Some of these remained un-repentant after being excommunicated for more than four years, partly because the sheriffs could be bribed into not delivering the writ *de excommunicato capiendo*, and partly because excommunica-tion had lost much of its terror for the laity, though it remained the the chief spiritual weapon in the bishop's armoury. Among the accusations made against Davies by Fabian Phillips was one charg-ing him with allowing widespread immorality to go unchecked in his diocese. Davies defended himself and his chancellor warmly against these charges. He denied strenuously ever having tolerated evil living 'in respect of any manner of gain, money, pleasure, or any other commodity'.[100] He admitted that bigamy and whoredom were frequent in his diocese; but, he argued, he could not be held responsible for that any more than Fabian Phillips, or any other justice, could be blamed for the 'felonies and other enormities' that happened to be committed about him. As evidence of his forwardness in detecting and punishing offenders, he claimed that five hundred persons were excommunicated in St. David's diocese every year.[101] As for the unsavoury case of Rhys Morgan and his sister, to which Phillips made specific reference, he contended that he had done everything within his power to get them tried and punished.

As thorny as any aspect of his relations with the laity were the struggles over the possessions of the Church. Rights of advowson were much sought after by the gentry, and were calculated to give rise to frequent contentions. On at least two occasions, Davies was pestered by rival claimants to the same living as the result of a disputed advowson. In the first instance, after examining the claims put forward by two alleged patrons of the rectory of Bishopston, he decided that both lots were spurious, and proceeded to induct his own nominee.[102] The second case could not be as summarily dismissed. It concerned the church of Llanddewibrefi, which became vacant in January, 1566, on the death of Bishop Rowland Meyrick of Bangor, who held it *in commendam*.[103] Davies collated his own chancellor, Lewis Gwynn, only to find that the earls of Pembroke and Leicester were presenting one Bowen. An added complication existed in the shape of a grant on behalf of Samuel Ferrar, son of the martyr bishop, Robert Ferrar. Davies rejected the grant of the earls as a manifest forgery; but he considered that of Ferrar to be authentic, though he could hardly admit it in view of his own collation.[104] In his predicament he turned to Archbishop Parker for advice. The archbishop's reply was vague and guarded, but Davies seemed to derive great strength and comfort from it.[105] The final outcome of the dispute is not certainly known, but there is good reason for thinking Davies to have been victorious.[106]

It is possible that the two earls continued the feud through the agency of one Cary, a groom of the Queen's chamber. This man shortly afterwards obtained a commission to enquire into concealed lands. Such a commission was a favourite device of the speculating landsharks, and covered a multitude of frauds and injustices.[107] It was on the allegedly collegiate church of Llanddewibrefi that Cary battened. The idea of founding a college on the site of the legendary synod of Llanddewi had first been mooted by Bishop Beck in 1287, but at the time of Reformation a Chantry commissioner reported that there was some doubt whether a true college had in fact been established. In 1569, Richard Davies insisted that it had never come into existence, and that the Court of Augmentations had given judgment to that effect in Edward VI's day.[108] Nevertheless, Cary informed the Queen that Llanddewi was a concealed college. For his reward he was allowed to lease the lands for £40 a year – a very happy bargain, since he was able to sublet them to the Vaughans of Trawscoed for £140 a year.[109]

His success whetted Cary's appetite. He next brought a writ of intrusion against the incumbent of Llanddewibrefi, but was at first rebuffed by the decision of a jury of 'substantial gentlemen out of Herefordshire', who, in 1567, found judgment against him; and declared the church to be 'no college nor concealed'.[110] But juries could be bought to 'swerve from the truth', by 'racking of evidence, and also by affection, fear, or favour', and in the following year another jury gave a verdict in Cary's favour. This brought not only Llanddewi into his net, but also thirteen other parish churches as parts and members of the supposed college. From the incumbents and farmers of these, he was claiming arrears of tithes amounting to £3,420, and in addition, £2,000 from Davies himself in respect of the parsonage of Llanarth and the chapel of Llanina. The dispute dragged out its tedious course until after the bishop's death, when the triumphant Cary, with characteristic rapacity, sued his widow for arrears of rent.[111]

One of the consequences of these frequent and bitter exchanges between the clergy and laity was that the former tended to become as shameless as their adversaries. Even the best Elizabethan bishops did not entirely escape the taint, while the administration of some 'rapidly degenerated into avarice and corruption'.[112] Davies himself has aquired an unenviable notoriety for making use of his office for private profit, particularly by selling collations. It was his successor, Middleton, who first averred that Davies had leased all the episcopal lands, granted away the advowsons of all livings worth more than £10 a year and allowed all the episcopal residences to fall into ruin.[113] The available records show, in fact, that there were about 130 livings within the bishop's gift in the sixteenth century and that Davies disposed of the rights of presentation in about 38 of them – so it would hardly be fair to describe this, as some authors have done, as 'most of the livings within his gift'.[114] To entrust the nomination of an incumbent to a laymen in this way was not the surest guarantee of a worthy choice. The lay patron often took the opportunity of presenting a client or relative without much regard to his suitability. In addition, he often took advantage of his hold over the nominee to extract a large sum of money, or a favourable lease for himself or his dependants. Davies must have been aware of these risks. The only excuse that can be offered for him is that he was not alone among his contemporaries in making these grants. That he has become more than ordinarily notorious for doing so is due to a number of reasons. It is partly because he was able to make a large number of grants during his unusually long episcopate; partly because the chapter records, not available before 1560, record all his deeds; and partly because Middleton gave him such a bad name. At the same time he cannot be entirely absolved from blame. He knew the value set on these privileges, and it would be straining credulity very far to suggest that he was so ingenuous as to part with them uncompensated, except possibly to members of Thomas Huet's family and his own. Advowsons granted to these two families accounted for well over a third of the total number of grants made. Davies's solicitude, and that of Huet, for his own family's interests was characteristic of the Elizabethan age, as it had been of an earlier Tudor generation.[115] Prelates, no less than squires, felt the pull of family interests. They knew the pinch of maintaining their children on reduced revenues, and tended to forget they were the trustees of an entailed inheritance and not the proprietors of a landed estate.

Hardly less prejudicial to the best interests of the Church was the wholesale leasing of episcopal estates and parish tithes. In this respect, too, Davies sought to provide for his relatives in a way that did him greater credit as a *paterfamilias* than as a bishop. All his sons were given extensive leases, two of them at a very tender age. In 1563, when his youngest son, Gerson, was hardly more than a baby, the lease of the prebend of Lampeter was drawn up in his name. It was subsequently confirmed and extended.[116] The second son, Peregrine, had been made archdeacon of Cardigan while still a boy. When he gave up his preferment a few years later, in 1568, he was compensated by being allowed to lease the living of Llandovery for 70 years.[117] He and Davies's eldest son, Richard, were joint lessees of a number of episcopal manors, including those of Brawdy and Painscastle with the prebend of Brawdy.[118] Nor did Bishop Davies overlook the claims of his wife and her relatives. Mrs. Davies leased the rectory of Ystrad in Cardiganshire until 1568, when it was transferred to her brother, Thomas Woodforde. Woodforde was also made receiver-general of the collegiate church of Brecon.[119] Both he and his brother, James, also benefited from their brother-in-law's openhandedness in his grants of advowsons. In all this Davies was behaving no differently from other prelates. His own chapter's records make it clear that it was quite usual for the clergy to oblige their kinsmen in this way. Indeed, as well-known and respected a figure as the precentor of St. David's, Thomas Huet, could be accused in the court of Chancery by the diocesan treasurer, Hugh Price, of having unlawfully kept the three seals of the chapter in his own possession and thereby being able to lease many valuable estates to his own profit.[120] We may therefore feel fairly sure that Huet and the chapter had no qualms about confirming their bishop's grant and leases. If Davies is to be reproached it must be for failing to rise above the general level of the age, not for sinking below it.

IV. Davies's Scholarship and Literary Pursuits

One of the most significant aspects of Richard Davies's cultural interests was his pride in the literature of Wales and his sensitivity to its classic charm. Sprung as he was from families of Welsh *uchelwyr* he shared their proud heritage of appreciation and patronage of the literary art. As a boy he may well have been initiated by his mother's kinsman, Gruffudd ab Ieuan ap Llywelyn Fychan, a gentleman-poet of more than average distinction, into some of the mysteries of a thousand years and more of bardic lore. It was in the poet's library, too, that he seems to have made his first contact with manuscripts containing Welsh literature. There is even an unsubstantiated tradition that the young Richard won an award at the Caerwys bardic eisteddfod of 1523. But it does not appear that he underwent any formal apprenticeship as a poet until he went to St. Asaph in 1560. There he is reputed to have sat at the feet of Gruffudd Hiraethog, a *pencerdd* (master poet) with many distinguished pupils. It is as well for Gruffudd's fame as a teacher that it does not depend on his episcopal pupil's verses. His surviving efforts are uninspired and suggest that he had not the skill or the leisure to woo the muse.[121] They are of interest only because they reveal the author's active as well as receptive delight in poetry.

He rendered greater service to verse as a patron than as a poet. As befitted a man of his birth and station he delighted to welcome bards to his hearth. At least two of the most notable poets of the age, William Llŷn and Siôn Tudur, both pupils of his own master Gruffudd Hiraethog, were among his honoured guests. If what they say is true, Davies's palace at Abergwili always offered an open door to members of their fraternity. Siôn Tudur described it as 'aber beirdd ai bir ai bwyd' ('confluence of poets with its beer and food').[122] His comrade, William Llŷn, was no less appreciative of the bishop's munificence, describing with equal gusto the wine, feasting and gold as well as the more spiritual delights of excellent preaching which he received there.[123] All this might easily be discounted as the conventional flattery of professional bards were it not reinforced by similar tributes from the north Welsh priest, Robert Middleton, who was not a professional poet and who would seem to have little to gain from insincere praise.[124] Even the Catholic poet, Hywel ap Syr Mathew, spoke no less warmly of the hospitality and patronage he received at Abergwili. Nor were the poets the only people to be welcomed there. Davies also invited scholars like Salesbury and Huet there, and he retained in his service 'younger brothers of the best houses in the country, to whom with his own sons . . . he gave good maintenance and education'.[125] All in all he must have maintained a stimulating and colourful household. Clerics and men of affairs, bards and squires, lawyers and scholars, all rubbed shoulders with one another; Renaissance scholarship was grafted on to the centuries-old poetry of Wales; sixteenth-century acquisitiveness went side by side with the hospitality of tribal society. Not the least remarkable feature was the conscious assumption by the Protestant bishop of the responsibility for maintaining hospitality, learning and literature, which had been shouldered in earlier ages by the religious houses.

Davies's cultural interests and contacts were not parochial, any more than his reputation. His prestige as a scholar stood high in an age when savants were by no means rare and he was consulted by the notably scholarly Archbishop Parker on more than one occasion on points of scholarship, as well as being chosen by the primate as one of the translators for the English Bible.[126] During the time that William Salesbury spent at Abergwili working on the translation of the New Testament into Welsh, Parker sent Davies and his collaborator a book written in a mysterious language.

Both were completely mystified by this esoteric work, now identified as an Armenian psalter.[127] In their replies to Parker both Davies and Salesbury, well aware of the primate's deep interest in the history of the Church in Britain, and especially of his desire to find in early British history authentic precedents for the practices and beliefs of contemporary reformers, kept him informed of their researches in the field of Welsh ecclesiastical history. Much of the information then sent him was later incorporated into Parker's own book *De Antiquitate* and also into Davies's Address to the Welsh Nation with which he prefaced the Welsh New Testament of 1567.[128] On another occasion, also, Parker got in touch with Davies for information. In 1568 he wrote asking for more details of Sulien, Davies's illustrious predecessor as bishop of St. David's in the eleventh century. Davies tried to satisfy his curiosity by translating into Latin a long extract from *Brut y Tywysogyon* ('the Chronicle of the Princes') containing references to Sulien and his family.[129]

A further interesting connection between Davies and leading humanistic circles is suggested by the overwhelmingly strong probability that Richard Davies is the original of 'Diggon Davie', the shepherd of the ninth eclogue in Spenser's famous pastoral poem, *The Shepheardes Calender*. It is known that Diggon was a real contemporary person and not a literary creation. All his characteristics fit Richard Davies perfectly. He was certainly a leading cleric and his speech characteristics were intended to show he was a Welshman. The similarity between the name 'Diggon Davie' and Richard Davies is completely typical of the way in which Spenser playfully modified the names of other bishops among his 'shepherds'. Davies was known to have been very friendly with some of Spenser's other leading patrons, notably Archbishop Grindal, Bishop John Young, and Sir Henry Sidney and his son, Philip. The internal evidence of the content of the eclogue also strongly attests that Spenser intended 'Diggon Davie' to be recognized immediately by all initiates as Richard Davies.[130] If this is in fact so then it places Davies near the centre of a major group of English humanists with strongly reformist, even Puritan, sympathies; not the extreme allegiance that wanted to move all the way towards the Genevan model, but the more moderate element which had experienced religious freedom in exile and which wanted to simplify the worship of the Church of England and 'purify' it of many of its surviving vestiges of 'papistry'.

The influence of the opinions of such circles can be traced to some extent in such evidence as we have of Davies's social and educational values. He shared their views of the importance of the new kind of reforming humanism as the basis of secular education and training,[131] and in particular its emphasis on the responsibility of the aristocracy. Davies's opinions come out most clearly in his published *Funeral Sermon* preached on the death of the earl of Essex in 1577. Having stressed that 'valiant and courageous noblemen' were 'bulwarks and walls of defence of the whole realm' he went on to single out the earl of Essex as a paragon of the virtues of the ancient classical world but grounded in the reformed religion. 'The wells of nobility are *Prudence, Fortitude, Justice,* and *Temperance:* the hill whence they spring is the fear of God or true religion', for the ability to 'discern betwixt true religion and the hypocritical false religion' was the necessary point of 'true nobility'.[132] In view of the bishop's admiration of the earl and the close similarity of their views, it was hardly surprising that they should both have been associated in 1576 in the founding of one of the new seminaries of their kind of Protestant humanism, the Queen Elizabeth grammar school at Carmarthen.

The fusion of the diverse elements in Davies's intellectual and religious convictions is best seen in his Address to the Welsh Nation and his translations of parts of the New Testament. In them the free play of the Renaissance scholar's skill in languages and delight in antiquities was shaped and directed by the convictions of an ardent reformer. Here, too, is seen the respect for learning with which Oxford endowed him, and, irradiating all he wrote, is that instinctive awareness of the genius of his own language given him by his upbringing and his poetic training. All this stood Wales in good stead, for there were but few men in Elizabeth's reign who had the desire and the knowledge to turn the Bible into Welsh. Davies may have taken the first steps during his stay at St. Asaph when he and Salesbury, as near neighbours, very probably came into close contact with one another. The act of 1563 seems to have been more likely to have been engineered by him than anyone else. Once the act had been passed he assumed the initiative for implementing its provisions and was, indeed, the only bishop to take a personal share in carrying out its terms. His qualifications for the task won the warm commendation of his colleague, William Salesbury, the greatest Welsh scholar of the century, from whom praise was praise indeed. Later critics have been no less generous in their tributes to his skill in handling the original versions of the scriptures, and the vigour and clarity of his Welsh prose.[133]

When Salesbury and Davies's first translation of the New Testament into Welsh was published in 1567 Davies wrote, as a preface to it, his well-known *Epistol at y Cembru* or Address to the Welsh Nation. It is an interesting and revealing document; but it is a curious work, full of unsound history, fervent Protestantism, and wholehearted patriotism. Its methods of reasoning are essentially those of the Middle Ages; it relies on the weight of its authorities, not the value of its logic, to convince the reader. Or, as Davies himself put it in another context, 'the credit and authority of things found out and committed to writing . . . depends on the first authors'.[134] The value of the Address for the student of literature or theology is negligible; but, though slight in substance, it is of considerable interest as an indication of its author's approach to contemporary religious and scholarly controversies (see also below, pp. 207-14). He was particularly anxious to prove to his fellow-countrymen that the Christian faith had originally been introduced to their ancestors, the ancient British, in pure and undefiled form by Joseph of Arimathea. It was then based firmly on the rock of Christ's teaching and the authority of the scriptures. It had been maintained intact in all its pristine purity despite the savage persecution of Roman emperors, the subversive wiles of Pelagian heretics and the on-slaughts of pagan invaders. Only at the end of the sixth century when Augustine of Canterbury introduced Romanish 'superstitions' and induced Anglo-Saxon rulers to force the Welsh to receive them at the point of the sword, did the Welsh fall from grace. Thereafter the floodgates were opened to all kinds of impurity and idolatry, and the Welsh sank lower and lower into the depths of ignorance and false faith. So low had they fallen that they, whose forefathers had been among the foremost to receive and welcome Christian teaching in apostolic times, were now among the last nations in Europe to receive it in its 'second flowering' as a result of the Reformation. Only repentance and acceptance of reformed teaching could restore to them the long-departed glory of early British Christianity. Throughout Davies stressed the central doctrines of the Reformation: that reformed religion was not an innovation but that it represented a return to the sanctity and simplicity of the Church of Christ and his apostles; that the overriding authority on which all belief and worship must be based was that of the scriptures; and that it was faith not works which justified men. The Address has rightly been stressed as a major turning point in the evolution of Welsh reformers' view of history.[135] It put forward two central arguments that were likely to be particularly congenial to contemporaries and which were certainly major influences on subsequent Welsh writers. The first was that the Reformation was not a brash innovation unrooted in tradition or early authority, The other was that reformed doctrine, far from being alien to Wales, was a return to its most glorious indigenous inheritance (see below, pp. 212-14).

Much of Davies's 'historical' information was derived from the tainted source of Geoffrey of Monmouth's *Historia Regum*. But although he accepted Geoffrey's work in substance he was often critical in details. For instance he was very suspicious of Geoffrey's account of the conversion of the whole island of Britain by Fagan and Damian, the emissaries whom Pope Eleutherius was supposed to have sent to Britain about A.D. 180 at the request of king Lucius son of Coel (see below, pp. 209-10). Remembering, perhaps, the disappointingly slow reaction to his own efforts as a reformer, Davies remarked caustically that the dramatically swift conversion of the whole island attributed to Fagan and Damian was improbable for no large and populous kingdom is converted overnight. In addition to the information culled from Geoffrey's work Davies used other chronicle sources like the *Brut y Tywysogyon* with which his antiquarian researches had made him familiar and about which he and Salesbury had been corresponding with Parker. Not the least interesting feature of the Address is the use which Davies made in it of the work of Welsh poets as *pièces justificatives*. Their authority, of course, he readily recognized was in no way comparable with that of the Bible; but he considered that he, like St. Paul at Athens, could properly liken an ancient poet to a prophet. This furnishes further proof – if that were needed – of the high place that the native literature held in his esteem. Furthermore, the use he made of it suggests that he expected a wide circle of readers to feel as he did.

His contribution to the actual translation of the New Testament was very modest as compared with that of Salesbury. It consisted of the First Epistle to Timothy, the Epistle to the Hebrews, the Epistle of James, and the Epistles of Peter. It has already received a good deal of attention,[136] and there is little that needs to be added here. It may suffice to quote the opinion of so eminent a judge of Welsh prose as W. J. Gruffydd that of the three translators of 1567 Davies writes much the most fluent Welsh; his, too, is the surest grasp of idiom and expression; characterized by the assurance of an author long accustomed to writing Welsh[137] – a remarkable tribute to a man most of whose adult life had been spent out of Wales! Nor was Davies's translation marred by the pedantry and the idiosyncrasies which lessened so much of the value of Salesbury's translation (see below, pp. 198-200). He was nothing like as erudite as his coadjutor, but neither was he as dazzled by the glory of the classics and he had a surer instinct for making his Welsh prose acceptable and intelligible to his fellow-countrymen.

Along with the New Testament of 1567 there also appeared the first Welsh version of the Book of Common Prayer, actually published a short time before the New Testament. For a long time this was either attributed solely to Richard Davies or was regarded as a joint work for which the bishop was mainly responsible. But examination of the text makes it quite clear that Salesbury was responsible for most if not all of it (see below pp. 197-8).

There is no doubt that the New Testament was regarded by Davies and Salesbury as no more than the first instalment of the translation of the whole Bible. Davies himself said so

in his preface of 1567 where he expressed the hope that the Old
Testament would soon follow. The needs of the people, as well as
the terms of the act of 1563, urgently called for it. But the hopes
of the translators never materialized. The reason for their failure
to finish the work has usually been given as an irreconcilable quarrel
over the meaning of a single word. Sir John Wynn, who first told
the story,[138] was prone to make mistakes in detail, and he may have
been quite wrong in his account of the origin of the disagreement,
if indeed there ever was one. But he would seem to have no obvious
reason to invent such a dispute, though he may have misunderstood
the real nature of it. If the two men did indeed disagree, it is likely
that it was for a more fundamental reason. That may have been
Salesbury's views about orthography. Salesbury's quirks over
language were very curious indeed (see below pp. 198-9), and it
would not have been surprising if Davies had urged upon his collaborator the need for making more concessions in the interests of
intelligibility. If he did, he would undoubtedly have found in
Salesbury a stiff and touchy opponent, unlikely to give way with
any grace or willingness. Disagreement between them may have
been smouldering for a long time before it finally flared up into an
open quarrel about the meaning of one word. The break between
the two men had a very different effect upon each. Salesbury, for
one reason or another, became an Achilles sulking in his tent
(see below. pp. 200-1). Davies proceeded to work on a fresh translation of some books of the New Testament. In this new translation,
surviving only in manuscript form among the Gwysaney papers, he
not only rejected Salesburian influences, but also began to translate
afresh some of the books assigned to Salesbury in the New
Testament of 1567.[139] All this seems to strengthen the suggestion
that he and Salesbury had quarrelled over the latter's opinions about
language. But it also seems to indicate that Davies, left to himself,
lacked the drive or the leisure, or both, to see a work through to
completion in the way that Salesbury could, either alone or in
collaboration.

In many ways it is sad that Davies was not able to influence Salesbury more strongly. If he could have done so it might not only
have led to the completion of the Old Testament but might also
have saved the New Testament and the Prayer Book from the
peculiarities that marred them. For Davies, if less of a scholar than
Salesbury, was also less of a pedant; and if he was much less versed
in the past history of the Welsh language and its literature, as
a shepherd of souls he was much more closely attuned to the practical needs of the parish priest and his parishioners. Yet, whatever
their mistakes or their failures, both he and Salesbury have a secure
place among that little band of pioneers to whom the language and
religion of Wales owe so incalculable a debt.

NOTES

[1] Archdeacon D. R. Thomas, in his *The Life of Richard Davies and Willam Salesbury* (Oswestry, 1902), the only biography of Davies, other than the valuable article in *The Dictionary of National Biography*, did not ignore Davies's exile or his activities as a bishop, but he did treat them as incidental to his main purpose, which was to show the extent of Davies's contributions to the translations.

[2] For details see C. Ashton, *Bywyd ac Amserau yr Esgob Morgan* (Treherbert, 1891), pp. 67-8.

[3] H. Grieve 'The deprived clergy in Essex, 1553-61', *Trans. Royal Hist. Soc.*, iv, XXII (1940), 145.

[4] *Acts of the Privy Council of England*, ed. J. R. Dasent (thirty-two vols., London, 1890-1907), III, 321, 328 and 361 respectively.

[5] *Calendar Patent Rolls, Philip and Mary*, 1553-8, ed. M. Giuseppi (four vols., London, 1936-38), I, 357.

[6] C. H. Garrett, *The Marian Exiles* (Cambridge, 1928), p. 15.

[7] Thus Knox was promptly required to leave Frankfort in 1555 when it was discovered that he had uttered seditious words concerning the Emperor in 1553. Knox himself accused his adversaries of having clung to their old 'shot-anchor' of 'non est Caesaris amicus' in order to be rid of him. Knox, *Works*, ed. D. Laing (Edinburgh, 1846-54), IV, p. 67.

[8] W. Whittingham, *A Brief Discourse of the Troubles begun at Frankfort* . . . Ed. J. Petheram (London, 1846), p. 155.

[9] Garrett, *op. cit.*, p. 20.

[10] Sir John Wynn, *History of the Gwydir Family*, ed. J. Ballinger (Cardiff, 1927), pp. 64-5.

[11] Garrett, *op. cit.*, p. 20.

[12] M. M. Knappen, *Tudor Puritanism* (Chicago, 1938), p. 145.

[13] Whittingham, *Troubles* p. 184.

[14] This list, the *Livre des Anglais*, is printed as an appendix in C. Martin, *Les protestants anglais refugiés à Genève au temps de Calvin* 1555-60 (Geneva, 1915).

[15] Ibid., pp. 47-8.

[16] Knox, *Works*, IV, p. 44.

[17] Garrett, *op. cit.*, p. 141.

[18] G. Baskerville, 'Married clergy and pensioned religious in Norwich diocese, 1555', *Eng. Hist. Rev.*, XLVIII (1933), p. 55.

[19] Whittingham, *op. cit.*, p. 60.

[20] Garrett, *op. cit.*, p. 141.

[21] Whittingham, *op. cit.*, p. 65.

[22] Ibid., p. 168.

[23] His first act was to address a letter to fifteen members of the church, among whom was Richard Davies, appealing to them to help him to conciliate the contending parties (Whittingham, *op. cit.*, p. 65).

[24] Horne was threatening an appeal to the magistrates to remove his opponents.

[25] Whittingham claimed that Chambers refused to give any more to those who opposed him and Horne (*Troubles*, p. 104).

[26] *Ibid.*, p. 117.

[27] Quoted in H. E. Jacobs, *The Lutheran Movement in England* (Philadelphia, 1908), p. 346.

[28] Of the exiles who became bishops during Elizabeth's reign, nearly all were drawn from members of the more conservative congregations, e.g. Horne of Winchester, Cox of Ely, Berkeley of Bath and Wells, Bentham of Coventry (all at Frankfort); Sandys of Worcester, Grindal of London and Canterbury (both at Strasbourg); Parkhurst of Norwich, Pilkington of Durham, and Jewel of Salisbury (all at Zurich). All the leading bishops of the first years of Elizabeth's reign had been in exile, with the exception of Parker, who had remained in England in hiding.

[29] B. M. Harleian MS., 595, ff. 79-92; cf. also Edward Owen, *Catalogue of Manuscripts relating to Wales in the British Museum* (4 parts. Cymmrodorion Record Series, no. 4), II, 159-60.

[30] Williams, *Welsh Church*, p. 283.

[31] C. Skeel, *The Council in the Marches of Wales* (London, 1904), p. 181; E. A. Lewis, *Early Chancery Proceedings relating to Wales* (Cardiff, 1937), p. 47,

[32] D. Wilkins, *Concilia Magnae Britanniae et Hiberniae* . . . 446-1718 (4 vols. London, 1737), IV, 237, 268, 293-4.

[33] P. Collinson, *The Elizabethan Puritan Movement* (London, 1967), pp. 168-176.

[34] *D.N.B.*, *s.n.* Richard Davies.

[33] B. M. Lansdowne MS., 8, ff. 193, 195, 199 and 202. Some of them are printed in M. Parker, *Correspondence* (Parker Soc., 1853).

[34] Lansdowne MS., 8, f. 193.

[35] *Journals of the House of Lords* (London, 1846), Volume I, *passim*; vol. II, 20-4.

[36] *Ibid.*, I, 610-13. Thomas Davies of St. Asaph was the only other Welsh bishop who was present at all. He attended the first two hearings. Scory of Hereford, also affected by the terms of the Act, was present at the second hearing.

[39] Ashton, *William Morgan*, p. 64. For Llwyd's part, see Geraint Gruffydd, *Llên Cymru*, IV (1956), 114-15, 233.

[40] R. Flenley (ed.), *Calendar of the Register of the Council in the Marches of Wales* (Cymmrodorion Rec. Ser., no. 8), pp. 109, 126, 187-9, 190.

[41] *Ibid.*, p. 139.

[42] *Ibid.*, p. 140.

[43] J. Phillips, 'Glimpses of Elizabethan Pembrokeshire', *Arch. Camb.*, v, XIV, 308-23, XVI, 269-83; vi, IV, 253-74; D. Mathew, 'Cornish and Welsh pirates in the reign of Queen Elizabeth', *Eng. Hist. Rev.*, XXXIX (1924), 337-48; E. R. Williams, *Some Studies in Elizabethan Wales* (Newtown, 1924).

[44] P.R.O., S.P. 12, vol. 126, no. 40.

[45] *Acts Privy Council*, VII, 265 *et. seq.* For the report of these commissioners, P.R.O. S.P. 12, vol. 39, no. 27.

[46] P.R.O., S.P. 12, vol. 126, no. 40.

[47] *Acts Privy Council*, VII, 279.

[48] R. Rawlinson (ed.), *The History of . . . Sir John Perrott* (London, 1728), p. 20.

[49] *Gwydir Family*, p. 64.

[50] Rawlinson, *Perrott*, p. 20.

[51] *Acts Privy Council*, VII, 375-6.

[52] Ibid., VII, 372-3, VIII, 11-2, 12-13, 41.

[53] Richard Davies, *Funeral Sermon preached at Carmarthen on the Death of the Earl of Essex* (London, 1577), no pagination.

[54] In his prefatory 'Address to the Welsh Nation' for the first Welsh New Testament of 1567.

[55] Cf. P.R.O., S.P. 12, vol. 107, which contains a series of reports, including those by William Gerard and David Lewis, on the state of Wales in 1576.

[56] *Acts Privy Council*, XI, 349.

[57] P.R.O. S.P. 12, vol. 110, no. 13; cf. also *BBCS*, VI (1931-3), 70-2. For details of Phillips's career, W. R. Williams, *The History of the Great Sessions in Wales*, 1542-1830 (Brecon, 1889), pp. 88-9.

[58] Quoted in Skeel, *Council of the Marches*, p. 110.

[59] The text of the accusations, with Davies's replies to them, will be found in P.R.O , S.P. 12, vol. 131, nos. 42, 42(1). Some extracts are published in Thomas, *Davies and Salesbury*, pp. 45-8.

[60] P.R.O., S.P. 12, vol. 131 no. 42.

[61] Both are bound in a single volume along with the register of Henry Morgan (1554-9). They constitute the second volume of St. David's episcopal registers and are now deposited in the National Library of Wales. A calendar of them, with analytical introduction, will be found in G. Williams, 'The episcopal registers of St. David's 1554-65', *BBCS*, XIV (1950), 45-54, 125-38.

[62] Henry Gee, *The Elizabethan Settlement* took 1565 as a deadline, but H. N. Birt, *The Elizabethan Religious Settlement* (London, 1907), showed that there were papist objectors after that date.

[63] For further details, *BBCS*, XIV, 125-38.

[64] *Ibid.*, XIV, 45-54.

[65] W. H. Frère, *The Marian Reaction in its Relation to the English Clergy* (London, 1896), p. 31 n.

[66] *Zurich Letters* (2 vols. Parker Soc., 1842-5), I, 45.

[67] *Ibid.*, I, 33; cf. also, pp. 11, 29, 40, 55, 77, 92.

[68] *BBCS.*, XIV, 125-38.

[69] *Camden Miscellany*, IX, 11-23.

[70] W. P. M. Kennedy, *Elizabethan Episcopal Administration* (3 vols. Alcuin Club, 1925), II, 145 ff.

[71] *Ibid.*, II, 146-8.

[72] *Ibid.*, II, 148-50. Bishop Robinson reported on similar practices in the diocese of Bangor, P.R.O., S.P. 12, vol. 69, no. 14.

[73] Kennedy, *Episc. Administration*, II, 149-50.

[74] Cf. the complaints of Bishop Berkeley of Bath and Wells (1560-81), P.R.O. S.P. 12, vol. 16, no. 27 and Strype, *Annals*, III, i, 481.

[75] P.R.O., S.P. 12, vol. 66, nos. 26, 26(i); cf. Thomas, *Davies and Salesbury*, pp. 41-3.

[76] P.R.O., S.P. 12, vol. 162, no. 29.

[77] *Zurich Letters*, I, 98.

[78] P.R.O., S.P. 12, vol. 66, no. 26(i); cf. Thomas, *Davies and Salesbury*, p. 39.

[79] Ibid., and S.P. 12. vol. 162, no. 29.

[80] Cf. note 78.

[81] B. M. Harleian MS. 595, f. 79.

[82] P.R.O., S.P. 12, vol. 66, no. 26(i); cf. Thomas, *Davies and Salesbury*, pp. 38-41.

[83] *Ibid.*, p. 42.

[84] *Ibid.*, p. 43.

[85] N.L.W., St. David's Chapter Acts, I, 52, 57, 89, 114, 241, II, 1. Cf. also W. B. Jones and E. A. Freeman, *St. David's*, pp. 338-41.

[86] Thomas, *Davies and Salesbury*, p. 43.

[87] *Funeral Sermon* (1577).

[88] P.R.O., S.P. 12, vol. 162, no. 29.

[89] *Cal. State Papers, Spanish, Elizabeth*, II, 147.

[90] Thomas, *Davies and Salesbury*, pp. 37-8.

[91] P.R.O., S.P. 12, vol. 118, no. 11(i).

[92] *Ibid.*, nos. 8, 10 and 11(ii).

[93] Cf. Whitgift's comments in his covering letter, *ibid.* no. 11.

[94] B. M. Lansdowne MS., 3, no. 4.

[95] P.R.O., S.P. 12, vol. 123, no. 11.

[96] N.L.W., St. David's Chapter Acts, I, 236.

[97] *West Wales Historical Records* (Carmarthen, 1912), VI, 30-1.

[98] See above, pp. 172-3.

[99] Thomas, *Davies and Salesbury*, p. 43.

[100] P.R.O., S.P. 12, vol. 120, no. 42(i).

[101] *Ibid.*

[102] N.L.W., St. David's Episcopal Registers, 1554-65, ff. 38-9.

[103] *D.N.B.*, *s.n.* Meyrick.

[104] *Parker Correspondence*, p. 67.

[105] *Ibid.*, p. 279.

[106] Lewis Gwynn was the incumbent sued for arrears of rent in 1567, see pp. 178-9.

[107] Many dioceses suffered badly from these commissions, Strype, *Annals*, II, i, 312, 513; E. Grindal, *Remains* (Parker Soc., 1843), p. 344.

[108] P.R.O., S.P. 12, vol. 49, nos. 35, 35(i). For the history of the collegiate church see G. Williams, *Ceredigion*, IV, iv (1963), 336-52.

[109] *Ibid.*   [110] *Ibid.*, cf. Strype, *Annals*, III, ii, 226-7.   [111] *Ibid.*

[112] W. H. Frère, *History of the English Church*, 1558-1603 (London, 1903), p. 191.

[113] He has been followed by later authors, Jones and Freeman, *St. David's*, pp. 337-8.

[114] *Ibid.*   [115] Williams, *Welsh Church*, pp. 320-4.

[116] N.L.W., St. David's Chapter Acts, I, 71-2, 229-31.

[117] *Ibid.*, I, 213-4.   [118] *Ibid.*, II, 60-3.   [119] *Ibid.*, I, 144-6, 163-4, 213.

[120] P.R.O., C3/57/6.

[121] Some are printed in Thomas, *Davies and Salesbury*, p. 16; others in my *Bywyd ac Amserau yr Esgob Richard Davies*, pp. 119-21.

[122] Thomas, *Davies and Salesbury*, p. 16.

[123] J. C. Morrice (ed.), *Barddoniaeth Wiliam Llŷn* (Bangor, 1908), pp. 166-8.

[124] Thomas, *Davies and Salesbury*, pp. 50-2.

[125] Wynn, *Gwydir Family*, pp. 50-2.

[126] Robin Flower, 'William Salesbury, Richard Davies and Archbishop Parker', and 'Richard Davies, William Cecil and Giraldus Cambrensis', in *N.L.W. Journal*, II, 7-14 and III, 11-14.

[127] Flower, *N.L.W. Journal*, II, 11.

[128]. *Ibid.* pp. 13-14.

[129] G. Williams, 'Bishop Sulien, Bishop Richard Davies and Archbishop Parker', *N.L.W. Journal*, V (1948), 215-9.

[130] V. B. Hulbert, 'Diggon Davie', *Journal of English and Germanic Philology*, XLI (1942), 349-67; P. McLane, 'Diggon Davie again', *ibid.*, XLVI (1947), 144-9; G. Williams, 'Richard Davies . . . a'r *Shepheardes Calender*', *Llên Cymru*, II (1953), 232-6.

[131] See D. Bush, *The Renaissance and English Humanism* (Toronto, 1939), ch. III; P. N. Siegel, 'English Humanism and the new Tudor aristocracy', *Journal History of Ideas*, XIII (1952), 450-68.

[132] *Funeral Sermon.*

[133] T. C. Edwards in *Trans. Liverpool Welsh National Society*, 1885-6, pp. 60-2; W. J. Gruffydd, *Llên Cymru*, pp. 54-5; Thomas, *Davies and Salesbury*, pp. 112, 145-7.

[134] *Funeral Sermon.*

[135] Saunders Lewis, 'Y ddamcaniaeth eglwysig Brotestannaidd', *Efrydiau Catholig*, II (1947), 36-55.

[136] Thomas, *Davies and Salesbury*, passim; Gruffydd, *Llên Cymru*, chs. iii and iv; and Thomas Parry, *Hanes Llenyddiaeth Gymraeg* (Cardiff, 1944), pp. 150-4.

[137] Gruffydd, *Llên Cymru*, p. 54.

[138] *Gwydir Family*, p. 64.

[139] Thomas, *Davies and Salesbury*, pp. 144 ff.

VIII. THE ACHIEVEMENT OF
WILLIAM SALESBURY

It is not often that a single individual can be said radically to have influenced the course of a nation's history. This must all the more rarely be true of a man who was not a king nor a chief minister, neither a soldier nor a statesman, but a scholar and a writer. Yet we believe that claim can, with justice, be made for William Salesbury. We shall try to show why in more detail later; but the essence of the case is this: that the primary reason why Wales retained an individual literature and culture of her own after the sixteenth century was Salesbury's vision of her need and the steps he took to meet it. Denbighshire has cause to feel the deepest pride in him as one of the greatest of her sons. The long and notable history of the county's literary tradition, second to none in Wales, was traced some years ago in a singularly brilliant paper by Professor Griffith John Williams.[1] In all that sustained and shining heritage, no one made a more potent contribution than William Salesbury.

Little purpose would be served in dwelling overlong on such biographical details as are available to us. Even by the scanty and unpretentious standards of biographies of other Tudor Welshmen, what information we have about his life is remarkably sparse. Professor W. J. Gruffydd's comment that William Salesbury's history is the history of his work, and that not much more can be said of him with certainty than that he was the author of Welsh books[2] remains profoundly true.[3] However, Salesbury's family name in itself tells us a good deal about him. It is one of the most famous in Denbighshire's history, and none of the county's clans is better known than these prolific, thrustful, intelligent and opportunist Salesburys. Admittedly, we can no longer accept so distinguished a pedigree for them as they once arrogated to themselves. True to the best genealogical fashion, they found for themselves an ancestor who was one of the Conqueror's companions. But that splendid and romantic forebear of theirs, Adam of Salzburg, has faded away in the light of modern research. Thanks to Mr. W. J. Smith, we can now trace them back to humbler yeoman origin in the lordship of Denbigh in the fourteenth century.[4] This makes their subsequent rise to swift and decisive supremacy in Tudor and Stuart Denbighshire the more, not the less, remarkable. Though obviously not Welsh by origins, the family showed a remarkable propensity for both absorbing and stimulating the literary and cultural traditions with which they were surrounded. As participants as well as patrons, they were to make a notable contribution to Welsh letters. Henry

Salesbury of Dolbeleidr was the author of a Welsh grammar (1593), Thomas Salesbury published Welsh versions of the Psalms by William Middleton (1603) and Edward Kyffin (1603), while William Salesbury was to become the most famous of them all.

William Salesbury did not belong to the main branch of the family at Lleweni. His grandfather, Robert, had belonged to it, but being a younger son, he had successfully found himself an heiress— Gwenhwyfar, daughter and heiress of Rhys ab Einion Fychan, of Plas Isaf, Llanrwst. Their son, Foulk, also of Plas Isaf, married Annes, daughter of William ap Gruffydd ap Robin, and by her had two sons, Robert and William. It seems unlikely that William was born at Plas Isaf, although his father had inherited it. He tells us in one of his books, *Llysieulyfr Meddyginiaethol* ('Medicinal Herb-book'), which remained unpublished in his own day,[5] that he was born in the parish of Llansannan, where his father may have had another and smaller house known as Cae Du. We do not know when he was born, but we should probably be safe in assuming that it was about the year 1520.

Neither do we know where he got his early education. The supposition that it was at Maenan Abbey has no better foundation than the old-fashioned assumption: 'When in doubt, attribute education to the nearest monastery.' But Maenan, in Salesbury's youth, was in no condition to have provided education—or edification—for anyone.[6] In the *Llysieulyfr* already referred to, Salesbury tells us that as a youth he spent some time in Lancashire. Possibly he received part of his education there. Certainly, he acquired enough of the rudiments of learning to proceed to the University of Oxford. Anthony à Wood tells us that he resided at Broadgates Hall,[7] though there is no record of his name or his degrees in the University registers. However, we know from a *cywydd* to him by Gruffudd Hiraethog that he spent some time at the University:

> Fo wyr dy gorff wrda i gyd
> foddion y saith gelfyddyd
> ystryw holl ssofestri hen
> yw/r/ dichell o ryd ychen.[8]

('Thy body knows, good man, all the ways of the seven arts, the trick of all old sophistry is the device from Oxford.')

Salesbury's father and his eldest brother both died about the time when he might have been expected to have been a student at the University, and he may have had to return home rather suddenly and unexpectedly. We know that some time between *c.* 1540 and 1546 he was involved in a dispute over land with his late brother's two heiresses. The quarrel may have derived some added bitterness from the fact that William Salesbury and his dead brother had married two sisters, daughters to Robert ap Rhys, and that William had 'put away' his wife Catrin. The dispute over the land was settled peacefully by arbitrators, of whom Ellis Price, William Salesbury's wife's brother, was one. The settlement may, however, have left a bitter taste in Salesbury's mouth, for in his introduction to one of the first of his published works, *Oll Synnwyr Pen* (1547), he referred with some animus to those 'who had deprived and despoiled him' so completely of his property. He was also involved at this time in a Star Chamber action, the details of which are almost totally obscure but which may be connected with this other dispute with his nieces.[9]

In addition to his spell at the University, Salesbury also spent some time at the Inns of Court. In 1550 he was at Thavies Inn, one of the Inns of Chancery, founded in the fourteenth century by a Welshman, John Davy, and afterwards much frequented by his fellow countrymen. There is also some suggestion that Salesbury was at this time in the service of Lord Rich.

The time he spent at Oxford and the Inns of Court could have been of crucial importance. This seems to have been the most likely occasion for him to have been brought into contact with the ideas and influences of the Renaissance and Reformation. It is improbable that he would have encountered such sources of inspiration in his native Wales; indeed, as far as religious doctrine is concerned, he tells us that in his youth he was brought up an 'earnest papist'. But of the circumstances in which he was introduced to these new seminal forces, or of the men he might have regarded as his mentors, we know nothing and appear to be able to know nothing. The fruits of such influences, however, began to appear increasingly in his works.

During the five years or so from 1547 to 1552 he was astonishingly prolific and versatile in his literary output. First he was able to publish three scholarly books of an essentially philological or literary nature: *Oll Synnwyr Pen Cymro Ynghyd* (1547), a collection of Welsh proverbs; a *Dictionary in English and Welsh* (1547), and a *Brief and Plain Introduction Teaching How to Pronounce the Letters in the British Tongue* (1550). He also produced two polemical works against Roman Catholics: *The Battery against the Popes' Buttress* (1550) and *Ban wedi ei Dynnu o Gyfraith Hywel Dda* (1550). He translated from a Latin version of Diadochus Proclus, *The Description of Sphere of the Frame of the World.* Finally in 1551, he published his Welsh translation of the epistles and gospels of the Book of Common Prayer under the title, *Cynnifer Llith a Ban* (1551). In the following year, 1552, he had completed the manuscript of his *Llyfr Rhetoreg* ('Book of Rhetoric'), but this may well have been meant only for circulation among the bards and not for publication. The sheer speed and volume of his publications between 1547 and

1552 must pose the question of whether Salesbury spent most of his time in London during these years. It is difficult to see how else he could have prepared so many works for the printers and particularly how else he could have seen them through the press. His output was such as almost to suggest that at this juncture he envisaged his career as that of a professional writer and publicist.

Some of the books he published during these years are of more interest and significance than others and deserve to be singled out for further comment. Probably the first to appear, and a book which vies with Sir John Price's *Yn y Llyfr Hwn* for the distinction of being the first Welsh printed book, was the Dictionary of 1547. Its title suggests an English-Welsh Dictionary: 'A Dictionary in English and Welsh much necessary to all such Welshmen as will speedily learn the English tongue'. But it is in fact a Welsh-English dictionary, based on a bardic word-list of a kind which was familiar enough among the Welsh poetic and literary fraternity in the sixteenth century. This apparent contradiction between the book's title and its contents led Professor W. J. Gruffydd to propound a theory that William Salesbury was distinctly ambivalent in his attitude towards teaching his fellow-countrymen to learn English. He contended that whatever lip-service Salesbury might pay to the desirability of Welshmen's learning English, a Welsh-English dictionary was no help for such a purpose; it was much more likely to enrich a Welshman's understanding of his own native culture. A more recent student of Salesbury's work, Mr Alun Mathias, dissents from this view. He holds that Salesbury, impressed by the output of English books embodying the New Learning, was sincerely desirous of helping his fellow-countrymen to master the English language. Whatever Salesbury's intentions, his dictionary may have attracted attention in influential quarters of a kind hitherto unsuspected, and not in England and Wales only. That ardent reformer, John Hooper, bishop of Gloucester, writing to his famous mentor, Henry Bullinger of Zurich, on 27th December, 1549, says

> Tell my excellent friend, Master Gessner, that there is on the road for him a Welsh dictionary, and some writings in the language of Cornubia, commonly called Cornwall.[10]

There can be no doubt that the dictionary in question was Salesbury's One cannot help wondering, also, whether this sheds some light. on Salesbury's religious associates during these years.

The other work published in 1547, *Oll Synnwyr Pen*, is even more important. It consists of a collection of Welsh proverbs, which Salesbury said he 'stole' from the poet and scholar, Gruffudd Hiraethog. Such 'felonious' practice need not perturb us; it was a common enough literary device and convention in the sixteenth century. It is the introduction to the book which is particularly interesting. There, Salesbury emphasizes the urgent need to gather together from dusty corners and cobwebbed cupboards, in which many of them lay mouldering neglected, all manuscripts containing Welsh literary treasures. The ultimate object of such an exercise would be to facilitate the translation of the Scriptures into Welsh, a literary task overriding all others in importance in Salesbury's eyes. That the Welsh language was a medium fit for the purpose, Salesbury had no doubt. Sufficient proof of that was provided by the existence of such a wealth of proverbial wisdom in the language, not unworthy of comparison with Erasmus's *Adagia* and the many other similar collections in the vernacular which had followed it. Mr. Saunders Lewis appropriately described this introduction to *Oll Synnwyr Pen* as the first manifesto of Welsh Protestant humanism. It reveals, at the outset of Salesbury's literary career, the profound four-fold preoccupation which was to dominate the whole of it: his passionate concern for the language and literature of Wales; his avid interest in the Renaissance; his deep desire that a Welsh Bible should make the Reformation a reality in Wales; and, above all, his synoptic awareness of the crisis with which the New Learning of the age confronted Welsh culture. Sooner and more clearly than anyone else, he became aware of the implications for Wales of the *zeitgeist* of the Renaissance and the Reformation: could the language and literature of medieval Wales be adapted, expanded and enriched sufficiently to become the medium of the new cultural and religious aspirations as other European languages had done? In the introduction to *Oll Synnwyr Pen*, he stated the problem with force and clarity. He added a blunt warning that time was not on the Welshman's side; it was an issue to which his own generation must find the outcome; any longer delay would be fatal. For the rest of his active life, Salesbury wrestled to provide the answer, and always one senses his acute awareness of the lonely rôle of the pioneer who has destiny and the prospect of disaster breathing hard down his neck.

The two short polemical works published in 1550—the *Battery* and the *Ban . . . o Gyfraith Hywel Dda*—are of interest chiefly because they reveal Salesbury's unmistakably Protestant sympathies. Both these publications were linked with major ecclesiastical and religious changes now being enforced by the State. The *Ban* is an attempt to justify the permission given to clerics to marry by an appeal to the provisions of the ancient Welsh laws associated with Hywel Dda. The *Battery* is an attack on the Romanist altars and the doctrine of the mass as a sacrifice associated with them. Its publication followed hard on the heels of widespread destruction of altars in the churches of England and Wales during the years 1549–50. Though the style and tone of the *Battery* are more restrained and dignified than those of many Protestant controversialists, the pamphlet nonetheless reveals its author as being wholeheartedly in sympathy with the reformist changes in religion being promulgated by the Edwardian regime.[11]

Of these changes, the most important was the publication of the Book of Common Prayer in 1549 and the enforcement of its use in all parish churches by an Act of Uniformity. No provision was made for a Welsh version; yet, without one, public worship according to the Prayer Book would be largely unintelligible in most Welsh parishes. Many men must have been aware of this: only one was willing to act. He, it need hardly be said, was William Salesbury. Working at top pressure he had, by 1551, produced his translation of the epistles and gospels, *Cynnifer Llith a Ban*. Dedicating it, in Latin, to the bishops of Wales and of Hereford, he administered a gentle implied rebuke that none of these reverend fathers in God had seen fit to require a translation. It had been left to Salesbury to 'free the Word of God from the fetters' in which, for most of the Welsh, it was shackled. He had been 'touched to the quick by the misery of those born in the same country and of the same people as myself—a people however ignorant of sacred knowledge yet burning more than most men with a fervent zeal for God'. He urged the bishops to give his book authorization for public use, and to depute the task of examining it to six learned men from each diocese. They do not appear to have acceded to his request. But the book was used, and copies of it survived the Marian reaction. In Salesbury's own diocese of St. Asaph, not suprisingly perhaps, there were still enough copies in 1561 for the then bishop, Thomas Davies, to require its use in the churches, and a record survives of the purchase of at least one copy from the diocesan authorities by Foulk ap Thomas, vicar of Llanasaph, for 2s.[12]

Cynnifer Llith a Ban has its faults. It shows signs of haste —and little wonder!—and Salesbury was content in some instances to translate from the English Great Bible rather than directly from the Greek. It is distinctly weaker in its translation of the epistles than of the gospels. Most serious of all, it bears all the marks of Salesbury's decidedly individual, not to say wrongheaded, views about orthography, about which more later. But it also represents a very remarkable achievement. It contained incomparably the most extensive biblical translations into Welsh so far undertaken. As pieces of Welsh prose, disregarding the quirks of spelling and mutation, parts of it were very good indeed, e.g. the parable of the Lost Sheep and Lost Piece of Silver or of the Good Samaritan.[13] Moreover, undertaking so ambitious a project had been a most fruitful training for Salesbury and, still more important, had established an invaluable precedent pointing to the urgent need for a Welsh Bible and Order of Service and also to the possibility of satisfying it.

After the death of Edward VI and the accession of the Catholic Mary, there comes a blank and mysterious episode in Salesbury's life. He had now revealed himself as a man of pronounced reforming sympathies, to whom the atmosphere of the new régime can have been anything but congenial. Tradition has it that he went into hiding at Cae Du in Llansannan. This may well have been true; certainly there are indications in the *Llysieulyfr* that he was at home in Wales in the year 1555. He was probably in scant danger of suffering active persecution for his opinions. As long as he exercised discretion and restraint, the influence of his family in north-east Wales was probably sufficient to protect him against anything worse than mild inconvenience and inward frustration. It is possible, even, that he was able to work off some of his frustration by continuing with his literary work. The speed with which he completed his translations in the 1560s is best explained, perhaps, by assuming that he continued to work on them in secret during his withdrawal to Cae Du in Mary's reign.

But if he did continue with any such activity, any hope of publishing it had to be put off until after Elizabeth's accession. Then Salesbury entered the most fruitful and rewarding phase of his career. In 1560, Richard Davies became bishop of St. Asaph and soon proved himself to be the Welsh prelate most unreservedly and actively in sympathy with Salesbury's own aspirations. The friendship between the two men ripened quickly. Though no direct links can be traced, it seems very probable that it was they who were responsible for the quickening pace of a succession of measures designed to secure the translation of the Bible and Prayer Book into Welsh: a petition of 1561, the translation of the litany into Welsh in 1562, and, most significant of all, the act of 1563 requiring the bishops of Wales and of Hereford to take order among themselves to provide a translation of the Bible and Prayer Book by 1567. The act was a major milestone; for the first time it gave official sanction and specific mandate for a Welsh Bible. Subsequent events pointed still more clearly to Davies and Salesbury's having been responsible for it. Davies invited Salesbury to his palace at Abergwili to expedite the work of translation. By 1567 they had between them managed to complete and publish a translation of the Prayer Book and the New Testament.

The Book of Common Prayer appeared slightly sooner than the New Testament. Though there is no indication in the Prayer Book itself of who was responsible for it, for a very long time the credit for translating it used to be given to Richard Davies. This was partly because his authorship was acknowledged by contemporaries like Bishop William Morgan and George Owen of Henllys, who might have been expected to have known the facts. Partly, too, it was because the fewness of the copies surviving into modern times has prevented many scholars from examining it. But we do not believe that anyone who has read the work closely and compared it with translations known to be by Richard Davies or William Salesbury can fail to assign it to the latter.[14] This is not the place for details of textual comparisons,[15] but two major considerations pointing to Salesbury's authorship can be indicated here. First, the Prayer Book is steeped in all the unmistakable marks of Salesbury's orthography. This in itself need not be conclusive, for Salesbury is known to have prepared for the press other work by Richard Davies and to have imposed his own orthography upon it. More decisive is the second consideration that comparison of the relevant passages in the Prayer Book with similar ones in *Cynnifer Llith a Ban* and those parts of the New Testament translated by Salesbury shows an almost word-for-word similarity. Either Salesbury was responsible for the Prayer Book, or Davies was an unblushing plagiarist who 'lifted' practically the whole of the scriptural parts of the Prayer Book from his coadjutor's translation of the New Testament. It is possible that some parts of the Order of Service may have been translated or, more probably, revised by Richard Davies, but these are small and do not in any way detract from Salesbury's responsibility for the bulk of the work.

He was responsible, also, for the greater part of the New Testament. Here there need be no doubts about the extent of his authorship, for the contributions of the three men who participated in the work were clearly established in the New Testament itself. Thomas Huet, precentor of St. David's, translated the Book of Revelation only; Richard Davies undertook five epistles—I Timothy, Hebrews, James and I and II Peter; William Salesbury did all the rest. To have been responsible for the Prayer Book and so much of the New Testament was a tremendous achievement for one man. Indeed, one of the reasons often put forward for Richard Davies's supposed authorship of the Prayer Book was that such an allocation of responsibility between themselves by the two collaborators would have been a rational division of labour in a task too great for one man to have completed in the time at their disposal. At this point it is, perhaps, worth reminding ourselves that Salesbury may have been working steadily to fulfil his life's great ambition since Edward VI's reign, and that the Act of 1563 was probably the final not the initial stimulus to his endeavours.

However great an effort the translations of 1567 may have required of Salesbury, they have had a very 'mixed press' from subsequent commentators. Some distinguished scholars have dismissed the work as almost worthless.[16] In general, though, there has been a willingness to acknowledge the pioneer importance of the translations and to concede that Salesbury was capable of writing very fine prose. Conversely, however, it is usually argued that these merits are vitiated by his extraordinary views about language and spelling. Criticism on this score began in his own age by John Penry and Maurice Kyffin, the latter declaring that such were the peculiarities in Salesbury's printed text 'that the ear of no true Welshman could bear to listen to it'.[17] Such criticism still continues on four counts. First, that Salesbury dressed up his Welsh words in unfamiliar Latin guise; thus 'eccles' for 'eglwys', 'Deo' for 'Duw' or 'discipul' for 'disgybl'. Second, he ignored the mutation of initial consonants, particularly the nasal mutation. Third, he retained too many archaic forms no longer intelligible to any but scholars. Finally—and more venial this—in his attempts to overcome the difficulty of dialect variations, Salesbury inserted a bewildering number of alternatives in the margins of his text. None of these criticisms lacks justification; but if we were able to summon Salesbury back to the bar of history to answer them, there is no doubt that he would offer a sturdy defence on all four counts. In answer to the first, he might well point out that scholars in many European languages were experimenting with different forms of spelling in the sixteenth century, that his intention was to show in the outward appearance of Welsh words their close affinity with the great languages of classical antiquity, and that of course he had no intention of changing the way in which Welsh words were pronounced. Similarly, on the second count, he could insist that he had no intention of not having the mutation of the initial consonants sounded, but that preserving the radical consonant would greatly help those scholars who were not Welsh to master the language –here, we think, Salesbury would always have insisted that he had his eye on the international scholarly public, and the earlier reference to the interest in his dictionary in Zurich suggests he may not have been unjustified in doing so. As far as archaic forms are concerned, Salesbury might, with reason, point out that with the benefit of four hundred years of hindsight he, too, might confidently judge what were and were not archaisms. Finally, on the question of dialect variations, he could reasonably affirm that in the absence of an accepted standard Welsh prose, he was anxious that men in all parts of Wales should not be debarred from understanding his translation because of differences of dialect.

There are two further points of criticism to which he might find it more difficult to reply. First there was the wide degree of inconsistency in his own practice in the matter of orthography; he is frequently capable of ignoring or overriding his own cherished principles. Furthermore, there was his failure to take into account the limitations in the training and equipment of the average parish priests who would, after all, be the key users of Salesbury's translation. Few of them were scholars, and many of them were ill-educated and barely literate. To expect them to indulge in the mental and

enunciatory gymnastics necessary to 'translate' Salesbury's scholarly idiosyncrasies into 'ordinary' Welsh intelligible to their parishioners was asking too much. It is at this point that the contrast
between Salesbury's attitude and that of Bishop Davies becomes
most marked. The latter knew only too well how modest were the
capacities of many of his parish priests and was not prepared to
sacrifice intelligibility in the parishes to increase prestige and interest
in wider scholarly circles.

Before leaving this subject of the translations of 1567, however,
there are two further points that are worth making. The first is
this: that no matter how bizarre or exotic the appearance of much
of Salesbury's Welsh is at first sight, it is quite extraordinary how
you get used to it in time and find yourself making the necessary
mental adjustments almost automatically. Only those who have
had to read Salesbury's books regularly and frequently over a
period can testify to this; but it suggests that perhaps, although his
translations occasioned murky obscurities and frightful blunders
for most Welsh priests, there were more than might at first be
supposed who were able to make effective use of the New Testament
and Prayer Book. That brings us to the second consideration,
which is, that all those who could strip away the surface difficulties
of orthography were able to penetrate to an undeniable excellence
underlying them in the translation itself. For make no mistake,
Salesbury was a master of Welsh prose, as Bishop William Morgan
recognized when he acknowledged him to be the pioneer of biblical
translation to whom Wales owed more than to any other. Morgan
recognized it in still more practical fashion by virtually adopting
Salesbury's translation in his own New Testament of 1588. If the
Authorized Version of the English Bible was basically Tyndale's
Bible, it is even truer to say that our Welsh New Testament is
Salesbury's.

When the New Testament was published in 1567, Davies and
Salesbury undoubtedly hoped that it would soon be followed by
a Welsh translation of the Old Testament. But their hopes never
materialized. Disagreement between the two men, if there was any,
may have been doubly unfortunate; not only did it prevent the
appearance of a Welsh version of the Old Testament before Morgan's
translation, but it may also have discouraged Salesbury from publishing any other Welsh books. In a letter writen to Gruffudd Hiraethog,
written some time between 1567 and 1575, he declared that he
would publish no more, and that for 'good reasons' ('iawn achosion').
But the eminent physician, Thomas Williams, writing in 1574, was
more hopeful of the prospects: 'we shall yet have (if God sees fit to
grant him life) many notable pieces of his work' ['e geir eto (os gwyl
Dvw vod yn iawn gael ono einioes) lawer o bethau arbenic oi
waith']. Thomas Williams's confidence may have sprung from his

having seen a manuscript version of the *Llysieulyfr*, which Salesbury seems to have been engaged in writing between 1568 and 1574. But, in fact, nothing further was published by him before his death, with the exception of a second edition of the Prayer Book—if he was indeed responsible for it—in 1586. There may be more than one reason for this silence. He was always a proud, moody, difficult man, just such a one as might be deeply sensitive to and hurt by what he might regard as unjustified criticism of his work. But a more compelling reason may have been simply lack of funds. He was no longer capable of the prodigious efforts that had supported his pen between 1547 and 1550. He had no great income of his own and we know of no wealthy patron on whom he might depend.

Whatever the reason for it, there was a long unbroken silence until his death. Just when that took place is unknown. In the past it has usually been assumed that he was still alive in 1594 and that he died some time between that date and 1600. More recently it has been suggested that he died about 1584,[18] though the arguments for such a date do not appear altogether conclusive. For our present purpose, it matters little which date we accept; all are agreed that after 1567, if we except the unpublished *Llysieulyfr*, he has no new achievement to his credit.

*   *   *

It remains now to draw the threads together in order to try to sum up the nature of Salesbury's achievement.

First he stands out as the clearest and most complete embodiment of the new Protestant humanism in a Welsh setting. He was a typical Renaissance polymath with a protean range of scholarly enquiry and equipment: linguist, lawyer, theologian, historian, scientist, litterateur, author and translator. But all this was firmly anchored in a profound knowledge of and love for the traditional culture and literature of his native Wales, revealed in his connexion with the bardic fraternity, the *eisteddfodau*, and the collection and study of Welsh manuscripts. It was because he had drunk so deeply and so avidly at both these springs that he was able to make his particular contribution to the life of Wales. This brings us to his second claim to distinction: that he saw more vividly than anyone else the crucial nature of the choice with which the language, literature and religion of Wales were faced in the sixteenth century. He made it plain that all three were at a fateful crossroads. One route led, as Salesbury saw it, to a bright and progressive future with all that was most alive and enterprising in Renaissance Europe. The other, along which an unchanged Wales was doomed to stagger, encumbered by the dead weight of an outmoded cultural and religious pattern, pointed only to stagnation and sterility. The issue was less stark and uncomplicated than Salesbury tended to present it, yet it undoubtedly existed. He did far more than anyone else to spell out its implications to his fellow-countrymen and to shape their response to it.

What was the nature of the choice as defined by Salesbury? As far as the language was concerned, the question was could it rise to the test of the Renaissance? Could it find within itself the dignity, resource and flexibility to become a fit medium for Renaissance learning, as the languages of classical antiquity had been and as the European vernaculars were then becoming? Could it express the whole range of new intellectual interest and achievement with which it had never been concerned hitherto? Inextricably linked with this was the choice for Welsh literature. Could it shed its decorative but tightly-constricting skin of medieval theme and custom? Could it assume the more expansive and variegated garb of Renaissance motifs? Could it free itself from the cramping limitations of oral tradition and manuscript circulation and aim at a wider and more sophisticated audience by means of the printed book? In so doing, could it serve the highest end of all—the spread of true religion? For Salesbury, like many another humanist, Catholic and Protestant alike, saw learning and literature as the handmaidens of religion. Their supreme justification was that they made the ways of God plainer and more intelligible to all men. Hence Salesbury's intense preoccupation with the translation of the Bible. Herein lay the supreme test for language, literature and religion. If this could be successfully acomplished, then Wales might emerge triumphant from the crisis confronting her. A Bible in the vernacular would prove more conclusively than anything else that she had the potential to become the cradle of a Protestant humanism expressed distinctively in Welsh.

William Salesbury, energetically though he laboured, did not wholly succeed in fulfilling his aspirations. He did not manage to translate the Old Testament; and even the New Testament and the Prayer Book were marred by the idiosyncrasies earlier noted. Yet his is the major credit for Welsh translations of the Scriptures; it was from him that the creative spark and the break-through came. It was he who had virtually to create the vastly extended range of theological vocabulary and expression, and to show that the task was well within the bounds of possibility, even if he himself did not entirely succeed. There is another respect, also, in which he may be said to have had no more than partial success: neither he nor other contemporary Welsh humanists were able to establish to more than a very limited extent the new Welsh prose and poetry of which they dreamed. The causes for their lack of success lie beyond the realm of any personal failure on their part; they must be sought in the social and economic condition of Tudor Wales, which was at this time almost certainly incapable of maintaining literary institutions of the kind to which they aspired.[19] But even in this respect, what they did manage to achieve was of decisive influence in the future. They did—and it was Salesbury more than any other in their midst who was responsible— contrive to secure official recognition of the need for a Welsh Bible and Prayer Book and the establishment of Welsh as the language of public worship. This was a turning-point of vital significance. It may have made all the difference to the survival of the Welsh language at all; it certainly explains its continuance as a medium of literary expression. It was its indispensability in religion which for the next two or three centuries justified the publication of most of the literature that appeared in the Welsh language. However meagre in volume that output may have been, it preserved the essential continuity of the Welsh literary tradition. The result was that by the end of the eighteenth century and the beginning of the nineteenth, when Welsh society had become prosperous enough to maintain a vastly extended range of printed literature, there was at hand a literary language which could readily be used for the purpose.

Such a development as we have just outlined is in some danger of being regarded as inevitable when viewed in retrospect. To recognize that it could very easily never have happened at all calls for greater effort of the imagination than has usually been exercised. But just consider for a moment two factors: the powerful attraction of writing in English on the one hand, and the active discouragements to publishing in Welsh on the other. Many Welsh-born authors had, in the sixteenth century, been writing in English with considerable success, and Salesbury early in his career was by no means the least effective of them. The prospects were extremely attractive: a powerful literary tradition extending its scope with astonishing speed and diversity; the possibility of reaching a wide and growing public; and the hope of gaining fame and influence and making money. Offset against that were the disheartening obstacles that any author publishing in Welsh had to surmount. Wales had no printing-press of its own; nor was there any hope as yet of establishing a heavy-investment industry like printing within the country. The 'public' an author could expect for Welsh books was bound to be very restricted in numbers and influence—not many people could at best read Welsh books, and there would be infinitely fewer who could afford to buy them. Worst of all was the apathy of so large a proportion of Welshmen concerning their language and literature;[20] not a Welsh humanist author but was sickeningly aware of it, and Salesbury was more deeply grieved by it than anyone. The temptation to yield to despair and to divert his abundant talent to a more rewarding medium must at times have been almost overwhelming. In assessing his achievement we ought not to forget these heavy odds stacked against it.

There may indeed be some who will ask: 'was the game worth the candle? Would it not have been better that Salesbury and others should have allowed the Welsh literary tradition to wither and devoted their creative energies to establishing an "Anglo-Welsh" literature in the Tudor period?' There were not a few in the six-teenth century who argued that it was a mistake thus to prop up the Welsh language. But to any Welshman with a conscience, such an attitude was a counsel of despair and a confession of moral bankruptcy: 'a allai diawl ei hun ddoedyd yn amgenach?' ('could the devil himself speak differently'), asked Maurice Kyffin. To Salesbury, any course of action which left the Word of God still in fetters for the vast majority of his countrymen was unthinkable. All credit to him and the handful of other Welsh humanists with a conscience sensitive enough and a vision sufficiently irresistible to make Welsh viable as the language of worship, learning and literature.

Some 400 years on from the appearance of the first Welsh New Testament and Prayer Book, we do well to honour the man who did by far the most to make it possible and whose life's greatest achievement it was. Nor could there be a better place to do so than in the heart of his own native county. For if Welshmen owe an immense debt to him, he in turn was under an equally great obligation to Dyffryn Clwyd and all it stood for in Welsh life and letters. His superlative feat was to graft the new and fecund stem of Renaissance learning into the ancient stock of Welsh language and literature. He might never even have thought of trying to do so had not its roots been so deep, virile and secure in the soil of his own native region.

NOTES

* The substance of this essay was delivered as a lecture to the annual meeting of the Society held at Ruthin on 13th March, 1965.

[1] 'Traddodiad Llenyddol Dyffryn Clwyd a'r Cyffiniau', *Transactions of the Denbighshire Historical Society*, I (1952), 20-32.

[2] 'Hanes ei waith yw hanes William Salesbury, ac nid oes dim llawer i'w ddywedyd amdano gyda sicrwydd ond ei fod yn awdur llyfrau Cymraeg.' *Llenyddiaeth Cymru: Rhyddiaith o 1540 hyd 1660* (Wrecsam, 1926), p. 34.

[3] D. R. Thomas, *The Life and Work of Bishop Davies and William Salesbury* remains the standard biography. But there exists an excellent M.A. thesis by Mr. W. Alun Mathias, 'Astudiaeth o Weithgarwch Llenyddol William Salesbury' (Cardiff, 1949). Mr Mathias also wrote the article on Salesbury in the *Dictionary of Welsh Biography*.

[4] *Calendar of Salusbury Correspondence, 1553-c. 1700* (Cardiff, 1954), pp. 1-6.

[5] It was published in 1916 by E. Stanton Roberts.

[6] See R. W. Hays, *The History of the Abbey of Aberconway*, chs. VII and IX.

[7] *Athenae Oxonienses*, I (1813), 358.

[8] Quoted by W. A. Mathias, 'Gweithgarwch Llenyddol', p. 12.

[9] The suit is P.R.O., St. Ch. 2/29/178. Only the bill of complaint survives. I failed to decipher enough to make sense of it, and so did Mr. Alun Mathias. But the late Bob Owen, reading perhaps with the eye of faith, was able to reconstruct quite a story from it, *Y Genedl Gymreig*, 31st October, 1932. A single *ex parte* statement of the kind contained in the bill should, in any event, be used with the greatest circumspection.

[10] *Original letters relative to the English Reformation* (2 vols. Parker Society, 1846), I, 73. Conrad Gessner was one of the ministers at Zurich with whom Hooper was friendly.

[11] I have given a fuller account of this interesting book in *BBCS*, XIII (1949), 146-50.

[12] N.L.W., St. Asaph MSS., SA/MB/14, f. 40*v*.

[13] Canon John Fisher in the introduction to his edition of *Kynniver Llith a Ban* (Cardiff, 1931), draws attention to the quality of these translations, but adds feelingly that Salesbury 'is at his worst in the Epistles, where he found (and who has not?) St. Paul's long and involved sentences very difficult to translate intelligibly', p. xxxiii.

[14] Mr. Alun Mathias and I, working at much the same time—he on Salesbury and I on Richard Davies—came to this conclusion quite independently of one another.

[15] Readers who are interested will find such comparisons in Mr Mathias's thesis or in my *Bywyd a Gwaith yr Esgob Richard Davies*, pp. 95-8, appendix C.

[16] Mr. T. Hughes Jones, M.A., of Wrexham, in a most interesting conversation at Ruthin, told me that the late Timothy Lewis was moved to tears in defending Salesbury against his detractors, of whom, it seems, no less Olympian an authority than Sir John Morris-Jones was one.

[17] The vexed question of whether Salesbury's text was so difficult as not to be read at all in the churches was settled by Professor R. T. Jenkins in his article 'William Salesbury yn y Llannau', *Y Traethodydd*, 1946.

[18] Alun Mathias, *D.W.B.*

[19] I have argued this case more fully in *Dadeni, Diwygiad a Diwylliant Cymru.*

[20] Professor R. T. Jenkins made the point admirably in a letter written to me recently, in which he says, 'The truth is, I fear, that the main body of Welsh speakers were not (and are not) willing to take trouble with the language or its literature. . . . And, of course, the main body of the English (except under compulsion from the Education Acts) are no better than we in relation to their language. But the great difference in the number of those speaking both languages has at all times ensured enough English readers to provide a sufficient "public" to maintain authors and books' (my translation).

IX. SOME PROTESTANT VIEWS OF EARLY BRITISH CHURCH HISTORY

There is no longer the need to labour the point that the men of every age tend to rewrite history in the light of their own needs and experience. Furthermore, the greater the contemporary turmoil, the more drastically are people likely to revise their judgments on the past; so that an upheaval as violent as the Reformation could scarcely fail to bring about a Protestant reinterpretation of history. When reformers sought to justify their teaching by reference to the doctrine and practice of the early church, this was in fact an appeal to history which meant that men must discover not only the nature of the early church, but when, where, and how, the medieval church had come to differ from it. Luther himself came to realize this. He wrote

> 'I for my part, unversed and ill-informed as I was at first with regard to history, attacked the papacy, *a priori*, as they say, that is out of the Holy Scriptures. And now it is a wonderful delight to me to find that others are doing the same thing *a posteriori*, that is from history—and it gives me the greatest joy and satisfaction to see, as I do most clearly, that history and Scripture entirely coincide in this respect.'[1]

It was well said of him that he had been

> 'enforced to awake all antiquity and to call former times to his succours ... so that the ancient authors both in divinity and humanity, which had a long time slept in libraries, began generally to be read and resolved.'[2]

The Protestants were led completely to reject traditional notions concerning the historical role of the church. The idea of its having grown steadily in grace and wisdom must be abandoned. Far from having increasingly revealed God's truth, it had persistently obscured it. To quote a favourite Protestant metaphor, the gold of the evangelical church had become cankered down the ages by the dross of papist superstition. Only an elect minority had held to the truth; chosen individuals, 'few in comparison of them that be called and come feignedly', but 'kept by the mighty hand of God against all natural possibility'. [3] This was a stupendous challenge! And a challenge that had to be grounded in history as well as in the scriptures.

Renaissance scholarship provided a further incentive. Its interest in ancient texts of all kinds, and its more exact knowledge of languages and manuscripts, had led to acuter standards of textual criticism. The application of them to some of the key documents on which papal claims were based had already resulted in some astounding revelations, the most notable of which, of course, was Lorenzo Valla's exposure of the Donation of Constantine. So it was not mere academic interest that prompted John Bale to urge

'some learned Englishman (as there are now most excellent fresh wits) to
set forth the English chronicles in their right shape, as certain other lands
have done afore them, all affections set apart. I cannot think a more necessary thing to be laboured to the honour of God, beauty of the realm, erudition of the people, and commodity of other lands, next the sacred scriptures
of the Bible, than that work would be.'[4]

Like many other reformers, Bale was convinced that most of the
surviving historical records had been too much coloured by the
prejudices of the pope's minions. 'For truly in those we have',
he wrote, 'there yet is vice more advanced than virtue, and
Romish blasphemy than godliness.' Yet Bale himself was capable
of rejecting the findings of Renaissance scholarship in favour of
fantastic and uncritical musings of his own.[5]

The first man in Britain to undertake the rewriting of sacred and
secular history from a Protestant standpoint seems to have been
William Tyndale. His *Practice of Prelates*,[6] published by Hans
Luft at Marburg in 1530, is of particular interest. In this book he
tried to prove how the papacy had steadily usurped more authority,
and in so doing had muddied the clear stream of Christianity with
superstition and idolatry. He claimed that the popes had enslaved
first the bishops and then the emperors, and that having received
their kingdom from the devil, they had distributed it among their
vassals, first making use of bishops and priests, then of monks, and
lastly of those most detestable of 'caterpillars', 'horse-leeches' and
'drones'—the friars. In the process they had created their own corpus
of law and set aside the authority of the scriptures by means of false
councils. Having then sought to show from the English chronicles
that the bishops were always in league with the popes against temporal authority, Tyndale ended his book with a long and bitter attack
on Wolsey, the latest and most obnoxious of papal tools. Coverdale,
too, told of

'great poison poured into the church whereby religion sore decayed. For
while the ministers of the word laboured more after riches than to perform
their office and charge, and to edify the church, they were pleased with super-
stitiousness instead of true religion.... Hereof cometh it that we now have the
abomination of the popes' power of pardons, of masses for the dead and
the quick, of merits, power and intercession of saints in heaven, of worshipping their bones on earth, of idols and vain ornaments, pomp and pride of
the church, of hired singing and praying in the temple, and of the whole
swarm of idle religious. All which things, with other more like fondness, are
nothing but new alterations, pervertings, and contrary to all old ordinances,
having no ground in God's word, and are clean against God, though many
hard-necked people are yet in a fury and brawl for such things, and will
make all the world believe that this their foolishness, alteration, and pervert-
ing of God's ordinance is the old faith.'[7]

In the course of the troubled and controversial years of the sixteenth century, Protestant authors in Britain became increasingly
interested in the early history of the church in their own country.

They were particularly anxious to prove that there had at one time existed in the island a church maintaining apostolic purity, entirely free from papal control and uncontaminated by romanist practices. The two crucial issues therefore seemed to be the origins of Christianity in Britain, and the perversion of the church as a result of Augustine of Canterbury's mission.

A number of hoary medieval traditions concerning the first introduction of Christianity into Britain were still current in the sixteenth century. Best known and most venerated of them was the legend which connected Joseph of Arimathea with Glastonbury abbey.[8] There were other less-known myths of the same kind in which St. Paul, St. Peter, St. James, Simon Zelotes, and others, figured.[9] There was also the testimony of Gildas, which seemed to suggest that the island of Britain had been converted during the reign of Tiberius.[10] Much more reliable was the evidence of Tertullian in his *Contra Iudaeos*, written about A.D. 208, that Christianity was already firmly established among the Britons even in places which were inaccessible to the Roman armies. The evidence of the legends, of Gildas, and of Tertullian and other early Christian authors, was distinctly tenuous, but the Protestants had to make the fullest use of it because of a dangerously circumstantial, and apparently well-documented, Catholic case that could be put forward. This claimed that the island had been converted as the result of a direct papal mission undertaken by Fagan and Damian, two missionaries sent by Pope Eleutherius in response to a letter from Lucius, son of Coel, king of the Britons, some time during the latter half of the second century.[11] Even though Eleutherius did seem to admit in his letter that Lucius was the vicar of God in his own country, that did not prevent Catholic apologists like Harding, Jewel's antagonist, from claiming Eleutherius as the apostle of the British, as Augustine of Canterbury was of the English, and thus to declare triumphantly that 'all the faith of the western part of the world came only from the bishops of Rome'.[12]

None of the Protestant authors seemed disposed to deny altogether the validity of the Eleutherius story. All they could do was to try to minimize its consequences by emphasizing the older tradition of independent apostolic conversion, and by crediting to the popes of the second century far less extravagant and ungodly pretensions than those of their successors. Pilkington, for example, insisted that Eleutherius's letter showed him to have agreed far more with the Protestant viewpoint than that of their adversaries.

> 'If true religion was stablished here by this pope' (Eleutherius), he wrote bitingly, 'why does this scavenger (Pilkington's Catholic opponent) sweep the streets with contrary doctrine to this pope and with false lies? These holy bishops of ours honour their pope in suffering for him that will never thank them and say they would have all to do the same: yet they themselves

are the first that teach and do contrary to this pope, and many other of the eldest sort, in all such things as please them; and so will correct him rather than follow the ancientest and best of them.'[13]

The puritan Thomas Cartwright was perhaps more severe on the Lucius-Eleutherius episode than any other of the sixteenth-century authors.[14] Unlike most of the Protestant authors, who upheld Geoffrey of Monmouth's *History* against Polydore Vergil's 'popish' criticisms, Cartwright treated the *vetustissimus liber* with marked irreverence. He pointed contemptuously to the childish errors which might frequently be detected whenever Geoffrey was talking of 'any matter of ancient time', and drew attention to the highly suspicious circumstance that in no author before Geoffrey was there any mention of the archflamins and flamins whom Lucius was sup- posed to have replaced with archbishops and bishops.[15] He accused Whitgift of having been so eager to uphold the episcopate that he had swallowed Geoffrey's tales uncritically, and actually seemed to be siding with Harding rather than Jewel in this particular issue.[16] Cartwright himself was inclined to dismiss altogether the whole story with its dangerous traditions of papal intervention and a royally-founded episcopate. Following Gildas, he believed that the faith had been received in the days of Tiberius,

'but that was not publicly nor universally by authority of prince, but of some few, and of those how? "Of some boldly, of some soundly," and how long? "Until the times of Diocletian the tyrant": which was after Lucius, at least 132 years.'[17]

Following the publication of Gildas's work by Polydore Vergil in 1525, its importance as a unique literary source for the state of the church in Britain in the period immediately preceding Augustine's mission was quickly recognised. Despite all his unflattering comments on his fellow-countrymen, many Protestant authors quite fell in love with Gildas. And understandably; for here was a fervent early reformer who not only inveighed in the grand manner against the shortcomings of contemporary religion, but who buttressed all his denunciations with an unfailing wealth of scriptural justification. Tyndale was greatly taken up with him. He saw in Gildas a God-sent prophet entrusted with the high task of rebuking his countrymen for having deserted the scriptures and followed the vain imaginings of men. In his famous book, *The Obedience of a Christian Man* (1528), Tyndale depicted Gildas as one of those true 'prophets and preachers', always sent by God 'before a general plague', 'to warn the people and give them time to repent'. Like Gildas, he saw in the Saxon invasions the awful punishment visited upon the Britons for their betrayal of true religion:

'Unto the old Britons . . . preached Gildas; and rebuked them of their wickedness, and prophesied both to the spiritual and to the laymen also, what vengeance would follow except they repented. But they waxed hard- hearted: and God sent his plagues and pestilences among them, and sent their enemies in upon them on every side, and destroyed them utterly.'[18]

But contention was bitterest concerning the role of Augustine of Canterbury in British history. Papalists here had a strong case to argue. The earliest and most important authority was the Venerable Bede, a witness favourable enough to Rome. Augustine was indisputably a papal emissary. He had been the first archbishop of Canterbury, and ever since his time the English church had shown a becomingly filial and steadfast deference to the pope. There was no denying, either, that Pope Gregory the Great had given Augustine authority over the other bishops in Britain, and if they had rejected his claim to dominion over them, within a hundred and fifty years or so their successors had been willing enough to submit to the pope. As one catholic apologist put it,

> 'This land being inhabited with Saxons, being Painims, Saint Gregory, pope of Rome, about the year of our Lord God 595, sent Saint Austin and his company, who by their doctrine and virtuous living planted the faith, and so established a true religion in England: the which faith and religion ever when the people have declined from it, they have felt great calamities as well by the hand of God, as by the conquest of the Danes, and after by the Normans; and sith the conquest from time to time.'[19]

Latest portent of the retribution they might expect for defection from the Catholic ranks had been the burning of St. Paul's in 1561, which event had impelled the author to utter his warning.

However, the Protestants thought they could find in the Augustine story some weak spots at which to hammer away. They insisted that Gregory had never had the right to invest Augustine with jurisdiction over the Celtic bishops. They seized on the archbishop's own weakness of character, making great play with Bede's story of his reluctance to stand when greeting the Celtic representatives. They found further proof of his arrogance and cruelty in Geoffrey of Monmouth's account of the massacre of two thousand monks at Bangor Iscoed by Ethelred, king of Northumberland, allegedly at Augustine's instigation. Yet all these things were of little account in their eyes as compared with the enormity of his wickedness in having been the first to introduce papist superstitions into Britain. His advent they regarded as the opening of the floodgates to the tide of Romanish impurities thereafter to flow in unimpeded. The most celebrated of anglican apologists wrote that

> 'the faith of Christ had been universally received and perfectly rooted in this realm many hundred years before this Augustine the monk was born. Indeed he brought in great heaps of strange novelties and superstitions, such as candles, candlesticks, banners and holy water, and other like shews, whereof the Church of God had no greet need. And yet have the same since been increased by other new devices, and vanities above measure.'[20]

Foxe likewise impressed upon 'the true and faithful congregation of Christ's universal church' that

> 'religion remained in Britain uncorrupt, and the word of Christ truly preached, till about the coming of Augustine and of his companions from Rome, many of the same Britain-preachers were slain by the Saxons. After

that began the Christian faith to enter and spring among the Saxons, after a
certain Romish sort,'

though admittedly this was 'somewhat more tolerable than were
the times which after followed'.[21]

This discussion of the early British church, together with the
still more absorbing problem of the authenticity of Geoffrey of
Monmouth's *History*, held a special attraction for Welsh scholars.
They saw a distinct connection between the two questions, since
both involved the vindication of the past glory of the ancient
British race, so long deprived of its rightful sovereignty by Saxon
'usurpers'. All ardent Welshmen, and especially those who were
Protestants to boot, must be deeply concerned in these matters
so nearly affecting the honour of their people and the truth of their
religion.

In close association with some of the leading Welsh scholars was
Matthew Parker, archbishop of Canterbury. Parker himself held
strong views on the subject of early British history. In response to
queries posed by Calvin soon after his consecration he stoutly
affirmed that the English episcopacy derived from Joseph of
Arimathea and not from the papacy,[22] and in the years that followed,
he was deeply interested in securing as much evidence as possible
for the existence in the early British and Saxon churches of practices
and beliefs of a Protestant complexion.[23] In the course of his en-
quiries, Parker came into touch with Richard Davies and William
Salesbury, the two most notable Protestant scholars in Wales. The
former was bishop of St. David's from 1561 to 1581 and the foremost Welsh ecclesiastic of his day, while the latter was probably the
greatest Renaissance scholar produced in Wales. Both were enthusiastic antiquarians sharing Parker's interest in the history
of the early church. In letters which passed between them and the
archbishop they kept him informed of the results of their investiga-
tions. They collaborated in the work of translating the New
Testament into Welsh for the first time, and it is in Davies's 'Address
to the Welsh Nation', which prefaced that translation, that the
fullest statement of the Welsh Protestants' version of early British
church history is to be found.[24]

In his 'Address', Davies maintained the usual themes of the introduction of Christianity into Britain by Joseph of Arimathea and
its desecration by Augustine of Canterbury. What gave his work
its interest was the particular twist he gave to evidence which he
claimed to have found in an old chronicle. This led him to descibe
how the Welsh had been willing enough to traffic with the Saxons
while they were still heathens, but so great was their abhorrence of
the superstitions introduced by Augustine that they would have
nothing to do with them after their conversion. Bent on keeping

their own faith undesecrated, the Welsh remained rigidly aloof until they were eventually forced to accept papist abominations at the point of the sword. The chronicle from which Davies got his information has not, so far as is known, been identified, but its ultimate source seems to be Aldhelm's letter to Geraint or Gerontius, king of Dumnonia.[25]

This markedly nationalist complexion which Davies put on the episode may well have arisen from his desire to get rid of two of the most serious obstacles to the spread of Protestantism in Wales. These were the prejudice against it as a new-fangled heresy and as an 'English' religion, uncongenial to Wales. The first of these objections was certainly not peculiar to Wales. English and continental reformers had often to rebut what Jewel called the 'high brag' of their opponents that 'all antiquity and a continual consent of all ages' was on their side, while Protestantism was 'but new and yesterday's work'.[26] Davies, however, felt confident of being able to prove that at the apogee of the ancient British kingdom its religion had been firmly grounded on the Protestant rock of scriptural authority. He would not, he told his readers, say a word about the 'dignity, esteem, and worldly fame, of the ancient British', he would merely remind them of 'one excellence that out-weighed all the others'—the people's 'undefiled religion, pure Christianity, and fruitful edifying faith'. This most priceless heritage they had been forced to relinquish and evil days had come upon their posterity. Learning decayed, the scriptures in their own tongue were lost, and the proud descendants of Brutus were ground beneath the Saxon heel. However, God in his infinite mercy had vouchsafed them a new opportunity of embracing, not a new-fangled error, but the ancient faith of their nation in its golden age.

Almost as devastating was the blow which Davies's account struck at those who insisted that Protestantism was something English and alien. He seemed to be turning the tables on them completely by showing that Romish religion, far from being in the national tradition of the Welsh, was something degrading imposed upon them by their enemies. He besought his nation to

'call to mind its ancient privilege and great honour, which sprang from its acceptance of the faith of Christ and the word of God, which it had received before all the islands of the world.'

This was its true spiritual patrimony, something in which the English had never shared before the Reformation. In accepting Protestant teaching, therefore, the Welsh were not embracing an alien faith but reavailing themselves of their 'once most glorious heritage'.

In the seventeenth century, Archbishop Ussher, in addition to upholding the Protestant view of the history of the church in Britain, was at great pains to clear the early Irish church from any possible taint of papistry.[27] He attributed to Polydore Vergil the origin of the idea that the pope enjoyed temporal power over Ireland by virtue of a special grant made to him at the time of its first conversion. It was a favourite Protestant innuendo that Polydore,

> 'being sent over by the pope into England for the collecting of his Peter-pence, undertook the writing of the history of that nation; wherein he forgat not by the way to do the best service he could to his lord that had employed him thither.'[28]

Ussher would go no further than to admit that St. Patrick had a 'special regard unto the Church of Rome, from whence he was sent for the conversion of this island',[29] a regard which Ussher concedes he himself would have had in those days.

> 'But that St. Patrick was of opinion that the Church of Rome was sure ever afterward to continue in that good estate, and that there was a per-petual privilege annexed unto that see, that it should never err in judgment, or that the pope's sentences were always to be held as infallible oracles; that will I never believe.'[30]

Nor could he ever believe other than that the 'religion professed by the ancient bishops, priests, monks, and other Christians in this land' was for substance the very same as that which was in his own day 'by public authority maintained therein, against the foreign doctrine brought in thither in latter times by the bishop of Rome's followers'.[31]

During the seventeenth, eighteenth, and nineteenth centuries, British historians continued to retain the essentials of the theory of an early Protestant church in Britain, although better-informed and more critical scholarship pruned it of its more palpably mythical accretions. Thus, for example, the legends about Joseph of Arimathea were disposed of in the 'honest atmosphere of the best seventeenth-century scholarship'.[32] Ussher had doubts about their authenticity; he was scornful of the Glastonbury traditions which he did not consider older than the time of the Normans, and full of late superstition.[33] Sir Henry Spelman voiced more serious criticisms,[34] Fuller was distinctly sceptical,[35] and Edward Stillingfleet, bishop of Worcester, finally disposed of them in 1685.[36] Yet although de-molishing this myth, Stillingfleet himself was no less anxious to provide the church in Britain with an apostolic founder than his predecessors had been, and this despite the characteristically shrewd comments of Fuller on the vanity which impelled churches to seek such illustrious origins.[37] The proofs which Stillingfleet offered on behalf of St. Paul as the founder of the British church[38] seemed so strong that they were accepted by Protestant historians down to the middle of the nineteenth century.

Similarly, though a second-century British king like Lucius, ruling in the midst of a Roman province, appeared so improbable

a figure to thoughtful antiquarians, it was not until well into the
nineteenth century that he finally disappeared. The difficulty of
finding a consistent chronology which would have enabled him
to be fitted into the pontificate of Eleutherius was noted by a
number of authors from Ussher onwards. There was the equally
awkward problem of explaining away the remarkable phenomenon
of his anomalous position with regard to the imperial authorities.
After the *animadversiones* of Spelman[39] against the letter supposedly
addressed to Lucius by Eleutherius, that celebrated document
became increasingly discredited. Yet, in 1708, Collier could insist
that 'that there was such a Christian king in Britain as Lucius about
that time is beyond question', while rejecting very firmly any
suggestion that Lucius had heard of the

> 'pope's supremacy and universal pastorship, that all controversy was to be
> determined there in the last resort and that the care of all the churches lay
> particularly upon that bishop's shoulders. At that time of day there was
> neither practice nor principles set on foot to give Lucius any such
> persuasion.'[40]

M. A. Tierney, as late as 1839, in his edition of *Dodd's Church
History*, wrote, 'Of the precise motives which influenced the conduct
of Lucius on this occasion, we can know nothing. The facts, however, remain undisputed. . . .'[41]

It was very slowly, too, that the prejudice against Augustine
disappeared. Protestants deplored his pride and were sceptical
of his miracles. With a characteristic quip, Fuller writes of his
first miracle, that of leaving his first footprint on a rock as in wax:
'the Romanists will cry shame on our hard hearts, if our obdurate
belief, more stubborn than the stone, will not as pliably receive
the impression of this miracle.'[42] It was a long time before Protestants
completely exonerated him from complicity in Ethelred's massacre
of the Welsh monks, though Foxe had long since given him the
benefit of what slight doubt there was.[43] Though they learnt to pay
tribute to his missionary work among the Anglo-Saxons, they
never quite forgave him for bringing in a religion

> 'spun with a coarser thread though guarded with a finer trimming, made
> luscious to the senses with pleasing ceremonies . . . . We commend his
> pains, condemn his pride, allow his life, approve his learning, admire his
> miracles, admit the foundation of his doctrine, Jesus Christ; but refuse the
> hay and stubble he built thereupon.'[44]

The deadly threat to church and state which earnest anglicans
saw in the demands for Catholic Emancipation at the beginning
of the nineteenth century gave a new significance in the eyes of
many to the notion of an early Protestant church. It now became
for them the most telling argument on behalf of maintaining the
establishment, and one which, if properly used, could be fatal to the
sophistry of those papists who maintained that theirs was after all the

true ancient religion of Britain. Nowhere was the idea of an early Protestant church more fervently proclaimed than in Bishop Burgess's *Tracts on the Origin and Independence of the Ancient British Church, &c.* (1815). Burgess, bishop of St. David's from 1803 to 1825, longed for the 'warning voice of Apocalypse'[45] to impress upon his Catholic contemporaries in Great Britain and Ireland that the ancient church of Britain was a 'Protestant church nine centuries before the days of Luther',[46] 'protesting against the corruptions of superstition, images, and idolatry, refusing all communion with the Church of Rome'.[47] Founded, 'beyond all controversy and doubt', by St. Paul,[48] 'it was fully established before the Church of Rome'[49] and was 'publicly professed and protected by a British king' (Lucius) before the end of the second century.[50] It was idle for some 'Romish writers' to 'pretend that the bishop of Rome had a right to obedience from this country, on account of Austin having planted Christianity here in his mission from the pope'.[51] All the more so when it seemed plain to Burgess, following his illustrious predecessor, Richard Davies, that the British not only rejected the 'authority of Austin' and the 'doctrine and usages of his church', but also refused to have any communication with the Saxons following their conversion.[52] Therefore, he asserted triumphantly,

> 'the popery of Britain constitutes the *middle ages* of the British Church. Down to the beginning of the seventh century, there was no trace of popery. . . . From that time to the reign of Henry I the British Church continued perfectly independent of the Church of Rome. From the reign of Henry I to the middle of that of Henry VIII (1115–1530) was the period of her subjection to the Pope.'

This he felt, should convince an 'unprejudiced mind that Popery obtained no establishment in this country but by usurpation'.[53]

Time, and the emergence of diametrically different conceptions of history, have softened the sharp edges of difference between sixteenth-century reformers and their opponents and thrown into relief their underlying similarity. From our point of view, the contribution of the Protestants to historical scholarship does not appear impressively original. As far as historical method went, they added little that was new. It is true that they did much to help in the search for old books and manuscripts, and in their preservation. They also gave a great stimulus to the scholarly ransacking of ancient authorities for new evidence concerning church history. But this avidity for historical material was created at least as much by the Renaissance as by the Reformation; and when it came to handling the evidence, there were times when many of the Protestant historians showed themselves to be too medievally-minded to accept the findings of more discriminating Renaissance scholarship, the outstanding example being their illfounded defence of Geoffrey of Monmouth's work against Polydore Vergil's iconoclasm.

Nor could the Protestants abandon the classical Christian conception of human history as part of a mighty cosmic drama, in which the creation of the world and the incarnation of Christ were the most significant episodes, and final redemption the end to which all history was moving. They emphasized that the only authentic revelation of that divine plan, of which human history was the unfolding, was to be found in the Bible. So it was not surprising that the relations between Jehovah and his people revealed in sacred history should have coloured all their thinking about secular history, and that their supreme concern was to find in it evidence of obedience to God being followed by prosperity, and deviation from his paths no less surely bringing disaster in its train. Within the framework of the Christian viewpoint, therefore, there was room for considerable difference of opinion, in emphasis and in detail if not in fundamentals. The Protestants' account of the rise of the papacy, for example, was very revealing. They had a shrewd appreciation of the work of the great popes, even if they did detest their achievements. Unhampered by the need to justify the enlargement of papal authority as a revelation of the divine will, they had a clearer sight of the human frailty that oftentimes underlay it, though of course they went too far in the other direction in attributing the whole diabolical phenomenon to the machinations of the Prince of Darkness.

They left their mark on British history, too, though many of their most cherished opinions have been scattered like chaff before the wind of modern scholarship. The Joseph of Arimathea legend and the Eleutherius story have long since been decently buried, and few would any longer be found to see in Augustine's quarrel with the Welsh bishops evidence of early Protestant opposition to papal encroachment. Yet however unhistorically they may have viewed the Celtic Church in some respects, their insistence that its representatives were rightfully proud of their own idependent religious heritage was of permanent value, for indeed they were not mere backwoodsmen rejecting Rome and clinging to their own tradition from nothing but ignorance and stubborn prejudice. In Wales it was an interpretation particularly acceptable and long-lived Only with great reluctance was it gradually qualified or given up, and even now, in much modified form, it is by no means entirely extinct. It gave fresh point and depth to that particular veneration in which the Celtic Church had always been held. The Reformation appeared to be vindicated as the highest fulfilment of the ancient prophecies that the glories of the earlier British Kingdom would, in the fullness of time, be restored. To many Welshmen of Tudor and Stuart times nothing could have been more gratifying to their patriotic confidence or a more lasting source of pride and consolation.

NOTES

[1] In the preface to Robert Barnes's *Vitae Romanorum Pontificum* (Wittenberg, 1535).

[2] J. M. Robertson (edit.), *The Philosophical Works of Francis Bacon* (London, 1905), p. 54; cf. T. D. Kendrick, *British Antiquity* (London, 1950), p. 115.

[3] William Tyndale, *Answer to Sir Thomas More's Dialogue* in his *Works* (Parker Soc., 1848), iii, 103.

[4] John Bale, *Selected Works* (Parker Soc., 1849), p. 8.

[5] Kendrick, *British Antiquity*, pp. 69-72.   [6] Tyndale, *Works*, ii, 240-344.

[7] Miles Coverdale, *Writings and Translations* (Parker Soc., 1844), p. 82.

[8] See A. W. Haddan and W. Stubbs, *Councils and Ecclesiastical Documents* (Oxford, 1869), i, 22-6.

[9] See James Ussher, *Britannicarum Ecclesiarum Antiquitates* (Dublin, 1639), pp. 5-12, for a convenient and scholarly summary of these surmises and hypotheses.

[10] Hugh Williams (edit.), *De Excidio* (Cymmrodorion Record Series, 1899), i, 20-2.

[11] The text of a letter supposedly written by Eleutherius to Lucius may be seen in John Foxe, *Acts and Monuments* (edit., S. R. Cattley and G. Townsend, 1837-41), i, 309-10.

[12] John Jewel, *Works* (Parker Soc., 1845-50), i, 279-80.

[13] James Pilkington, *Works* (Parker Soc., 1842), pp. 514-5.

[14] *The Second Replie of Thomas Cartwright agaynst Maister Doctor Whitgifte's Second Answer* (London, 1575), pp. 472-5.

[15] *Ibid.*, p. 475.

[16] *Ibid.*, p. 472; for Whitgift's position, see *Works* (Parker Soc., 1851-3), 128-30.

[17] Carwright, *Second Reply*, p. 475.

[18] Tyndale, *Works*, i, 143.   [19] Pilkington, *Works*, p. 515.

[20] Jewel, *Works*, iv, 778.   [21] Foxe, *Acts and Monuments*, i, 516.

[22] G. W. Child, *Church and State under the Tudors* (London, 1890), p. 204.

[23] See W. W. Greg, 'Books and bookmen in the correspondence of Archbishop Parker', *The Library*, xvi (1935), 247, ff.; Robin Flower, 'William Salesbury, Richard Davies, and Archbishop Parker', *National Library of Wales Journal*, ii (i) (1941), 7-14; and G. Williams, 'Bishop Sulien, Bishop Richard Davies, and Archbishop Parker', *ibid.*, v (iii) (1948), 215-9.

[24] A translation of the 'Address' may be found in A. O. Evans, *A Memorandum on the Legality of the Welsh Bible* (Cardiff, 1925), pp. 83-124.

[25] F. M. Stenton, *Anglo-Saxon England* (Oxford, 1943), pp. 63-4

[26] Jewel, *Works*, iii, 84.

[27] *Discourse of the Religion Anciently Professed by the Irish and the British* (London, 1631). I am indebted to Professor D. B. Quinn for drawing my attention to this work.

[28] *Ibid.*, p. 89.   [29] Ussher, *Discourse*, pp. 65-6.   [30] *Ibid.*, loc. cit.

[31] *Ibid.*, introduction, no pagination.

[32] T. D. Kendrick, *British Antiquity*, p. 112.   [33] *Antiquitates*, p. 12.

[34] *Concilia, Decreta, Leges, Constitutions, &c.* (1639), p. 11.

[35] Thomas Fuller, *The Church History of Britain* (1655), pp. 6-8.

[36] *Origines Britannicae* (1840 edit.), pp. 6-12.   [37] *Church History*, p. 4.

[38] Stillingfleet, *Origines*, pp. 39-49.   [39] *Concilia*, pp. 35-6.

[39] Jeremy Collier, *Ecclesiastical History* (1708), i, 17.

[40] Quoted by Kendrick, *British Antiquity*, p. 113.

[41] *Church History*, pp. 53-4.   [42] *Acts and Monuments*, i, 339-40.

[43] Fuller, *Church History*, p. 68.

[44] Burgess, *Tracts*, p. 106.   [45] Burgess, *Tracts*, pp. 142-3.

[46] *Ibid.*, p. 106.   [47] *Ibid.*, p. 54.   [48] *Ibid.*, p. 56.

[49] *Ibid.*, p. 142.   [50] *Ibid.*, p. 96.   [51] *Ibid.*, p. 103.

[52] Burgess, *Tracts*, p. 279. Cf. Henry Soames, *The Anglo-Saxon Church* (1835), pp. 311-2.

INDEX

A

Aberconway, abbey of,	38, 46, 155; see also Maenan.
Aberdaron rectory,	46.
Abergwili,	118, 121, 127, 134, 167, 181, 197.
Absenteeism; see Non-residence.	
Acts of Parliament:	
Supremacy, Act of 1534,	40, 111.
Supremacy, Act of 1559,	141, 143, 146.
Uniformity, Act of 1549,	49.
Uniformity, Act of 1559,	54, 141, 146.
Union, Act of 1536,	14, 18, 19.
'Address to the Welsh Nation,'	61, 182, 183, 184, 185, 212.
Advowsons,	177, 179, 180.
Anglesey,	43, 53, 54, 143.
Anglesey, archdeacon of,	53, 54.
Anglicanism, Anglicans,	13, 15, 21, 26, 27, 28, 161; see also Established Church.
Anglo-Saxons; see also Saxons,	61, 184, 215.
Aragon, Catherine of,	40, 71, 76.
Arches, Court of,	77, 78.
Athequa, George de, bishop of Llandaff,	92, 93.
Augmentations, Court of,	48, 98, 99, 129, 178.
Augustinian Canons,	37, 124.
Augustine of Canterbury,	184, 209, 210, 211, 212, 215, 216, 217.

B

Bangor, bishops of,	35, 41, 53, 54, 125, 143, 144, 178.
cathedral,	35, 36, 37, 44, 48.
chancellor of,	52.
chapter of,	147.
diocese of,	35, 36, 40, 41, 42, 45, 51-4, 59, 60, 144, 148, 165.
friary,	37, 38, 39, 46, 47.
grammar school,	59.
Ban wedi ei Dynnu o Gyfraith Hywel Dda,	193, 195.
Bardsey Abbey,	20, 37, 46.
Barlow, John,	112, 113, 114, 115, 116, 119, 120, 121.
Roger,	112, 119, 121, 122, 128, 129, 130.
Thomas,	112, 121, 122.
William, bishop of St. David's,	80, 111-124, 125, 128, 131, 133, 134, 143, 163, 164.

C

I

J

K

L

M

N